The
Strength
of a Story

How to Earn the Eyes and Ears
of Any Audience

CARMEN MARIANO ED. D.

Fulton Books, Inc.
Meadville, PA

Published by Fulton Books 2021

ISBN 978-1-64952-913-8 (paperback)
ISBN 978-1-64952-915-2 (hardcover)
ISBN 978-1-64952-914-5 (digital)

Printed in the United States of America

Dedication

I don't have many heroes. My father, Luigi, deserves to be one of them. God has blessed me in many ways. His greatest blessing was to make me my father's son. Why? Find each of the stories I have written about my dad and you will know!

I admire a hero named George, as well. I admire his pride, his principles, his energy, and his ethics.

George was the head custodian in the first school I ever served. He worked in that same school for sixty years. George never taught a subject. He taught much more. Everyone who knew George loved him and learned from him, *and everyone knew George*!

Like Luigi, George's worth and wonder will be found in some of the stories that follow.

Last and not least came Ronnie.

John F. Kennedy once said, "Do not pray for easier lives. Instead, pray for stronger men." Ronnie had no easy life. Instead, he was among the strongest of men.

All three of those men have been my heroes and remain my compass. My goal is to be like them—nothing more, nothing less.

Yogi Berra once said, "If you don't know where you're going, you might never get there!" Thanks to Luigi, George, and Ronnie, I know where I am going—or at least where I want to go. I want to go to heaven and spend eternity in their company.

The most meaningful quote in this book is not mine. It came from Mark Twain and says this, "Every person's life celebrates two important dates. One is the date on which that person was born. The other is the date on which that person *finds out why*."

Luigi, George, and Ronnie showed me why I was born.

I was born to be like them!

Sincerely,
Carmen Mariano

Contents

Acknowledgments

Every morning, I buy two bagels at Dunkin' Donuts. When the cashier gives me my change, I express my superficial appreciation by saying "Thank you!"

Now I must use those same small words to express my heartfelt indebtedness to the people who have given life to the memories that follow.

DeeDee, for being my wife, my fellow student, my love, my life, and my favorite company, thank you.

Ma and Dad (in heaven), for believing in the transformational value of education and for believing in me, thank you.

Natalie, for being my sister, my inspiration, and the smartest woman I know, thank you.

Nonnas, Tadones, aunts, uncles, friends, those who helped me write my stories, tell my stories, or live my stories, thank you, thank you, thank you!

Introduction

What you are about to read is not a book. It is a conversation. These words should be spoken, not written. I wish they *were* spoken.

I wish I was speaking to you right now. I wish we were sharing a classroom or coffee table, so I could speak and you could agree (or argue!) with what I say.

Then I could learn from your words as you might learn from mine.

Yes, speaking *would* be better. But for now, writing is all I have, so I will write!

I will write about the world's greatest gifts.

Those gifts never stop giving!

They give meaning to our words, muscle to our messages, and magic to our memories.

What *are* those gifts?

Those gifts are *stories*!

Quoting the smartest woman I know, "*A picture is worth a thousand words, and a story is worth a thousand pictures.*"

We learn through stories, we laugh through stories, and we live through stories. Stories give our words wings. They give our speeches strength. They help us understand, illustrate, illuminate, and inspire.

Telling a story changes another's world. *Hearing* a story changes our own. Stories are the part of life that sticks to our ribs. They are "the spaghetti and meatballs of Sunday night supper!"

I will tell many stories that are true and that happened to me. I will tell other stories that did not happen to me. They may have happened to someone else or no one.

Someone once said that "when we steal from one person, we call it plagiarism, and when we steal from many people, we call it research!" I "researched" the stories in this conversation that are not mine, and I thank every author, artist, editor, and storyteller who let me!

I am a married man with no children and a lot of tread on my tires. I have been blessed with my faith, family, friends, feelings, memories, and more.

Because I have no children, I need something to bear witness to my blessings, not because *I* deserve *credit* but because *God* deserves *thanks*. I hope this converstaion and its stories will bear that witness and give that thanks.

Stories are valuable, and they come at a cost. Every story told here costs the space of another story! As my stories multiplied, I was left with too many stories and too little space!

Many of my cousins, uncles, aunts, friends, neighbors, and more will go unnamed and unnoticed because this conversation is not long enough.

How did I choose *some* stories and not *others* to be told? I simply read the stories! Then I listened for laughs, looked for smiles, felt for tears, and asked for advice!

As I added stories, I tried cutting the ones I liked least, but I liked even *those* stories too much to cut! I felt lost, so I did what I always do when I feel that way.

I asked my biggest fan and best friend, DeeDee, to *find* me! Dee reminded me of the many times she has heard me speak. She has heard me give eulogies, commencement addresses, keynote speeches, and more.

She has heard me facilitate workshops for hours. She has heard me *lead* seminars for days!

Every time I speak, DeeDee listens, but she *never speaks*! DeeDee never *tells* me what she *thinks* of what I *say* or how I *say* it.

At least she never did—until the day we were with friends celebrating a twenty-fifth wedding anniversary and I was asked to give the toast. It took *thirty seconds*!

When I finished, I returned to my seat next to DeeDee. As I sat down, after giving that thirty-second toast, DeeDee broke her silence. That's right, she leaned over, smiled, and said, "Carmen, that was the *best speech* of *your life*!"

"Are you trying to tell me something?" I asked Dee after she raved about my very few words!

"Yes," she replied. Then she looked me in the eye and said, "Carmen, if you want everyone in your audience to love any speech you give, just be sure to *start* it with two very popular words."

"What words are those?" I asked.

"*In conclusion*!" DeeDee answered.

I will follow DeeDee's advice! I will start by making you a promise. It is the *same* promise that *Elizabeth Taylor* made to every one of her eight former husbands.

That promise is this: "*I won't keep you long*!"

I will write this book and have this conversation "one *short* story at a time! Where will we start? *With meaning*!

Chapter 1

Giving Meaning to Our Words

The English language is like stale bread. It is hard!

We spend lots of time and energy trying to find *meaning* in what we say, write, read, and hear.

Sometimes the message we send gets misunderstood, distorted, exaggerated, or worse! What do I mean? Let me show you some (yes!) *stories*!

Landscaping

Last summer, I read an ad for a landscaping company. It went like this: "Don't kill yourself in your garden. Let us do it for you!"

What did that company *mean*?

Lumber

I bought some lumber at Home Depot a few weekends ago. When the cashier told me the price, I said, "Boy, lumber is expensive, isn't it!" The cashier smiled, nodded, and said, "Of course, lumber is expensive. It doesn't grow on trees, you know!"

What did that cashier *mean*?

Washing Machine

A stranger was walking down the street and noticed a man struggling with a washing machine at the front door of his house. When the stranger volunteered to help, the homeowner was overjoyed. Together, the two men tried to move the bulky appliance.

After several minutes of fruitless effort, the two men stopped and stared at each other in frustration. The homeowner was exhausted. When he finally caught his breath, he said, "Well, it looks like we'll never get this washing machine into my kitchen."

To that, the stranger replied, "*In?* I thought you said you wanted to get it *out!*"

Another search for meaning!

Dog Bites?

A man moves into a new town. After getting settled, he walks down to the town square to make some friends. He sees an old fellow sitting on the curb with a dog beside him. The new man in town walks over and asks, "Does your dog bite?" The old guy looks up at him and says "Nope."

So the new fellow reaches down to pet the dog, but when he does, the dog nearly rips his arm off. The new man in town jumps back quickly and says, "I thought you said your dog doesn't bite!"

The old guy looks up and says, "I did. But that ain't my dog!"

As I said, the message we send can get misunderstood!

Election Day

Last November, my niece Amy went to vote in the presidential election. When she walked into the gymnasium being used for the balloting, an elderly female volunteer greeted Amy and asked for her name. "My name is Amy Fagerlund," came my niece's reply.

"How do you spell it?" pursued the senior helper.

"F-a-g-e-r-l-u-n-d," replied Amy.

"Did you say it starts with an *s?*" asked the volunteer.

"No," replied Amy. "I said *F* as in Frank!"

"Frank?" challenged the senior. "How can your name be Frank? Aren't you a girl?"

The English language *is* hard. Just ask Amy!

What Bill?

There is a story that I was told came out of the Kennedy White House early in JFK's second term. It seems that the president was becoming increasingly frustrated by the many requests he was getting for appropriations he could not afford!

As the president and his fiscal managers reviewed these never-ending requests, a budget officer addressed the president at a distance.

"Mr. President, I must alert you to another unforeseen expense that has surfaced," bellowed the officer.

"What is it related to?" replied JFK. "The Defense Bill," responded the officer. At his wit's end, the president snapped back, "Oh, the hell with it. Just *pay* the Goddamned thing!"

The English language strikes again! It *is* hard! Just ask JFK!

Words can help, but not enough! We deserve *more* than words to help us use English. *We deserve* stories!

So stories will be our secret. Stories will be our strength.

Stories will help us give *meaning to our words*!

Did you say you need some examples?

Examples, here we come! Let's tell some stories that give meaning to the word *faith*.

Words of Wonder

Like many of the words, we will be "having a conversation" about *faith. Faith is a word of wonder*! It is one of the *most meaningful* and familiar words in our language. If I asked if you knew what *faith* meant, you would probably say yes, but if I asked you for its *meaning*, you might...wonder!

Try it. What is faith? What does it mean? How would you define it? How would you describe it?

Even a dictionary doesn't always help. It might define a word using *other* words, but defining a word might not help us *understand it, own it, or share it.*

A definition might help us *learn* a word of wonder, but it might not help us *live* that word.

I looked up *faith* in the dictionary, for example, and found the word *trust*. Then I looked up *trust* and found *faith*!

Did either of those definitions help me learn or live the other?

I wonder!

A student in my Catholic high school once asked our chaplain if he understood God. Kiddingly, the chaplain replied, "If you understand him, he must not be God!"

The same is true for words of wonder! Their name says it all. *They make us wonder*! Thus, we need something beyond a dictionary to find meaning in such words. We need *stories* to find that meaning.

A word of wonder is hard to define with other words and easier to define with a story.

Still not sure? What if I told some *stories* that gave the word *faith* more meaning than a definition or a dictionary ever could? *Would that help*?

It would depend on the stories I told, right? Yes.

So try these stories! They are all about *faith*. See if they help you give meaning to that word.

Faith

The Rope

A group of botanists went to the Italian Alps to collect specimens of a rare and valuable flower. One morning during their search, they walked through a small village high in the mountains and came to a cliff.

From there, the botanists looked over a green valley. In that valley, they spotted the flower they had been looking for.

Now these botanists *wanted* that flower, but from the cliff upon which they stood, it was a sheer drop of several hundred feet to the valley floor, and none of the botanists were brave (or nimble!) enough to make that descent!

As they discussed their problem, the scientists noticed that a small boy from the nearby village was listening with interest as the men discussed their situation.

One of the men turned to the boy and said, "Young fellow, have we got a deal for you! If you will let us tie this rope around your waist and lower you over a cliff so you can dig up one of those flowers, we'll pull you back and give you fifty dollars."

The boy thought for a moment then ran away—apparently frightened at the prospect of being lowered over such a steep cliff by a rope. Within a short time, however, he returned. He brought a man with him. The man was small and looked older than he was. He was bent and gray with hands gnarled and disfigured by hard labor.

Upon reaching the botanists, the boy pointed to the old man and said, "This is my father. I will go down into that valley and get your flower for fifty dollars…if you let *him* hold the rope."

That boy gave his *faith* to his father. Do you know the *meaning* of the word *faith* yet? Do you own the word? Have you lived the word?

I Knew You Would Come

I heard a story from the Vietnam War about a company of United States soldiers who were caught in a crossfire by a larger force of Viet Cong. Half of the Americans were killed before they could take cover. The other half hugged the ground but began to die as quickly as the Cong could reload their rifles.

The young lieutenant commanding the company was lying next to a medic when he heard a wounded soldier groaning ten yards away. The medic looked up at the soldier then turned to the lieutenant.

"Don't even think about trying to help him," said the lieutenant as Cong bullets filled the air. "You won't get to him alive. Even if you do, he will die before you can help him."

"I must try," said the medic as he rose and ran to the dying soldier. The medic was shot three times before he got to the soldier. The lieutenant ran to both men and made it unharmed. "I told you not to do it!" he scolded the brave medic. "Now I will lose you both."

"It was worth it, sir," retorted the medic.

"What do you mean?" asked the lieutenant.

"When I got to him, he was alive," explained the medic. "And just before he died, he looked at me and said, '*I knew you would come.*'"

That soldier *had faith* in that medic, just as the boy did in his father. Do you understand the word *faith* now? Do you own it? Have you lived it?

It's Your Turn!

Once upon a time, a family of European refugees was driven from their homes by invading soldiers during World War II. Their only chance of escape was over the mountains that surrounded their village.

But an elderly man was part of that family, and he was not sure he could make it over the mountains.

"Leave me behind," he told his son and daughter-in-law.

But they would not. Finally, the old man agreed to try, and the family set out after dark toward the mountains.

As they walked, the three adults took turns carrying their one-year-old baby.

After several hours, the grandfather stopped, sat on a large rock, and hung his head. "I can't make it," he said. "You must go on without me."

"Yes, you can!" his son implored him. But the old man refused to move.

Finally, the son said, "You must come. We need you. *It's your turn to carry the baby.*"

With that, the old man's eyes lit up.

"Let's go!" he said. He picked up the baby and headed up the mountain. The rest of the family followed.

They all reached safety that night, including the old man and the baby, all because the old man's son had *faith* in his father.

Were any of my stories strong enough to help you understand the word *faith* better than any dictionary or definition ever has? I wonder!

Faith in the World

As we travel to and from work, we show faith in the people of our world every day, and none of those people let us down. If even one did, I might not be writing this, and you might not be reading it. What do I mean? Think about it!

Every time you and I drive a car, we show faith in all the other drivers who are using the opposite lane of the *same* road that we are!

Yes, we have *faith* that those other drivers will stay on their side of the yellow line! If even one of those drivers does not stay in their lane, kaboom! I might not be writing this, and you might not be reading it!

There was a time when our first trip to a friend's house began with writing directions on the back of an envelope or the palm of our hand.

Not anymore!

Now we just listen to the female voice that floats through our dashboard! Even if that voice sends us down a dark dead end or over a dangerous dirt road, we obey that voice! Why? Because we have faith in that voice! We have faith in our GPS!

If "she" is wrong, I might not be writing this and you might not be reading it!

Faith in Friends

Yes, every day, we have *faith* in our world.

We also have *faith* in our families *and* our *friends*.

When friends make us a promise, we have *faith* in their word. If those friends break their word, we stop seeing them as friends!

If there was a recipe for friendship, its first and most important ingredient would be *faith*! When it comes to friendship, faith is the cherry on your sundae, beef in your burger, and sizzle on your steak.

We have faith in our friends or we have no friends at all!

Faith in God

And what about God? Do we have *faith* in him? I found the answer to that question in many stories. One of them is about a man named Todd.

Todd

On the morning of September 11, 2001, Todd Beamer earned enough faith from the passengers of Flight 93 to lead them in over-whelming their captives, crashing their plane, giving up their lives, and saving the Pentagon.

You have heard the story. Todd's last words were "Let's roll!" and the Lord's Prayer. With those words, Todd earned enough *faith* to lead a handful of his fellow passengers on a road to heroism and heaven. Yes, Todd put his faith in God's prayer, and God put his grace in Todd.

Todd was not a pilot, so he could not save the plane he was on. Still, he *did* save the *building* that Tod's plane was programmed to destroy. He saved the Pentagon and its twenty-six thousand occupants by causing his plane to crash into a meadow in Pennsylvania.

The Pentagon survived. Todd did not. He died a father, son, husband, and hero. Each of Todd's fellow passengers died heroes as well, thanks to the *faith* Todd earned from them and the followers they became.

Faith in Each Other

A baker in a little town bought his butter from a nearby farmer. One day, the baker suspected that some bricks of butter he bought from the farmer were not full pounds, so he weighed them.

The baker was right. The bricks weighed less than a pound. So he approached the farmer.

"You have been cheating me!" said the baker.

"That can't be" retorted the farmer. "I have balances, and I measure every brick of butter I sell."

"What do you balance the bricks *against?*" asked the baker.

"The one-pound loaves of bread that *you* sell *me!*" retorted the farmer. What happened? The farmer's faith was broken by the baker and faith "takes years to build, seconds to break, and forever to repair."

So that farmer may never have faith in that baker again. Do you understand the word *faith* yet? Have you wed the word faith yet? Have you lived it? I wonder!

Faith in the Truth

Like faith, *truth* is a word of wonder. We use it a lot as if we know what it means. Often, we really don't know.

People deserve the truth. So *have faith in the truth and earn faith with the truth*!

A man of questionable character dies and awaits a place in heaven.

As he enters heaven's waiting room, the man notices thousands of clocks hanging from every wall in the room.

"What are all these clocks for?" the man asks the angel in charge.

"There is a clock on these walls for every person who has ever lived," replies the angel.

"What does each person's clock represent?" the nervous man pursues. "The more someone lies, the faster that person's clock runs," explains the angel.

"Whose clock is that?" asks the man as he points to one whose hands are not moving at all. "That clock belongs to Mother Teresa," replied the angel. "She never lied, so her clock never moves!"

"There is another clock in the corner moving almost as slowly as mother Teresa's," observed the man. "Whose clock is that?"

"That clock is Abraham Lincoln's," replied the angel. "He almost never lied, either!"

The man continues to look at the clocks as he gets more and more nervous. He is bothered by one clock that seems to be missing from the wall.

"Where is *my* clock?" asks the man.

"Oh," the angel hesitates, "yours is hanging in God's office. *He is using it for a fan!*"

That man does not own the meaning of the word truth. Do you? Did my story help? Just in case it did not, let's read more stories that add meaning to the word *truth* and to other words of wonder like *family, friends, feelings, strength, success, sacrifice, food, fun,* and *more*! Let's start *with family*!

Family

Yes. *Family* is another word of wonder. Why? Think about it. We all have families that make us wonder…and wonder…and *wonder*!

You wonder how your sons and daughters could possibly be related to each other and still be so different. You wonder how your *mother* ever fell in love with your *father*. You wonder how your *father* ever fell in love with your *mother*!

You wonder why you get along with your friends so much better than with your brothers and sisters. You wonder how you all shared one bathroom for so long growing up without *killing each other*!

You wonder how your children were able to earn your love so completely and still *drive you so crazy* at the same time!

My best friend is divorced from his first wife. They had two children together. He and his second wife have three other children and five grandchildren. Who are the members of my best friend's family? Do you wonder?

Yes, when it comes to families, you wonder…and wonder… *and wonder*!

I will tell some *stories* about *my family, your family, other families,* and *every family* that will help give meaning to that word!

The Express

I saw a rerun of *The Express* last year. It is a movie about Ernie Davis, the first Black athlete to win the Heisman Trophy.

Ernie was a spectacular running back in high school, so more than fifty colleges recruited him. One of those schools was Syracuse University.

22

Ernie's grandfather (and legal guardian) approached the Syracuse coach at a recruiting session and asked, "If my grandson goes to your school, what will you do for him?"

The coach answered by boasting about his school's impressive academics, expansive campus, renowned athletics, significant endowment, and more. Ernie's granddad stopped the coach in midsentence. "No," the grandpa interrupted, "I didn't ask you what *Syracuse* will do for Ernie. I asked what *you* will do for him. What will *you* teach him? What will he learn from *you*? That is what matters. It's the coaches, not the college. *It's the people, not the place.*"

Ernie's grandfather was right. "It's the people!" Good people make good schools—*and* good families!

It has been said that "lucky parents who have fine children usually have lucky children who have fine parents." Parents and children who come from good families are lucky. *I am* lucky, and my family *is* good!

Another Special Movie

One of my favorite movies is called *Stand and Deliver*. It tells the inspirational story of Jaime Escalante, a high school math teacher who led his class of poor, Hispanic students from Southern California to the highest cumulative scores in the history of the National Advanced Placement Calculus Exam.

In one scene from this special movie, two of Mr. Escalante's teenage students were riding home in a car, that a third student was driving on a clear winter night after a basketball game. As they rode, one boy looked up at the sky. Then he pointed and said, "Wow! Look at all the stars."

The other boy looked up paused and said, "What stars? I don't see any stars."

The first boy insisted, "Of course, you do! You must see those stars!"

The second boy insisted back, "No, I don't. I don't see any stars at all!"

The first boy shook his head and said, "Stop kidding me. You *must* see all those stars."

"No, I don't," said the other boy, "and neither do you. What you see instead is the **light** that **left** those stars many years ago and is just now getting close enough to earth for us to see. Many of the stars that sent that light have changed in size or shape, in age or location since they sent their light, but their light is *still shining* on us."

We all know people like those stars. Over time, they have changed in many ways, but their light will shine on their friends, on their families, and on our world forever. We will be better and our world will shine brighter, thanks to them.

My grandparents, parents, sister, wife, aunts, uncles, and cousins have shined that kind of light on me. I am better, thanks to them, and my life has been brighter, thanks to them.

Each member of my family and every family has strengths *and* weaknesses. They all *can* help, they all *will* help, and they all *need* help *shining*!

The Porcupine's Dilemma

A minister named John Ortberg uses a story to reflect on a condition that lots of married people and families have to deal with. The reverend calls the condition "The Porcupine's Dilemma."

Reverend Ortberg explains that every year for a short time in late autumn, female porcupines briefly "turn their fancy to love!" When they do, the male porcupines in the area approach the females.

Now these males need to get close enough to help the females "make good things happen!"

Still, *we are talking about porcupines*! So if a male tries too hard or gets too close to a female, they will *both* get hurt! Family members are like porcupines. The closer they get to each other, the more they can help, *and* the more they can hurt each other!

Vulnerability is a necessary part of loving—*inside* a family *or out*! Families share so much time and so much love with each other they cannot help but wonder, "How do I get *close enough* without getting *hurt?*"

Are you answering? Are you *wondering*? If so, good! Because *family is* a word of wonder! It makes us wonder...and wonder...*and wonder!*

Out of Ham

A woman visited a judge one day to ask him about getting her husband out of jail. After a long wait, the wife was ushered into the judge's chambers, where she made her request.

"What is he in for?" asked the judge. "For stealing a ham, Your Honor," the wife replied.

"Well," said the judge, "that doesn't sound too bad. Tell me, is he a good husband?"

The woman thought for a minute then replied, "Not really, Judge. The fact is, in the twenty-plus years that we have been married, he has never shared a kind word or gentle thought with me."

"Well, is he a good worker?" asked the judge, "No, Your Honor," said the woman. "I couldn't say that. In fact, he is pretty lazy. He has never been able to hold down a job for more than a week or two!"

"Well then, is he a good father to your children?" the judge pursued.

"No," said the wife. "He is pretty mean to the kids."

"Ma'am," said the judge after a pause, "may I ask why you want a man like that to be released from prison and put back in your house?"

The woman paused then replied, "Well, Judge, it's like this. We are almost out of ham!"

Every person in a family has a place. Every person plays a part and fills a need. So in your family, play a part and fill a need. Stay close to each other. Just remember that the closer you get, the more you can help, *and* the more you can hurt!

Blossom, Bloom, Share

One day, while contemplating "the porcupine's dilemma," my eyes fell on a rosebud in my mother's flower garden.

Now picture a rosebud. It has color, but little else, because its petals have not opened.

They have not shared themselves with each other or with the world.

As time passes, some buds remain closed. Eventually, their stem weakens and bends, leaving the rose to turn downward and die.

Other buds do better. They blossom. They bloom. Their petals share their beauty. And each petal's beauty is different.

"Families are like roses," I told myself as I looked at my mother's garden. "They can remain closed. They can keep from sharing themselves with each other or with the world. If they do, they will die with their heads bowed, their growth stunted, and their beauty hidden forever, even from each other."

As a family member, don't hide your beauty or bow your head. Instead, bloom and blossom. Share yourself. Play your part. Fill a need. If you do, the result will be beautiful.

The Puzzle

I watched a fourth-grade class begin on one cold winter morning. As an assistant superintendent, I was observing the class while it was being taught by a first-year teacher.

"Has everybody looked at our puzzle?" asked this new and excellent teacher as she pointed to a large picture of the class that hung from behind the teacher's desk.

"Yes!" screamed five or six of her little students.

"Who is missing?" the teacher pursued.

"Bill and Jill are absent!" replied most of the kids in unison.

"Phil, could you take their pieces from the puzzle so we can all look at their empty places and think of them for the rest of the day?" asked the teacher.

Phil immediately went to the puzzle and removed two pieces containing Bill and Jill's pictures that had been part of the full class display.

"Our class will not be the same without them today," reminded the teacher.

Great message; no class is complete without all its parts.

No *class* is complete without everybody.

No *family* is complete without everybody either.

Every Goodbye

Ten years ago, two of my father-in-law's cousins came to visit. They stayed for two weeks. When they left, my father-in-law said, "Well, this is goodbye until we meet in heaven."

As I listened, it hit me. Future trips would not be in their future! The cousins were too old. The trip was too far. My father-in-law knew he would never again visit Finland, and his family would never again come to America.

It was hard. It was sad. It was true.

After his cousins left for the airport, my father-in-law turned to DeeDee and said, "You know, all our goodbyes should be like that one because we never know when our next goodbye will be our last one!"

Yes, it is always the right time for the last goodbye, not so it will be sad but so it will be special. Every goodbye should be special."

My father-in-law was right. Special goodbyes are what it means to be a family.

The Tailor

A tailor was once asked, "How do you make your wedding gowns so beautiful?"

He replied, "It's easy. I just put *brides* in them. Brides," the tailor continued, "make gowns beautiful. Just like children make homes beautiful and students make schools beautiful."

Yes, people make things beautiful. Families make things beautiful. Families make *life* beautiful. Families make beauty. They spread beauty. The word *family* is *always* plural! When a family *does* anything, *makes* anything, *wants* anything, or *needs* anything, it does so as to *more than one person*!

Thomas Edison

Thomas Edison once said that "you can burn my buildings and close my plants. As long as you leave me my people, together, we will rebuild and flourish. But if you take my people, then no matter what else you give me, I *have nothing*." Edison knew how much he needed people; just like families do!

It's true; families are valuable to people, and people are valuable to families. The people of a family should be given attention and made to feel important.

What do that attention and those feelings look like? Another story, here we come!

The Hawthorne Effect

In 1927, the Western Electric Company's plant in… *Hawthorne*… Illinois, experimented to see how certain working conditions affected production. They started with lighting.

First, the researchers improved the lighting in one of the shops, and guess what! The workers *in* that shop produced more than they had before the improvements were made.

But further studies revealed that the workers in a shop that got *no change* in their lighting increased *their* production, too!

Then the researchers went into another shop and *decreased* its lighting. Guess what happened to that shop's production?

Let's find out! By reading from the diary of one of the people who were there, in Hawthorne, Illinois, in 1927!

> The test group is given increased light. Its output goes up. Good; that was to be expected. But the output of the control group (without one candle power of extra light!) goes up, too! This was not expected. It was contrary to common sense. Indeed, it was completely screwy!

Screwier Results!

> "Still, screwier results were to follow!" continued the diary.
>
> "Light for the test group is now *decreased* below that of the control group. Its output *goes up again*! What in heaven's name is going on?

The research staff was forced to conclude that intensity of light was not a factor in production!

To verify this, the testers in the Hawthorne Project put two workers in a locker room with *no light at all* except what came through a crack under the door. Those workers increased output *even in the dark*!

The reason for this result, so contrary to the doctrine of scientific management and common sense, was there, plain to see, but the investigators had not yet gone far enough to see it.

> "Our conclusions," continued the testers, "after 21,000 case studies, were as follows:
>
> Underneath the stopwatches and bonus plans of the efficiency experts, the worker is driven by a desperate inner urge to find an environment where he belongs and has a function. Where he sees the purpose of his work and where he *feels important!*"
>
> "Yes, in what was later termed the Hawthorne Effect, the researchers discovered that it was the *attention* paid to the workers and not the amount of lighting that increased their production!
>
> The workers were *given attention*. They were made to feel important, and they responded by working harder."

People are important, especially to their followers, friends, and families. If they are made to feel that way, they will produce more, and they will work harder. That is a fact, but don't take it from me. Take it from the Western Electric Company in Hawthorne, Illinois!

Brad

As you have undoubtedly noticed, one of my favorite words of wonder is *family*! A special student and friend named Brad feels the same way about *his* family!

Brad and I met thanks to the Harvard Graduate School Leadership Program. Brad served as an intern there. I worked as his adviser.

This fine young man and future leader comes from Atlanta and was telling me about his family shortly before Thanksgiving last year.

"Do you miss them?" I asked.

"A lot!" Brad replied as he nodded.

"Will you use any of your winter vacation to visit them?"

Again, Brad answered with a nod and a yes.

"What else will you use your break for?" I pursued.

"I will look for a job," Brad answered.

"Where will you hope to work next year?" I asked.

"Here in Boston," Brad said.

"Won't that mean you will miss your family even more than you do now?" I pushed. "I mean, you won't see much of them while you are living eight hundred miles away, will you?"

"Doctor," Brad replied, "eight hundred miles are nowhere near enough to keep me away from my family. I love them much more than that and will drive or fly to see them a lot!"

Brad's words made me think of how much more *my* family should mean to me than miles. I love them. I miss them. Still, I see them much less than I should. Natalie lives less than an hour away. Still, I seldom visit her.

That will change, thanks to Brad. I have aunts and uncles who are in their nineties whom I almost never see. That will change, thanks to Brad.

Great lessons. Maybe *I* should be paying *Brad* tuition instead of the other way around!

Morris and Esther

Here comes another story about a family. This one is thanks to Morris and Esther!

You see, Morris and his wife, Esther, went to the State Fair every year, and every year, Morris asked Esther if he could take a ride in the stunt airplane that was a big feature at the fair.

Every year, Morris would say, "Ester, I'd like to take a ride in that airplane!"

"I know, Morris," Esther would reply, "but that airplane ride costs fifty dollars, and fifty dollars is fifty dollars."

One year, the couple went to the fair and Morris said, "Esther, I am eighty-five years old. If I don't ride that airplane soon, I might never get another chance!"

"Morris," Esther replied, "that airplane ride still costs fifty dollars, and fifty dollars is fifty dollars!"

The pilot overheard the couple's conversation and made a deal with Morris and Esther. "Folks," the pilot said, "I will take you both up for a ride. If you can both stay quiet for the entire ride and not say one word, I won't charge you for the ride, but if you make any sound of any kind, it will cost you fifty dollars."

Morris and Esther agreed, and up they went!

The pilot did all kinds of twists and turns, rolls and dives but not a word was said and not a sound was made. The pilot did all his tricks again and, still, not a word or a sound came from the couple!

When the plane landed, the pilot turned to Morris and said, "By golly, I did everything I could to get one of you to make a noise, but you didn't!"

"Well," Morris confessed, "I must admit that I was going to say something when Esther *fell out of the plane* a few miles back, but fifty dollars is fifty dollars!"

Make sure that you stay closer to your family than Morris did to Esther!

Remember that "families *are* nothing without people, and they *have* nothing without people. They *earn* nothing, *succeed* at nothing,

31

and *celebrate* nothing without people." The word "family" is *always plural*!

Why They Live

A teacher in my former school system attends motivational seminars a lot. One September, she wanted me to join her. I wanted to go but had to decline. She asked me again, and again, and again.

Each time she asked, I really wanted to go with her. Still, it seemed that every time she invited me, I had to say no. Thankfully, she wouldn't give up, and finally, we connected!

As my friend and I found our seats, the speaker began. "Who has brought a guest tonight?" she asked. My friend and others raised their hands. "That means none of you will hear a word I say all night!" continued the speaker. "Because you will be too busy worrying about what your guest thinks of me than you will be about anything else! You will watch your guest more than you will watch me. You will find a smile on your guest's face, or you will find no smile at all!"

Thinking back on that speaker's words, I realize how much they remind me of my parents—or of *any* parents.

Any parent lives to see light in the eyes of a son. Any parent lives to feel warmth in the heart of a daughter. Any parent lives to see light and feel warmth in the eyes or heart of a child!

That is why parents live. It is who parents are. It is a wonder of the word *family.*

Holding Hands

Once upon a time, a little girl and her father were crossing a bridge. The father was concerned for his daughter's safety, so he turned to her and said, "Sweetheart, please hold my hand so that you won't fall into the river."

The little girl thought for a moment then said, "No, Daddy, *you* hold *my* hand instead."

"What is the difference," asked the father?

"If I hold your hand and something happens to me," the little girl replied, "there is a chance that I may let your hand go. But if you hold my hand, I know for sure that no matter what happens, *you* will *never* let my hand go!"

Faith and family are words of wonder. Their meanings can be found in the hands of that little girl and her father.

People have *faith in* their families.

They even have *fun with* their families! Sometimes, people even *make* fun of their families, like Bob Hope, who once said, "I grew up with six brothers and learned how to dance while waiting for the bathroom," or Phyllis Diller, who advised parents to "always be nice to your children because they will choose your rest home!" or Cary Grant, who claimed, "My family is temperamental. They are half temper and half mental!"

Even someone called *Anonymous* had some fun at "family's" expense with these words, "Insanity runs in my family. In fact, it gallops!"

No harm, no foul! But all kidding aside, the meaning and message of a *family* go far beyond quips or comedy.

Everything They Had

A great musician was once asked if she inherited her talent from her parents. "No," she replied. "They could not play or sing a single note."

"What, then, did they give you?" the musician was asked.

"Everything they had," she replied.

My family gave me just that. Each member gave me all the love, laughs, wisdom, worries, smiles, support, aggravation, *agita*, problems, solutions, questions, and answers they had!

My family also gave me a *blanket*!

My Blanket

There are few feelings more wonderful than the new warmth of a spring day. After months of winter, the first warm day of spring changes our lives.

We open windows. We turn down thermostats. We remove blankets from our beds.

While we sleep, however, the weather changes because it's only spring and not yet summer. The temperature drops. It gets cold again. Winter returns, if only for a few hours at a time.

Because we went to sleep with windows open and no blankets, we get cold. We become uncomfortable.

Eventually, we awake, close the windows, and run for a blanket. We pull the blanket tightly to ourselves, and we cuddle in it. We even wiggle a little to help the blanket warm every nook of our cold body.

At times like those, we have no better *friend* than that blanket. We have no better *gift* than that blanket.

My family has been my blanket. When I felt cold, they made me feel warm. When I felt afraid, they made me feel safe. When I felt sad, they made me feel happy. When I felt sick, they made me feel better.

There will be more cold nights and more cold feelings. When those nights and feelings come, I will reach for my blanket and it will always be there.

I have faith in my blanket as I do in my family. My blanket is full of warmth. It is also **full** of **stories**, and all those stories have helped give *meaning* to the word of wonder we have talked so much about. Those stories have helped give meaning to the word *family*!

The Gift of Language

One *gift* that my Italian family *could* have given me but did not was language. It's true. All my grandparents, both of my parents, most of my aunts and uncles, and even some of my cousins spoke Italian before they learned English.

Still, even after earning a doctorate in education, I never learned to speak a second language. I regret few things in my life, and *I do regret that.* I regret that speaking only English made me feel isolated from those family members and friends who spoke only Italian.

I wish I could have my early years back and use them to learn more languages. I have no doubt that doing so would have brought me even closer to my family.

Speaking another person's language is like reaching for their hand and holding it until your whole conversation with them is over.

It makes that person's friends feel like family and makes that person's world feel like *home*.

Home

Home is another word of wonder! We use it all the time, but what does it mean? You have heard the expression "It's good to be home" often, but *where* is *home*? Is it defined by the four walls within which you live, or is home your neighborhood or your community?

Home for me used to be in Braintree, Massachusetts.

That was *before* I got off a plane in Miami, Florida, after spending two weeks teaching in Brazil and before I landed in New York City after two weeks of teaching in Costa Rica and before I landed in Dallas, Texas, after spending two weeks teaching in Mexico.

When I landed in each of those cities after being in each of those countries, I felt like I had *come home*! I felt like I *was* home.

I didn't have to wait to arrive in Braintree to be home; I was in the United States of America, so I *was home*! Thanks to my travels, the meaning of the word *home* has changed. "Home" has become my country more than my kitchen. It has become my refuge more than my residence.

Lord Nelson

Horatio Lord Nelson was one of the most decorated and revered admirals in the history of the British Navy. During the Napoleonic War, Nelson was ordered to seek and destroy a much larger French frigate than was the British man-of-war he commanded. Nelson chased the larger and faster French ship across the Atlantic to the coast of Brazil and beyond.

Eventually, he got close enough to fight. When he did, Nelson prepared his three-hundred-member crew for the coming battle by calling them onto the main deck and saying, "Gentlemen, before we fight, I want you all to close your eyes and *think* of *home*."

His men did what their Admiral asked, "Now," Nelson said, "I want you to open your eyes and *look* for home."

All three hundred men turned their eyes across the Atlantic toward England. Nelson responded by saying, "Every one of your eyes is wrong. You should not look *out* or *up* for home. Instead, you should look *in* and *down*. For *this ship* is your home, and you must fight for this ship as if it were your home, or you will have neither a ship *nor* a home."

Nelson's message? Home is not a place. It is a feeling. Home is wherever we *feel* it is. So do me a favor. *Feel* like you are *home* right now! Feel like this book is your home because it is meant to be.

Feel like all the stories we share are part of *your family's home* right now because they are meant to be. I am not *telling my* stories; I am *sharing our* stories with you because you deserve to own them as much as I do.

We have memories that match, smiles to share, and ties that bind. My stories belong to us all.

Thanks to the magic of our memories and the strength of our stories, I have traveled the same roads you have in different vehicles. I have sailed the same sea you have in different vessels.

All that traveling has brought us home. I truly hope that you find your home and your family in this book and its stories!

The Other Puzzle

We have all heard about the little boy who was home alone with his father on a rainy Saturday afternoon. He drove his dad crazy looking for things to do. The dad gave him crossword puzzles, which the boy did in no time. He gave him brainteasers too, which the boy completed immediately.

Finally, at his wit's end, the dad had an idea. He pulled out an old magazine and paged through it looking for the most complicated picture he could find. He stopped at a map of the world. It could not have been more detailed.

The dad ripped the page out then got a pair of scissors and cut the page into lots of very small pieces. "Come here," he called to his son. "Take all these pieces and put them back together to make a map of the world."

The boy nodded and left the room. Dad stretched out to take a

The boy nodded and left the room. Dad stretched out to take a nap with a proud look on his face. He was sure his son would not be back for a long time.

Instead, the son was back in a flash.

"All done!" he announced.

"You can't be done!" the dad argued.

"Here it is!" said the boy.

And there it was! The puzzle was all done. Somehow, the boy had put the entire map of the world together in no time.

The dad asked him how he did it.

"It was easy, Dad," said the boy. "See, on the other side of the map, there was a picture of a family. *I just put the family together and the world took care of itself.*"

That little boy was right. Together, we can take care of the world by taking care of our families. *Families are that valuable and that powerful!*

Our Invisible Thread

Our world takes better care of us when we take better care of ourselves *and* our *families*!

We are all connected by an invisible thread. When any one of us suffers pain or loss, the thread breaks. When that happens, someone in my family takes the new ends of that broken thread and ties them together. When that is done, two things happen. The thread gets shorter, and the thread gets stronger.

That thread has broken many times within my family. When it has, we have all tied it back together. That has brought us closer and it has kept us stronger.

In the words of Kendall Hailey, we "might never have introduced ourselves to our relatives, had life not done it for us."

Without life's introductions, what would you have lost? Without your family and without your thread, how different would your life be? How empty might it become? What did you *get from* your family? What were you *given by* your family?

Try this story.

A Hundred-Hundred Proposition

I once asked my father what the secret was to his long and happy marriage. He said, "It takes hard work times two. You and your wife have to work together."

"You are right," I replied. "A good marriage is a fifty-fifty proposition."

"No, Carmen," Dad answered back, "a good marriage *is not* a fifty-fifty proposition. It is a *hundred-hundred* proposition! A good marriage takes *all* you have *all* the time. It takes all your wife has too!"

Salt Water

I once heard a man say that being married is like drinking salt water. If you don't like the taste, there are two things you can do.

First, you can try to take the salt out of the water. (That would be *very* difficult!) The other is you can keep pouring fresh water *into* the salt water until the taste of the salt is gone. That works!

Try it. Spend your marriage being good to each other.

When something goes wrong, *keep* being good to each other! Keep pouring fresh water *into* the salt water until the taste of the salt is gone.

Be good to each other—*always*!

When one of you hurts the other, don't try to remove the hurt. Instead, flood the hurt with healing. Keep pouring fresh water *into* the salt water until the taste of the salt is gone.

Be good to each other—*always*!

Almost half of America's marriages *have* failed or *will*.

That means almost half of the American adults who have chosen a spouse will change their choice before they die—maybe even before they wake up tomorrow!

On its *easiest* day, being and staying married is *hard*! That is because my father (as usual) was right. Marriage "*is* a hundred-hundred proposition." It takes *everything*. It takes *all we have*!

In marriage, we must *give* everything we have and *take one* thing back. In marriage, what one thing must we take? We must *take responsibility*!

Take Responsibility

Successful husbands and wives know that! They know they cannot *control* anything unless they take responsibility for it, so they *take responsibility for everything*!

Years ago, while I walked to an afternoon class that was being held in a small community college, I passed a close friend who was also on his way to teach.

"Have a good class," I said as my friend walked by.

"If I don't, it will be my fault!" replied my friend.

No wonder that friend was such a good teacher! As a teacher, he *took responsibility* for being good! As a teacher, he took responsibility for everything!

If you are a *spouse or a teacher*, be like my friend! Take responsibility for everything!

Beautiful Flowers

Years ago, On the *Today Show*, one of the hosts interviewed a woman who was celebrating her 102nd birthday. Throughout the interview, the woman continually watered and pruned a table full of potted plants that sat in her living room.

After posing many questions about her diet, exercise, and other living habits, the host asked the old lady, "What is your secret for living this long and staying so alive?"

She responded, "If anything happened to me, who would take care of these beautiful flowers?"

That old woman had given herself responsibility. It made her feel important, and it kept her alive. It also kept her flowers alive for as long as she was! Whether you have flowers or a family, take responsibility for everything!

Bad News

When a man came home from work one night, his wife greeted him with bad news. "My car has water in the carburetor," she said.

"What are you talking about?" asked the husband. "You don't even know what the carburetor looks like."

"I am telling you. My car has water in the carburetor," insisted the wife.

"And I am telling you, you don't know enough about cars to know that," said the husband. "I'll go look at it myself. Where is the car?"

"I drove it into the lake!" responded the wife.

Be like that man's wife. Take responsibility for your car *and* your family! Take responsibility for everything!

Safety Patrol

When I was in the fifth grade, my teacher put me on the safety patrol!

I got a white belt and a badge. My post was on a street with lots of cars and lots of kids!

I made every car and every kid stop when they reached my post. I wouldn't let anyone *walk* by until I checked for *cars*. I wouldn't let anyone *drive* by until I checked for *kids*!

It was a hard job, but boy, did I feel responsible!

Responsibility is a key to a good safety patrol! It is also a key to a good marriage!

My cousin and I went out for a beer recently. He said kiddingly that he had something to tell me. "My wife and I have decided that we don't want to have any children," my cousin confessed with a wink and a smile. "We will break the news to both of them tonight during dinner!"

If you are a parent, don't be like my cousin! Take responsibility for your children! Take responsibility for everything!

Relentless

As a mother, father, wife, or husband while you are trying so hard to be responsible, try to be *relentless* too!

Dr. Seuss

Dr. Seuss was relentless. His first children's book was rejected by twenty-three publishers, but he never gave in. Dr. Seuss was relentless!

Babies

Babies are like Dr. Seuss. They are relentless as well! What do I mean? "Think about it!" Have you ever seen babies learn to walk? If so, what happens? Yes! They get down on "all fours," throw their bums into the air, then arch their backs, and lift their heads to the sky. Finally, they take a step with one foot and fall!

That sequence happens again and again and again. Then it happens again, again, and again! At the end of every sequence, where is the baby? Yes! The baby is on its bum and the floor!

Now tell me, what is that baby doing while it is on its bum and the floor? Is it crawling out of the room, wrapping itself into a blanket, and quitting? Is that baby sulking in a corner, sucking its thumb, and crying? Is it screaming at its mother or yelling, "Momma and Dadda, I just can't do this! I quit! I give up! I give in!"

No? Why? Because, as we said, babies are relentless! They will not stop trying to stand up *until they stand up*! They will not stop trying to walk *until they walk*!

As a husband, wife, brother, sister, or any kind of family member, be like babies. Be like Dr. Seuss. Be relentless. Never, never, never give in. Believe in your family. Believe in yourself.

Albert Einstein

In 1905, the university of Bern rejected a doctoral dissertation. The professor who reviewed it said the work "was irrelevant" and that its author "was a dreamer." Albert Einstein wrote that dissertation. He could have given in. He never, never, never did. Albert was relentless!

Victor's Uncle

Victor Borge once said, "Don't be like my uncle. He tried to market a variety of soft drinks. He gave them names from *1-up to 6-up*. Then he quit. Some other guy kept going with my uncle's idea. He just added one more 'up,' called the new drink '7-up' and did great!"

Guess who was relentless, just like babies, Dr. Seuss, and Albert Einstein! Yes! Victor Borge (not his uncle!)!

If you are married, try being *responsible* and *relentless*!

Rudy

In a movie called *Rudy*, the main character gets discouraged by his continuous rejection at the hands of Notre Dame University. He stops into church one day to pray for more patience (and for more faith!) There, he comes upon a priest he knows and asks for advice.

"I am not sure if you will ever get in or not," admitted the priest. "In fact, I am only sure of two things in life. One is that there is a God and the other is that *He* is not *me*!"

Like that priest, I am not God! I cannot make miracles, predictions, or even promises. Still, I *can believe that* the future of our marriage and our family has its best hope of success if DeeDee and I do all we can to help each other be *responsible and relentless*.

Quantity and Quality

Ever since Dee and I have been married, I have been proud of our family's "two Rs!" What do those letters stand for? Yes! *Responsible* and *relentless*!

Ever since that day, I have also been proud of our family's "two Qs!" What do those letters stand for? Yes! I have also been proud of our family's *quality* and *quantity*!

My parents took care of our quality, and my grandparents took care of our quantity!

What do I mean? Well, for starters, let's talk about my "Tadone" Carmine! He was my dad's father and had twenty brothers. Yes, my Tadone Carmine had *twenty brothers*!

That means Tadone's immediate family had twenty-three people in it and could singlehandedly provide enough people for two baseball teams, a manager, coach, groundskeeper, cheerleader, and a hot dog vendor!

Yes, Tadone Carmine taught me something about *quantity* when it came to a family! He also taught me something about *quality* as did all my grandparents and both of my parents.

Tadone Carmine

He was a caring husband, a good father, and a *wonderful grandfather*! He taught me how to grow a tomato, kill a chicken, swear in Italian, and most of all, *spoil his grandchildren*!

Tadone Carmine was not educated, but he was respected, loved, open, and honest. As is the case with most Italian men, it didn't take much to "earn" a piece of Carmine's mind!

You didn't have to encourage him, ask him, or pay him to hear what he was thinking! Most of the time, he would just *tell you* loudly and clearly! Although he did not speak English well, my Tadone Carmine always got his points across.

If *he* didn't understand something *I* said, he would smile, and smile, and smile until I said it in enough different ways for him *to* understand!

If *I* didn't understand something *he* said, he would say it louder and louder; then slower and slower!

If I *still* didn't understand, he would yell, and Tadone Carmine yelled even more than he smiled!

He smoked two cigars every day, and he chewed many more. He trimmed the fat off all his meat, *then* he *ate* the *fat*! He would not eat cheese unless it was moldy.

He loved hot peppers, raw eggs, salt pork, the skin of a turkey, *any* kind of whiskey, and *every* kind of wine!

He insisted that my parents had named me after him even though we had *different names*!

The Little Flower

Tadone reminded me of his hero, Fiorello LaGuardia (a.k.a. The Little Flower). As you may know, he was the first Italian American citizen to be elected to the United States Congress and the first Italian mayor of New York City.

Like *my* first name, *Fiorello* is a name usually reserved for Italian girls, not boys, and it means "Flower!" Despite such feminine overtones, The Little Flower struck a powerful presence and commanded a magnetic following. As I implied, that following included my grandfather!

Like my Tadone, Mayor LaGuardia understood the value of family.

He vigilantly cared for the safety and protection of his wife and daughter. Despite such care, they both died tragically of different diseases while they were much too young.

"My wife and my child both died before me," LaGuardia once lamented, "so I am here as mayor to help bring up some of the homeless children of New York in any way I can."

When the New York newspapers declared a strike against their publishing houses, LaGuardia went on the radio every Sunday morning to read the comic strips to the children who could not follow the comics "in person" because of the strike. "Children need to smile," Fiorello explained. "I want to help them do that."

God bless my Tadone Carmine! He commanded my respect just as he earned my love. *I* felt about *him* the way *he* felt about *Mayor LaGuardia*!

The Players and the Program

My mother's parents were my Tadone Raffaele and my Nonna Lucia. They both grew up across the street from each other in the little Italian town of Torre Dei Passeri (a.k.a. The Tower of Sparrows).

It was the *same town* that my *father's parents* grew up in, as well! So they were all friends before they became family and all family before they became friends!

Yes, my roots all grew from the same Italian tree!

My mother's family couldn't match Tadone Carmine's for size. (I mean, twenty brothers is a lot of brothers!) But my mom's parents gave it a good Italian try! They had ten sons and six daughters before their thirtieth wedding anniversary!

Yes, my mother's parents averaged more than one baby every two years—*for thirty years*!

You can't tell the players without a program, so I have listed all the names and nicknames of my mother's and father's brothers, sisters, and in-laws on the early pages of the appendix. I hope all those names don't confuse you as much as they used to confuse me!

You will find *a lot* of names and nicknames there because my mother's family had *a lot* of kids! Once, my uncle Johnny (Ma's brother) explained his family's population explosion by saying, "I guess my mother just never got a headache!"

"Things got pretty crowded," remembered my uncle George one Christmas, "Five of us slept in one double bed. Every night, we all had to sleep on our side, not on our back or stomach but on our side, and it always had to be the *same side*! If *one* of us rolled over, we *all* had to roll over!

"I slept closest to the wall," reflected Uncle Leo. "That meant if I had to use the bathroom during the night, I had to crawl over four brothers to get there. The truth be told, on many nights, I just lay in bed and peed in my pajamas!"

"At dinner," Uncle Albert added, "we had more children than chairs, and when the poultry truck came by, we had more chickens than children!"

Aunt Minnie

Nonna Lucia had a neighbor (and sister!) we called "Aunt Minnie." She delivered Nonna's first thirteen children. (Only the last three were born in a hospital!) In fact, when Nonna Lucia's only set of twins were born, a doctor delivered my uncle Jimmy and never noticed his little sister!

As the doc left the room, Aunt Minnie said something like "Not so fast" in Italian then went back inside Nonna and found my little aunt Jenny!

Pray for Them All

My uncle Bill was my mother's third oldest brother and the first one of my uncles to enlist in the service during World War II. Nonna Lucia watched six other sons and two sons-in-law enlist after Bill.

During the Korean conflict, Uncle Al Kelly, who is my aunt Gloria's husband, served overseas as well.

Nonna and her daughters prayed every night for the safe return of her sons, their brothers, and their husbands.

Their prayers were answered for all those boys who left home. Yes, all those boys came back safely. One of the few who never left home, however, never returned.

During World War II, my uncle Natale (a.k.a. Ned) was working two miles from home at the Fore River Ship Yard. Because he built warships at the Yard, Ned never had to leave Quincy Point, so Nonna Lucia was sure he was safe and didn't think he needed her prayers.

My Nonna was wrong. One day, while standing on a scaffold beside a large warship that was being built in the Yard, my uncle lost his footing and fell to his death—just two miles from home.

"I should have prayed for them all," said my Nonna Lucia every time she told that story. "Carminuzzo," she would say, "always pray for your family, and when you do, *pray for them all.*"

Ironically, my dad's brother Americo (a.k.a. another Uncle Mike) was killed in a car accident shortly after he returned home from the war, as well.

"Pasqualina should have prayed for them all," said my Nonna Lucia when she first learned of Americo's death.

Yes, Nonna Lucia wanted to pray for every one of her children. She also wanted to cook, clean, love, and care for every one of them, but there were just too many children and not enough Nonna to go around!

Nonna's Help

So Nonna got some help. From where? From her daughters!

Yes, Nonna's daughters became their younger brothers' mothers!

I asked my uncle Chick about this phenomenon one day. As I said, Chick was one of the youngest (number fourteen) of the family's children and the first to be born in a hospital!

Nonna must have been running out of gas by then, but it was okay because a replacement stepped up to the plate and hit a home run.

"I was six years old," remembered my uncle Chick, "before I realized that my sister Helena *wasn't* my *mother*! She took me everywhere," Chick went on. "If I was good, she gave me prizes. If I was bad, she gave me hell. She was a perfect mother even though she was only my sister!"

Funny and wonderful. Nothing would have made my mother prouder than hearing those words from her little brother (or should I say son?) Nothing could have made *me* prouder either.

Thank you, Uncle Chick, and thank you, Ma.

Christmas Eve

During World War II, one of my mother's younger brothers (Jimmy) was in the Coast Guard and was stationed in the Philippines. Today, he is convinced that he was there to support the invasion of Japan, which would have killed him and thousands of other American soldiers and sailors had the atomic bomb not been dropped before the invasion was necessary.

One Saturday night, while on shore leave, Uncle Jim met a machinist who was working on army transports that were clustering in the Philippines before the rumored invasion of Japan.

When the machinist asked where my uncle was from, he replied, "Quincy Point, Massachusetts," and the machinist replied, "There is another guy from Quincy on one of those ships in the harbor."

Hearing this, my uncle immediately "commandeered" (a.k.a. stole!) a small Coast Guard boat and used it to find the guy from

Quincy on one of the larger crafts in the harbor. Who *was* "that guy"? Yes, he was my father: Luigi!

Coincidently and amazingly, my dad was also in the Philippines to prepare army freighters and troop carriers for what he was also sure would be an attack on Japan.

My dad and my uncle drank (and drank!) together during that Christmas Eve of 1943, and they started a tradition that has lived to this day.

On that Christmas Eve and thanks to that tradition, my Uncle Jim and my dad became the best and oldest friends in our family! They had a drink from that first Christmas Eve in the Philippines until Dad died in 2008. Yes, no matter where they were, my dad and my uncle had a drink every Christmas Eve *for sixty-five years!*

In 2009 (the year my dad died), we kept that tradition alive when I visited my uncle at his home in Quincy and had a drink with him in my father's memory.

My uncle Jim is ninety-five years old, and I am seventy-three. We have never missed a drink on Christmas Eve since my father died, and Dad had never missed one with Uncle Jim while Dad was alive!

After our toast last Christmas, someone at the party asked Uncle Jim and me what we will do when one of us dies. My uncle looked at me and said, "Well, Carmen, I will just have to find someone to replace you!"

Somehow, I am sure he is not kidding!

Nonna Lucia

I am also sure that Nonna Lucia is in heaven *praying* that my uncle Jim and I will *never die* and that our faith, family, strength, and stories will continue. That is how I remember my Nonna Lucia. She was always praying...and praying...and praying.

And when she wasn't praying, she was giving! Her giving reminded me of another story about another special "giver" just like Nonna!

Special Sandwiches

On one Saturday morning, my wife, DeeDee, her best friend, Lorna,
and Lorna's mother spent some time making sandwiches. When they
finished, they wrapped the sandwiches in wax paper and bundled
them in brown lunch bags.

Then Lorna's mom asked Lorna and Dee for a ride to the park
near her house. When they arrived, Lorna's mom took all the sandwiches out of the car and began distributing them among the many
trash barrels that were peppered throughout the park.

"Why would you do that?" asked Lorna of her mom. "These are
fresh, clean, nice expensive sandwiches! Why would you put them in
the trash?"

Lorna's mom, of course, had an answer!

"Lots of homeless people visit this park every day," Lorna's mom
explained. "They are all hungry, but many of them are too proud to
beg for money or food. Instead, they grovel for scraps from those
barrels. Today when they grovel, they will find the sandwiches you
made, and they will have a nice lunch instead of scraps."

Lorna's mom would have loved Nonna Lucia, and Nonna Lucia
would he loved Nonna's mom!

Caviar

Have you seen the movie *You've Got Mail?*

It came out years ago. It's the one where Tom Hanks and Meg
Ryan both own book stores near each other and fight for the biggest
piece of the neighborhood's business.

By the movie's end, Tom and Meg fall in love, but in a scene
before that, the two of them end up at a cocktail party, where Meg
scolds Tom for scraping as much caviar from a plate full of crackers
as he can!

"Don't be so greedy!" Meg admonishes Tom.

"But I like caviar!" Tom retorts.

"Everybody likes caviar!" replies Meg. "But that gives you no
right to hog it all for yourself!"

My Nonna Lucia was like caviar! Everyone loved her, so everyone (her children, sisters, family, friends, neighbors, priests, and more!) fought over some time with her. Even Tadone Raphalle had to compete for his wife's time and attention!

16 Blocks

I watched a fascinating movie while working out one afternoon. It is called *16 Blocks* and stars Bruce Willis. Bruce plays an alcoholic cop who must bring an informant to a grand jury that is "holding court" *sixteen blocks* from the cell that holds the informant. Six dirty cops (one whom Bruce's informant plans to inform on!) go to *many* lengths to keep those sixteen blocks from being traveled.

Along the way, Bruce's informant (named Eddie) is wounded by a policeman's bullet. Undaunted, Bruce carries Eddie toward the courthouse.

Eddie loses consciousness. Bruce shakes him awake. "You're not dying on me, are you?" asked Bruce.

"I don't know," replies Eddie. "I never died before, so I don't know what it feels like."

All of us are like Eddie. We have never died before, so we don't know what dying feels like. But we *do* know what *living* feels like. To truly live, we must give. We must care. We must share.

That is how my Nonna Lucia lived, and that is why she was so loved. Why did people love Nonna so much? Because she loved them even more! Try this!

Nonna's Words and Wonder

Earlier, we talked about words of wonder. We said they are words we use as if we know what they mean even though we don't always know! They are words like *faith, family, friends, feelings, home, love, beauty, strength, sacrifice, success, responsibility, relentless,* and *more.*

We have said that those words are popular. We use them a lot. In fact, those words can be *too* popular!

Sometimes we use them so much, they lose their power. They lose their…wonder!

Now for just a minute, pretend you have never heard any of those words before. Picture a mother, a wife, and a friend, whose love was so full of *beauty, strength, success, sacrifice, wonder,* and *more* than those words felt fresh and new in your mouth as you spoke them.

Extravagant, Extreme, and Extraordinary

Are you picturing? Congratulations. Now you have some idea of how it felt to be loved by my Nonna Lucia. You have some idea of "A Mother's Love" as it was found and felt by her family and friends.

In Jeff Smith's *The World Among Us*, God's love is referred to as "extravagant, extreme, and unbounded."[1] My Nonna Lucia's love was all those things.

She loved beyond her means. That made her love extravagant.

She loved beyond her limits. That made her love extreme.

She loved beyond her bounds. That made her love unbounded. My Nonna Lucia loved and loved and loved.

She gave and gave and gave. What is more, she taught *my mother* how to love and how to give like Nonna did!

One of the things Nonna taught my mother to give was a smile. My mother gave lots of people lots of smiles. Some of those people spent their winters in Florida!

My parents spent lots of time in Florida after they retired. While there, they lived in a large apartment complex. Quarters were close in the complex, so the neighbors annoyed each other from time to time!

Once, a neighbor was especially upset with an elderly gentleman who kept his motorized wheelchair parked outside on his rented front lawn within sight of the upset neighbor.

"Why can't he take it inside?" the upset neighbor would ask while having a drink with my mother on her deck. "He is ruining my view. He is violating his lease!"

Through it all, Ma would just smile, nod her head, and say nothing. Finally one night, the complainer snapped and really yelled at my mother. "Don't you have anything to say about that god-damned wheelchair?"

Ma paused for a moment, looked down at her healthy legs, and said, "Yes dear, I do. I thank God it's not *mine*!"

I thanked God *with* my mother—and *for* my mother many times and for many smiles.

Some people spend their lives on themselves. My mother never did.

She was too much like *her* mother to do that. Nonna Lucia never said no to a neighbor, a friend, or a member of her family. If they needed a place to stay, Nonna found them one.

If they needed a meal to eat, Nonna cooked them one. (Yes, Nonna Lucia did teach my mother how to love, give, *and* cook!)

She found room in her home and her heart for anyone her children brought through the door.

To Nonna, when it came to her friends and family, "Her answer was yes, no matter what their question!"

Everyone who *stayed* with Nonna *ate* with Nonna. They ate with her children too! In Nonna Lucia's, house, food was a language. It added love and laughter, warmth and welcome to her kitchen like no words ever could. "Always leave something for our company to eat," Nonna would say to her own family.

Her children never disobeyed that order. If a guest was at their table, Nonna's children would never take the last piece of *anything*!

Instead, they would leave it for the guest.

Our Daily Bread

Whether there were cupcakes for dessert, doughnuts for breakfast, or hamburgers for lunch, no one in Nonna's family would take a whole one or the last one! Instead, they would break one in half, eat that half, then break another.

When only halves were left, they would begin breaking those halves into quarters, and so on until they were only sixteenths! Then (you guessed it!) they would *eat the sixteenths*!

Nonna was always watching, and they knew she wanted something to be left over for their company, even if were only one-sixteenth of a doughnut!

That story reminds me of the Our Father. That prayer contains a line that asks God to "give *us*…this day…*our* daily bread." The line does not ask God for *my* daily bread or *your* daily bread. It asks for *our* daily bread.

Yes, the *only* prayer Jesus *taught* is not for *any* of us. It is for *all* of us. It is a prayer of the community. It is a prayer of *unity*.

My Nonna Lucia said that prayer and lived that prayer every day.

Math Class

Some time ago, a nun I met told me about some elementary school students in Haiti. Their school had been destroyed in an earthquake, so they went to class outside, in a dried-up riverbed.

Their teacher, who is a US missionary, chose that spot because the bed was full of smooth, small stones left by the river's water before it disappeared.

Since the children had no desks, they had to sit and study on the ground and the smooth stones offered more comfort and cleanliness than soil would.

One day, the teacher was conducting a lesson on addition and subtraction.

She picked nine stones from the riverbed and gave one to each student.

As she did, she kept track of how many stones were left in her hand. ("Nine minus one equal eight, etc.") Finally, she looked into her empty hand (the one from which she had been taking the stones) and said, "Oh, look! I gave you all my stones and now have none left for myself."

A moment after their teacher said that, every one of her young students took their stone from their hand and offered it back to the teacher.

"God bless them," the teacher said to me much later.

"They could each have simply taken another stone from the riverbed because there were hundreds still there. Instead, they offered me *their* stone."

Those children could have been my Nonna's children. They were given the same gift. They were given the gift of giving.

Mother Teresa

Mother Teresa once told the story of a man who came to one of her missions in India and said, "There is a family with many children living nearby. They have not eaten for days." Hearing that, Mother Teresa took some rice and went to feed those children.

When she reached their tent, she saw how hungry they were. Mother Teresa gave some rice to the children's mother and expected her to start feeding it to her young family right away. She did not.

Instead, the children's mother got a bowl and put half of the rice in it. Then she disappeared behind the tent.

The mother came back minutes later with an empty bowl.

"Where did you take that rice?" Mother Teresa asked.

"To my neighbor," she said

"Why?" asked Teresa.

"Because *her* children are as hungry as mine," replied the mother.

If that Indian mother was Italian, she could have been my Nonna Lucia. No matter how many mouths she had to feed, she always found more food. Then she found more mouths!

She gave and gave and gave.

Our Future President

When Calvin Coolidge was campaigning to be our country's president, a wealthy family attended a high-powered fundraiser being held in honor of Mr. Coolidge. After they came through a receiving line to meet the future president and leave him a check, the father of that rich family turned to his teenage daughter and asked what she thought of this man who would hold the highest title in the land.

"I really like him!" the daughter replied.

"Why?" asked the dad.

"Well," replied the daughter, "yesterday, I cut my finger on a knife in our kitchen, so I put a Band-Aid on it. Later, when I held out my hand for the president to shake, he noticed the Band-Aid and asked what happened and how I was doing. Anyone who cared that much deserves to be president!"

My Nonna Lucia could have been president. She cared that much for *everybody's finger!*

I read a story in *Reader's Digest* years ago about a prospective father-in-law who challenged his daughter's fiancé like this: "Young man, are you able to support a family?"

The surprised groom-to-be replied, "Well, no, I am just planning to support your daughter. The rest of you will have to fend for yourselves!"

Nonna Lucia did not think like that bridegroom! She supported a lot of families, and her own was only one of them!

Not So Poor

Ronald Reagan once told this story about his childhood.

"We were poor," the president began. "We lived in a small town in Illinois. I think the difference between then and today is that the government didn't keep coming around telling us we were poor, so we didn't know it! Also, my mother was always finding friends who had less money than we did and helping them," continued the president. "That made us feel pretty rich! Come to think of it," ended President Regan, "my mother changed how we looked at being poor!"

Nonna Lucia was like Mrs. Regan. She kept finding (and making!) friends who were poorer than her family and helping them, so her family felt rich!

And Nonna Lucia's family really *was rich* because it *had* Nonna Lucia!

As I mentioned a dozen or so pages ago, my Nonna had a husband and sixteen children, and she cooked for all of them every day. Think about that! My grandmother fed eleven men and more than half that many women every day—three times a day!

As Nonna's middle child, my mother had lots to do. While her oldest sisters were at work and her other sisters were cleaning the house, my mom helped Nonna cook.

Even with help, it was no small task! The family ate at two different tables, in three different shifts for every meal.

"We were like a restaurant!" remembered my mother. "It reminded me of the Navy, only with better cooks!" recalled Uncle Chick.

My Nonna Lucia gave new meaning to the Italian saying, "La mia casa e la tua casa." Her house was truly everyone's house!

It did not have enough bedrooms, bathrooms, or kitchens, but Nonna never sent a friend away, no matter how little room she had or how long the visitor needed to stay.

My aunt Mary was the oldest of the sixteen children and had friends from work stay over "the house" all the time.

One of Aunt Mary's friends stayed for so long, her mother started mailing my Nonna rent checks!

"I thought my mother had *adopted* Mary's friend," said my aunt Gloria. "Our family just kept getting bigger!"

Nonna Lucia didn't just bring people into her *house*. She brought people into her *family*. She knew of their strengths and sacrifices. She knew of their wants and weaknesses.

FDR's Funeral

Actually, FDR's funeral was more like a motorcade.

His casket was placed on a huge locomotive, covered with American flags, and sent on a journey from coast to coast so that every American citizen could pay their respects by lining the rails in the president's honor.

There is a story about that event. It seems that while a newspaper reporter waited for the locomotive at a station in the Midwest, he noticed an old man standing in front of him whose eyes were welling up with tears.

Eventually, according to the story that old man actually began to cry even before FDR's locomotive ever reached the station!

"Excuse me, sir," offered the reporter to the man, "I can't help but notice that you are crying. You must be taking Mr. Roosevelt's death very hard. Did you know him?"

The old man looked down, shook his head, and replied, "No, I didn't know him, but *he* knew *me*."

This story and its ending remind me of the one I told you some pages ago about Calvin Coolidge and his attention to a little girl's injured finger while the president was on the campaign trail.

FDR, Mr. Coolidge, and Nonna knew everybody!

Not everyone who stayed in Nonna Lucia's house knew her, but she knew them *all*.

A Special House

Some years ago, DeeDee and I visited a home for unwed homeless mothers called "Friends of the Unborn." Fifteen pregnant mothers live there from the time they conceive until their baby is one year old.

These young mothers have no husband and no home. They cannot afford to buy food, pay bills, own a car, or pay for day care. Everything they cook and eat is donated. They spend their time caring for their babies, studying for classes, and praying for a better future.

They are special young women, living in a special old house. "When we are not worrying about the health of the babies and the care of their young mothers, we worry about the roof and the oil burner!" said the director to Dee and me during our visit. "If those two things are working, we worry about something else. Today, it is the dishwasher!"

At Thanksgiving, the girls ate what others gave them, as they always do. When they finished, "their cups runneth over." Lots of food was left uneaten.

"We should give it to our neighbors," said one of the young mothers to the others. Since the home is in a residential neighborhood of Quincy, there were lots of candidates.

The girls picked two elderly women who lived across the street from the home. They made gift baskets and baked pastries and then delivered their gifts to the old women as if they were in more need than the young mothers were.

Last year, they had been given more frozen turkeys than they could store in their freezer, so they gave some to another homeless shelter down the street! That is right; these young women have nothing but their babies and still somehow found a way to give much more than they had to people they thought had less.

When the mothers heard of a hurricane in Florida that devastated so many families, they collected some of the baby supplies that had been donated to them and sent them to the young victims of the storm.

They each had hands that were empty before they gave. Still, they found something in those hands to give.

That is what my Nonna Lucia did and taught us to do. God bless her, and God bless those young mothers.

Another Special House

Feeding all the mouths my Nonna did was never easy. Once, my uncle Pop, the oldest boy, remembered how tough things got during the depression.

"My father kept making more kids and making less money!" lamented my uncle.

"But he would never ask for help. He just made my two older sisters get more jobs and told my mother to put more water in the soup for supper! He also told my mother to stay away from the welfare office!" continued Uncle Pop.

"I will always find a way to take care of us," my Tadone Raffaele would promise his family. "As long as *we* have a *garden* and our *neighbor* has a *cow*, we'll be okay!"

During many strikes at the shipyard, lines of unemployed shipbuilders would form in front of my grandparents' house.

They were all friends of my grandfather and, because he was a foreman, came to ask him if he could find them a job. They also came because my Nonna always *fed* them while they waited in line to talk with my grandfather!

You would think that having so many family members and friends might dilute the love Nonna Lucia and Tadone Raffaele felt for each one of them. Not so!

Nonna and Tadone had twelve children before they lost one. Jenny, the little twin girl who almost got left behind by the doctor who was supposed to deliver her, died shortly after she was born.

Jenny was an infant, and my Nonna did already have twelve children. Still, she and my grandfather were devastated by their baby's death.

"It was amazing," reflected my aunt Gloria, "that after celebrating the birth of so many children, my parents still mourned Jenny's loss as much as they did. It was as if she was their only child," continued my aunt. "But that was how they treated us all. To my parents, we were sixteen families with one child in each family instead of the other way around. Imagine my parents' love."

That reminded me of something a priest once said to me about the crucifixion. "Christ suffered and died to redeem *all* of us," said that priest. "And he would have done the same thing to redeem *any* of us."

That is right. Our Lord would have suffered every part and every pain of his passion to redeem any person he ever loved, and God loved every person he ever made!

Imagine God's love. Imagine my Tadone's love. Imagine my Nonna's love.

Family Grave

Before my little aunt Jenny could be buried, Tadone Raffaele had to find a gravesite for her. Eventually, he bought one in Quincy's Mount Wollaston Cemetery.

The site is a big one, but not big enough for Tadone's and (especially) Nonna's needs.

It seems that much of the site was taken by Nonna Lucia's distant relatives, neighbors, or friends who came by Nonna's house for coffee or saw her after Mass on Sunday and said, "Luci, please help me! Some people I know in my family or neighborhood just died, and I need a place to bury them!"

Nonna, of course, never said no!

Nonna's Glass

Nonna Lucia never said no to anyone about anything. She welcomed anyone who was alive into her house, and she welcomed anyone who was dead into her cemetery plot!

When my Tadone Raffaele died, the family site was so full of Nonna's relatives, neighbors, and friends there was no room left for Tadone!

Yes, Nonna gave more than she had, and the more she gave, the more she had! Her glass was never half empty or half full.

It was always very full. It was always *completely* full!

Just be Happy!

A friend of mine has a son who played hockey in high school. "He played well but could have been much better if he worked harder," said my friend in his son's presence.

"When he really tried, he was a star," my friend continued. "One night, he played so well he was even named Player of the Game by his coach!"

Then my friend turned to his son and announced, "You could have won that award after every game if you had only tried harder."

"Dad," asked the son as he listened to his dad, "why don't you just be happy that I won it on *that* night?"

That story made me think of my Nonna Lucia's full glass. It also made me think of our first dog. She, like the other three, was a little poodle. They were all named after cereals: Maypo, Wheatie, and CheeRio. (The next one will be Honey Bunch!). For years, DeeDee and I left Maypo alone every day, all day, because we both worked.

Still, when we got home too many hours later, Maypo celebrated! She wagged her tail. She licked our faces. She welcomed us home!

That little dog did not resent the time we spent away. She did not scold us for our absence. Instead, she celebrated our return.

Her glass was never half empty or half full.

It was always *very* full. It was always completely full, just like my Nonna's!

Nonna's Embrace

I once read a book written by a priest with cancer. In it, he compared our relationship with God to that of an infant and its mother. "Watch the infant in the presence of its mother," the priest wrote. "It reaches out for her. It stretches its little arms and body in the hope of embracing the mother."

But it can't. Its arms are too short. Its body is too small. Try as it will, the infant cannot embrace its mother.

But that is all right because the infant does not have to.

Why? Because the *mother* embraces the *infant*!

The minute the mother realizes that the infant wants to be embraced, the mother *creates* the embrace for them both! So it is with us and God. We cannot embrace God, but we don't have to because God embraces us!

My Nonna Lucia found a way to make all her relatives and visitors *feel embraced*! She even reached out to all her living relatives in Italy and found a way to make them feel embraced from Quincy!

And my Nonna was not alone! Many young Italian men and women immigrated to the United States. They did not want to leave their homes, but they and their families were just too poor to stay.

Many young fathers and mothers could not find jobs in Italy that would pay enough to feed their children. So they moved to America and "embraced" their hungry families from thousands of miles away!

Truth be told, rather than watch their children starve, young Italian fathers would even scrape the plaster from their bedroom walls and add it to the flour their desperate young wives used to make pasta.

My sister Natalie once wrote an article for a magazine about that kind of starvation being faced by African tribes while the people of America enjoyed wealth and comfort. That was Africa. It was also Italy.

As you know well by now, Natalie is a doctor. No, not a doctor of education like I am. As my mother always said, "Natalie is the *real* doctor in the family. She is a doctor of medicine!"

So Natalie has always been concerned about the well-being of people, especially children.

Nat's article expressed that concern. It went like this:

The Cost of Eating Less

One Sunday morning, I turned the page of the Boston Globe and found myself staring at an emaciated child in Rhodesia eating the bark of a tree. The caption told of how thousands of starving children in African forests are scavenging for food like wild animals.

My eyes could not stay focused on the image and darted quickly to the opposite page. That page held a full-page advertisement for a health club. It beckoned the reader to spend hundreds of dollars for the opportunity to burn unwanted calories and fat, using state-of-the-art equipment while enjoying air-conditioned comfort.

I *wondered* what the Rhodesian child's mother would think about people who pay money to burn unneeded calories, while her baby eats bark off a tree...

Natalie Mariano, MD

Again, that was Africa. Again, it was also Italy.

While many young men were leaving Europe for America in search of *freedom,* many young men were leaving Italy in search of *food*...for their families.

Often, the young men of Italy went to America alone, leaving their families behind. These decisions were more than difficult.

They were painful. They were pathetic.

Think about it. These men were forced to choose between watching their children starve in Italy and spending years away from those children so they could make money for food in America.

While their husbands were away, their young wives were so haunted by their absence they faithfully set an empty place at the dinner table every night.

Special Stories

There are many special stories *about* Italians but *not limited* to Italians! You know that well, dear readers, because *your own family*, Italian or otherwise, has told *their own stories*! They have made their own mark, hewed their own history, and molded their own memories *with* such stories.

As I have said many times on many pages, this conversation and its stories are *ours*, not mine. None of us own them. *All* of us *share* them.

Their Families' Eyes

The family remains the center of our country's universe and the apple of our country's eye. In fact, every American parent I know has spent their life looking at the world *through the eyes* of their family!

Those eyes are important! Why? Because the eyes through which we look at the world *change that world*!

Maypo's Walk?

As I recently said, DeeDee and I have had three poodles, and a fourth "is on the way!"

One was fourteen years old when she died. Her name was Maypo.

For all of Maypo's fourteen years, every night when DeeDee came home from work, she put a leash on Maypo and took her for a walk.

One day, DeeDee took Maypo outside and put the leash on her but left her in the front yard for a minute while DeeDee took some bundles from her car.

When DeeDee finished unloading the bundles, she went to get Maypo in the front yard. But Maypo was gone. DeeDee called for Maypo and searched the yard but found no Maypo.

Holding back her tears, DeeDee ran up the street and around a corner. DeeDee found Maypo three blocks away. Maypo was walking on the sidewalk, dragging her leash behind her. She was following the exact route she and DeeDee followed every night. Maypo had simply started her walk (leash and all!) without DeeDee!

Until that day, whenever I saw Maypo on her leash and DeeDee walking behind her, I saw *DeeDee* walking *Maypo*.

But *since* that day, when I saw *the same thing*, I *saw Maypo walking DeeDee*! Yes, how I looked at DeeDee and Maypo changed, so what I saw them doing changed. My eyes changed, so my world changed.

Candy Canes?

You have all heard the story (true or otherwise!) of a candymaker in Indiana who wanted to make a Christmas candy in honor of Jesus Christ. He began with a stick of white hard candy to symbolize the sinless nature of Jesus. Thinking the candy was somewhat plain, the candy man decorated it with red stripes, to symbolize the blood Christ shed on the cross.

The candymaker made the candy in the form of a "J" to represent the name of Jesus. To the candymaker's dismay, his "J" was never seen by the people who bought his candy. Instead, people saw a cane—*a candy cane*!

Instead of symbolizing Christ, the candy cane became a very *popular* but *meaningless* Christmas decoration. All because of the way *people looked* at the man's candy!

The man *made* a "J." But people *saw* a cane. And the candy *became* what the *people saw*! Their eyes changed, so their world changed.

Great story, true or otherwise!

Lucky Not to Care?

My father and I visited my mother's grave soon after she died. As we walked through the cemetery, I commented on the terrible shape its roads were in. "You would think the city would fill in all these potholes," I lamented.

"Why should they?" kidded my dad. "There is no one lying dead in this place who can vote, complain, or even care!"

Speaking of caring, I have another question for you!

Another Question

What is the first thing that any mother wants to do when she feels cold?

Yes! She wants to put *sweaters on her children*, not on herself but her children. And every parent reading this would do that same thing if every child of theirs would let them!

"Parents are only as happy as their saddest child." Those words, once again, came to me from the smartest woman I have ever known (guess who!), and they are true!

Why? Because parents care. In fact, they care, and care, and care. As I said, every parent sees the world through the eyes of their family, and when their eyes change, their world changes.

The Changing Room

Once, my Natalie (The "Real Doctor!") became a patient. She needed some tests and had to go into the hospital to get them. Natalie wrote an article for the *Journal of the American Medical Association* about her time in the hospital. She called it *The Changing Room*.

In her article, Nat explains that when she arrived at the hospital to be admitted, she went into a little room to change out of her lab coat, stethoscope, and "doctor's clothes" into a johnny, a plastic bracelet, and paper slippers. "I changed more than my clothes in that room," Nat wrote. "I changed from a doctor to a patient, and I never forgot how different the world looked through my eyes when

I changed. Seeing the world through the eyes of a patient," Nat finished, "made me a much better doctor."

It seems that parents can be like doctors. Seeing the world through different eyes can be good for them all.

Anthony's Hat

A mother was walking with her young son on the beach one summer morning when, suddenly, a huge wave washed onto shore and pulled the little boy out to sea.

The mother lost sight of the boy immediately and began to cry. She then fell to her knees and prayed, "Dear God, please bring my little Anthony back to me. If you do, I promise to be forever grateful."

A few minutes later, another enormous wave crashed on the shore. When it ebbed, it left little Anthony behind in the sand. The mother leaped from her knees and bounded toward the boy—they embraced for a long time with the mother squealing, "Oh, Anthony! Anthony! You are back! You are back! Thank you, God! Thank you, God!"

Then she paused, stepped away from the boy, and examined him to be sure he was *all right*.

Next, she fell back to her knees, looked to heaven, and said, "Dear Lord, I hate to bother you again, but when little Anthony left me, he was wearing a hat!"

Anthony's hat helped his mother see the world through Anthony's eyes, and that was good for Anthony *and* his mother!

More Sand

A little girl's grandfather got sick and was rushed to the hospital. By the time the little girl arrived, her grandpa was in the emergency room, unconscious and being prepared for heart surgery.

"Will he be okay?" the girl asked her grandpa's heart surgeon. "If he stays alive overnight," replied the surgeon, "he has a good chance. Just pray that God will give your grandpa enough time to get his heart rate back to normal."

When the girl looked at her grandpa lying next to her, she noticed something on his nightstand. It was an hourglass. The last time she had seen it was in her grandpa's house. One of her parents must have brought it to the hospital to keep her grandpa company.

She immediately asked her mother to drive her home.

When she got there, she visited her sandbox in the backyard. She filled a bag with the box's sand and turned to her mom.

"Mom, could you bring this back to Grandpa as soon as you can? The nurse said he needs time. We don't have any time, so we'll have to give him some sand instead."

None of us have enough time. We'll have to pray that God will give us something else instead. We'll have to pray that God will give us something *more* instead.

Yes, all parents want *more* for their children. My parents were no different. The parents reading this book and having this "conversation" are no different either.

Family is truly is a word of wonder. We have told many stories proving that! Those stories speak of the value of any family, the strength of every family, the sacrifices of many families, the blessings of my family, the burdens of other families, the sadness of countless families, and more!

We now will leave *family* and *find friends*!

Friends

Friends are the family we get to choose.

Friends are also the family we get to *change*!

Remember, we do not often choose our family, but we *do* choose our friends. Thus, if we stop liking our friends, who can we blame? I guess we should blame ourselves, right?

Then again, why blame anyone? Instead, why not *keep liking* our friends? When it comes to our friends, why not decide that "failure is not an option!"

Why not decide that (in the words of the one-million-plus greeting cards in print throughout the world) *friends are forever*!

When it comes to making friends, we should have two rules. They remind me of the "menu" that my father used to keep on the wall near our kitchen table. That menu looked like this:

Menu
1. Take it.
2. Leave it.

And my friendship rules would look like these:

Friendship Rules
1. Make friends.
2. Keep friends.

Would those rules work? Well, they have for our high school girls' basketball team!

Our girls' basketball program is very successful. Our players, of course, deserve much of the credit, as do their parents.

Their coach is very understated about the part he plays in the team's success, but he deserves lots of praise, as well.

He turns good athletes into outstanding players and outstanding players into a superior team. This very special man also turns teammates into friends and friends into families.

What is more, he does that in life as well as he does it on the court!

"Examples?" you ask. Consider this.

The coach, myself, our wives, and some parents were having an off-season party on the pool deck behind my house when the coach complimented Dee and me on how much he enjoyed the views, vistas, climate, and comfort of the setting we shared.

"I just put in a new patio," the coach related. Your deck looks new as well. Ours came out really nice," he continued, "but it is a little different from yours."

"How so?" I asked.

"Well, the size and shape are similar," the coach explained. "But the location is different."

"Where did you build yours?" I asked.

"In my front yard!" replied the coach.

"Why did you do that?" I asked, unable to keep my surprise from my voice.

"We wanted to get closer to our neighbors," the coach explained, and we just thought having the patio *in front* of the house would encourage families on the street to come over and visit more than they would if the deck was *out back*!"

Thanks to that coach and his patio, friendship rule number 1 was done!

He and his patio *made friends*!

Take it from that coach. Friends don't have to share the same family to share the same feelings. They don't have to share the same lineage to share the same love.

All that makes *friend* another word of wonder! We call lots of people "our friends" without really defining the word just like we consider lots of people "our family" without ever checking their bloodlines or inspecting their birth certificates!

So what *are friends* and *family* and how do they differ?

We...wonder!

Some friends are even closer to us than "official" family members!

That makes comparing friends to such members far from reliable and close to impossible! Have you ever tried to measure the "distance" between you and any friend? How did that distance compare to the one between you and your closest family member?

Who is closer? Do you...wonder?

We all have friends who make us laugh more or cry less than some family members do. We also have friends who are easier to be with and harder to be without than many of our family!

In the end, many of our brothers, sisters, and cousins are ambidextrous! They are "great family," *and* they make great friends. Now and then, we even can name a true friend who is *not* a member of our family!

Friend or Father?

One day, a little girl strode proudly through her backyard, baseball cap in place, toting her ball and bat. After a minute, she took her batting stance.

Then she tossed the ball in the air, swung, and missed. Undaunted, she picked up the ball, threw it into the air, and missed again.

She swung at the ball again, and again, she missed. She paused a moment to examine the bat and ball carefully. Then once again, she threw the ball into the air. She swung hard and again missed the ball.

Just then, the little girl's father, who had been observing the entire scene, walked by and addressed his daughter.

"Wow," the dad exclaimed. "What a *great pitcher* you are!"

That father was his little girl's friend. He was also her family.

You know people who are both. You love people who are both.

What do some of my real-life family and friends look like?

I will answer with more stories!

Good Kid, Good Friend

He was eighteen or so and was an athlete for sure. He might have played for a high school or a college. Then again, he might not have played a sport at all.

I met him at a rink, so if he played a sport, I might guess it was hockey. Then again, I couldn't be sure because he was in a wheelchair.

He was leaving the rink's men's room as I approached. I watched with interest and respect. His work was not easy. The men's room door he used was oversized, ironically to accommodate people with challenges like his, and his wheelchair was more of a burden than a benefit for the chore he faced.

He used one hand to push the door open while the other pushed one of the chair's wheels forward. Four or five maneuvers later, he and his chair had cleared the door enough for him to look up and see me coming toward him.

When he did, he spun the chair around and pointed it back toward the men's room. He then spun on both wheels and forced his chair back into the door.

It was all painfully slow and difficult but effective.

By the time I reached the door, he had opened it for me and had positioned himself flush enough to the door for me to walk by him and his chair.

I tried to catch him in the middle of his effort and tell him I could do it myself, but he dauntlessly waved me off and said, "Oh no. This is a heavy door! I want to help!"

I made a good friend that day. I never saw him or his wheelchair before or since and still don't know his name, but he had to be my friend. Who *but a friend* would have done as much as he did for me?

Anne Marie

Before I tell you about my friend Anne Marie, let's begin by agreeing that "life is not fair, but God is." It's true. God gives us chances to choose. Those choices have consequences. That is fair. God is fair.

Life is different. Life does not always give us choices. Sometimes life gives us sadness, smiles, freedom, or failure, whether we choose any of those things or not. Again, life is not fair.

If you don't believe me, just picture an inspirational, charismatic, uplifting, magnificent, and magnetic woman lying in a coffin at fifty-four years old.

She should still be alive making people laugh, love, learn, and lift. Instead, because of brain cancer, her smile will never light up a room again, and her star will never light up the sky again.

Much of that is not fair. Much of life is not fair.

What stories can I tell you about this woman and this friend? For starters, you should know that her name was Anne Marie, and she was a principal, first of an elementary school and last of a middle school. She was good at being both. In fact, she was *much* better than good at being both!

Neither job was easy, but Anne Marie made them both look that way.

In fact, when it comes to kids, *nothing* is easy, especially when those kids are in middle school! Middle school kids remind me a lot of one of Harry Truman's best quotes:

> I have found that the best way to give advice
> to your children is to find out what they want to
> do and *advise* them to *do* it!

Middle school kids *will do* what you want them to but only if they *want* to! The kids in Anne Marie's middle school were no different!

They were a constant challenge; but not to Anne Marie!

She had fun making those thirteen-year-olds obey her. Impossible? Absolutely! Accomplished? Absolutely…by Anne Marie!

"Carmen, you promised us stories!" you say. You are right! So stories, here we come!

I lived some of those stories with Anne Marie. Other stories came to me thanks to Anne Marie's many friends. Especially Kathy and Marcia. I offer my thanks to them all!

June Is Tough

The month of June is always tough in any school. Kids can see the summer coming. They can hear it. They can smell it. They can even taste it! All that doesn't leave much of their senses left for school!

In June, kids come to school more undressed than dressed! The boys wear shorts, T-shirts, and sneakers—little else. The girls just wear little—no else!

On one June day, a televised weather forecast with the world's biggest, hottest sun painted on it brought Anne Marie to her school's auditorium with all her teenage girls.

As soon as her audience was settled, "AMZ" mounted the stage, took the mike, and greeted everyone.

Her words were short and hilarious.

How Do I Look?

"Ladies, with the hot weather upon us, I thought I should remind you of our dress code here at Broad Meadows Middle School. It is very simple. No matter what the weather is like and no matter what your wardrobe is like, our code goes like this. Every morning for the rest of the school year, each of you will open your closet door, take out the outfit you plan to wear that day, hold it up to a mirror, and look at that outfit for a long time. Then after that long look, you will close your eyes and picture me, Mrs. Zukauskas, wearing it. Yes, I mean you will picture me, your 190-pound principal, wearing that outfit!

"Now, ladies, be sure you understand. When you take that outfit out of your closet, you will be *planning* to wear it, but before you actually *do* wear it, you will *picture me* wearing it! Then ask yourself this question, "How will my outfit look on my principal?' and 'How will my principal look in my outfit?' If you are not absolutely sure that your outfit will look perfect on me and that I will look perfect in it, *do not wear that outfit*! Do you understand that ladies?" continued Anne Marie. "Good, then I will see you tomorrow."

The Belly Button

Most of Anne Marie's girls got her message after that assembly. Still, a few didn't. One "fashion plate" in particular needed additional reinforcement!

Two days before school was dismissed for the summer, this future model came to school in a halter top, short shorts, and a bare belly button.

Ann Marie noticed her and her belly button in the corridor, promptly brought her into the office, and reminded her of the assembly just days before.

"She got nasty and complained about how hot it was," recalled Ann Marie, "so I called her mother. I told her that her daughter was underdressed and I needed Mom to come to school that afternoon and take her daughter home!

"When the mother challenged me over the phone," said Ann Marie, "I kind of knew where all this was going. The mother arrived just before dismissal," continued Ann Marie. "As she walked into my office, I saw how right I was. Guess what the mother was wearing? Yes! A halter top, short shorts, and a bare belly button!

"We have a rule about clothes in school," explained Anne Marie to the mother. "Our girls can only wear things to school that their principal would look good in…and *I am their principal!*"

That mother gazed at all 190 pounds of Anne Marie. Then she smiled and said, "I get it! No more belly buttons!"

Don't Be Too Great!

As you have begun to see, Anne Marie was very generous with her wonderful wit. It was not reserved for her students either. She was happy to share it with anyone, including yours truly, her assistant superintendent!

One night, for example, she invited me to speak at a PTO meeting on some new learning materials the school system had just purchased.

Anne Marie, much like my wife, DeeDee, was nervous about how long I would speak. So for safety's sake, before I began to address the audience, she pulled me aside and said, "Carmen, I know you will great tonight, but please don't be too great for too long!"

When I replied with a puzzled look, Anne Marie explained like this, "The cupcakes I brought for after the meeting are my favorites, and I don't want them all to be gone by the time you finish talking!"

Yes, my friend Anne Marie poured gifts of laughter and more on others but saved very little for herself.

No, life is not fair. Just ask anyone who knew and lost Anne Marie.

Paddy and Elly

Once upon a time, a monk was walking down a dirt road. After a while, he came upon a traveler walking on the same road in the other direction. The traveler was a young man, and he looked tired, dirty, hungry, and sad.

"Can I help you, my son?" asked the monk to the traveler.

"Yes, Padre, you can," replied the man.

"I have no money and need food for myself and my young family. Anything you could give would mean the world to us!"

With that, the monk opened his knapsack and reached for a loaf of bread, a block of cheese, and some dried meat. As he did, the traveler could not help but notice a beautiful diamond that sat in the monk's knapsack next to his provisions.

As the monk took the food from his knapsack, the young traveler could not take his eyes off the stone. Finally, he said, "Padre, I am ashamed to ask you, but if you could find it in your heart to give me that diamond, I could trade it for silver and use that silver to care for my family for the rest of our lives."

Without hesitation, the monk *gave* that traveler his diamond. The traveler thanked the monk and went on his way.

Three days later, the monk was walking along the *same* dirt road and came upon the *same* traveler in exactly the *same* place.

"My son," said the monk "I can't believe we meet again."

"I have been waiting for you, brother," said the traveler.

"Why?" asked the monk.

"I must give you back the precious stone you gave me," explained the traveler.

"Why?" asked the monk again.

"In the hope that you will give me something much more valuable in return," said the traveler.

"My son," replied the monk, "what could I, a poor monk, possibly give you that would be more valuable than that diamond?"

"Brother," said the young man, "please give me *whatever it is inside you that let you give me that stone in the first place.*"

That monk had a gift. He had the gift of giving.

So do my cousins Paddy (short for Patricia) and Elly. They are close to my age and have touched more young lives than I could ever hope to.

What is more, the education that Paddy and Elly have given has been special. Yes, they have given their lives to *special education*. Paddy and Elly are truly *special* educators, special cousins, and special *friends*!

For almost fifteen years, Paddy directed a school for brain-injured children. Her work was heartwarming. It was inspirational.

Elly inspires, as does Paddy. She does so in a more "traditional" classroom setting called *inclusion*.

Inclusion

Inclusion is a form of special education that draws rave reviews from most instructional circles. It allows schools to place students who have legally recognized special needs into "mainstreamed" (nonspecial ed) classrooms.

Lessons are planned together and delivered together. In Elly's words, "Inclusion at its best makes it impossible for a classroom visitor to identify who are the special ed students and who are the special ed teachers!

"One day early in the school year," Elly described, "I assigned our inclusion class their first novel. In the spirit of inclusion, of course, every student was given exactly the same novel. I told all the kids to buy the book over the weekend and bring it to school on Monday," Elly continued. "I also told them to be sure to put a cover on the book because it was a paperback and without a cover would disintegrate in a week.

"On Monday morning," said Elly, "the class came in with their books. All were covered but one. I approached the special needs student whose book was bare.

"'Where is your cover?' asked Elly. 'In my locker,' the student replied. 'Why isn't it on your book?' Elly persisted.

"'Because I want to take the book to the cafeteria at lunchtime today so all my friends can see that I am reading the same book they are,' replied the student. 'Then I will cover it. Please say I can do that,' ended the student.'"

Elly, of course, complied.

Yes, education faces many problems.

Inclusion just might be a solution to some of them.

Teachers as special as my cousins Paddy and Elly might be another.

My Cousin Vinnie

Paddy had an older brother named Vin. He lived in Hawaii and, before he died, battled a difficult form of cancer, coupled with Alzheimer's disease. On Mother's Day weekend of last year, Paddy endured the five-thousand-mile journey to visit Vin in the hospital. She heard things were not going well, and Pat wanted to "be there" with Vin, his wife, daughter, and four-year-old granddaughter.

"Of course, Vin was our top priority," remembered Pat, after returning home, "but his family needed me too." Pat never stopped giving and giving.

"I think I was a calming presence," Pat offered in what I am sure was a major understatement. "Plus," Pat went on, "we laughed and laughed…a lot! I think that helped too." (Another understatement, I am sure!)

Paddy stayed close to Vin and his family for almost five days. In that time, in Paddy's words, "He knew who I was but could not remember my name."

Weeks later, I asked Pat if she was sorry she made the trip. "Not at all," replied Pat. "I got to visit with him even though he didn't get to visit with me."

As Pat spoke, I remember my dad's visit to Uncle Ed (coming soon!), and I thanked God for the wonder of my family.

Blood or Not

A few years ago, on national television, a proud young woman told a story. It was about her father and her family.

"We only had one car," the woman began, "so sometimes my dad had to hitchhike and walk long stretches during the thirty-mile trip home from the shipyard where he worked. On one rainy night," the woman continued, "Dad was very late getting home, and my mom got worried. We piled into the car and went looking for him—and we eventually found Dad making his way along the side of a dark road.

"He was soaked and shivering in his shirtsleeves. When Dad got in the car, Mom asked if he'd left his coat at work. He explained he'd given it to a homeless man he'd met on the highway.

When we asked Dad why he did that, he turned to us and said, "When I left that man, I knew my family would be coming for me and would bring me whatever I needed to stay warm, so I was happy to help that man stay warm too."

Sounds a bit like that wounded soldier in Vietnam, doesn't it? He knew the medic would come just as this young woman's father knew his family would come.

The dad knew that if he acted like a *friend* to that homeless man, his *family* would act like a *friend* to him!

So genes or not, the dad did what a family member would do for their father!

Like the monk on the dirt road, families and friends *give*. That *makes* them family. That *makes* them *friends*.

Amazing Grace

Yes, that is the name of a song. It is also the name of a person who was for me another special cousin and another special friend.

What kind of person? You tell me. What pictures does the name *Grace* draw for you?

Soft? Silent? Sedate? Strong?

Not this Grace! This Grace was anything but those things! Instead, she was brash, bold, entertaining, and energetic! And yes, she was also *giving*. Just like Paddy and Elly were.

My cousin Grace was the daughter of my dad's sister Rose. Yes, in our family, *grace* and *rose* were two beautiful *words* and two beautiful *names*!

Similarities ended there. My aunt Rose said very little. My cousin Grace said very much, and what Grace said was a riot!

According to her daughter, among Grace's last words was this advice to that daughter, "Don't sniff Viagra. It will make your nose bigger than it already is!" If you asked her what happened to her first (of three) husbands, she would say, "He went out for a quart of milk and never came back. His name was Jack and 'Jack hit the road' without me having to tell him!"

Grace was anything but graceful! She was irreverent and funny. She earned people's attention, and she earned people's smiles. In many ways, Grace is a word (and person) of wonder. So it would be right for me to tell a story that helps give meaning to both.

Her granddaughter read the story at Grace's funeral.

You may well have heard it before. It is called *Footprints* and goes like this.

Footprints

One night, I had a dream. As I was walking along the beach with my Lord, across the dark sky flashed scenes from my life, for each scene, I noticed two sets of footprints in the sand, one belonging to me and one to my Lord.

After the last scene of my life flashed before me, I looked back at the footprints in the sand. I noticed that at many times along the path of my life, especially at the very lowest and saddest times, there was only one set of footprints.

This really troubled me, so I asked the Lord about it.

"Lord, you said once I decided to follow you, you'd walk with me all the way. But I noticed that during the saddest and most troublesome times of my life, there was only one set of footprints. I don't understand why when I needed You the most, you would leave me."

He whispered, "My precious child, I love you and will never leave you. Never, ever, during your trials and tests. When you saw only one set of footprints, it was then that *I carried you.*"

The grace of God is always with us. When we need his strength, his help, or his spirit, that grace picks us up and carries us through our trials and tests.

My friend and cousin Grace did that for many. She did it for me.

My friend and cousin Grace gave us grace! She walked with us when we needed her company, and she carried us when we needed her strength.

She gave us the gift of grace. She gave us the gift of *grace*!

More than Plays

Our drama program does more than produce plays.

It makes friends.

Years ago, I visited play practice. Eighty of our students were in our auditorium on a Thursday afternoon preparing for the next month's spring show.

"Let's start with a circle," said the teacher who gives the program its soul.

"Alex, take us through it."

With that, one of our seniors and most gifted actors lead his castmates through some stretching and breathing exercises, then the teacher said, "Good. Now before we think of the show, let's think of each other. Look at someone. Tell them something. Whisper it in their ear. Make what you tell them something that helps them get through this practice or through this day."

Somehow, the students did just that. They united. They bonded. They became one.

Days later, I was in the cafeteria with the other teacher (husband of the first) who makes our drama program happen. I told him how impressed I was with the circle.

"Yes," he said, "it's pretty special, and kids never forget it."

"Last week," he continued, "an alum of the program who graduated *six years ago* walked into the auditorium just as the circle started. No one knew he was coming. In fact, no one knew him at all, except my wife and me. He walked onto the stage and took a place in the circle, joining hands with the students on either side of him. The activity was a little different, but yes, the kids united. They bonded. They became one.

"After the circle," ended the teacher, "I greeted the alum and asked him what brought him to us that day."

"I drove three hours to get here," he said.

"Why?" asked the teacher.

"I lost my dad six weeks ago, and I just needed to be with friends and family" came the reply.

That alum had never met any of the students in the circle before. Still, he drove three hours to be with them because he needed to be with "friends and family."

Our drama program does more than produce plays. It makes friends.

Tim

When he was in high school, Tim wrestled for me and captained our team.

I admired him, respected him, and trusted him. I still do.

In the prime of his life, Tim committed an act of courage and character. He gave one of his kidneys to his sister.

Like another friend of mine named Lucas, whom you will hear about later, Tim saw an organ transplant as the best source of light for him to offer in a time of darkness and disease.

"Both of her kidneys were failing," Tim explained, "but she would never have asked me to help, and I would never have offered. Instead, my sister got my mother to ask me, and who could ever say no to *their mother*?"

"Were you afraid?" I asked as we embarked on one of the most intimate conversations of our lifelong friendship.

"Not until I lay naked on a gurney in the hospital corridor just before the operation!" replied Tim. "As I looked at the ceiling waiting for the tranquilizer to kick in, I whispered to myself, '*What the hell am I doing here?*' If I had clothes on or even nearby, I would have been dressed and out of there in a heartbeat!" Tim confessed. "But I didn't, so I stayed!"

"How did you feel after it was over?" I asked. "And how do you feel now so many years later?"

"Well, it all went fine, so I have no regrets," answered Tim. "True confessions, though," he continued, "I would have been okay with it even if it had ended badly because it made me very proud. Whenever I think of what I did," Tim continued, "I whisper to myself, 'If you never do anything else good in your life, at least you did that!'"

And there is more! I have known Tim very well for fifty years.

For most of that time, I *had no idea* what he had done for his sister! Neither did most of his other close friends.

Tim never talked *about* what he did.

In fact, when I first heard of Tim's gift, it made me think of the man who managed a lighthouse on Cape Cod.

He turned his light on every night at sundown. He did so quietly with no fanfare, no drum roll, no cannon fire, and no fireworks.

Still, every night, all the people on Cape Cod saw that man's light go on. It simply needed to shine to be seen. Such is Tim's light and his gift to his sister.

I will forever admire Tim for having done something he can forever point to and say, "At least I did that!" He will never have to question the value of his life. What is more, he will never have to *prove* that value.

I will admire him even more for letting what he did *simply save, simply serve, and simply shine* for his sister.

Matthew Kelly once said that "great lives belong to men and women who see life as a generosity contest."

Tim sees life that way. Thanks to him, so do his sister.

Brian

"Jesus never asked to be admired. Instead, he asked to be *followed*. His goal was not *admiration*. It was *imitation*."

A priest said that to me and others months ago in a sermon he gave at the start of Lent. Then that priest said this, "Ask yourself what Jesus would do or what Jesus would say anytime at all. Then spend Lent *saying* that and *doing* it! Spend Lent," ended the priest, "*imitating Jesus!*"

It all made me think of Brian. He is over fifty and was always the guy whose "grass was always greener!"

He had retired very young with a beautiful wife, two radiant daughters, and (in his words) "more money than God!"

That all changed two summers ago. While riding his bike, Brian felt a lump in his chest and had trouble swallowing. The whole thing hit him in minutes with no warning.

A week later, Brian had a diagnosis: stage four cancer in his stomach and esophagus. Even with surgery, chemotherapy, and radiation, his prognosis was grim.

Before the lump, Brian *lived* on a golf course ("or two! or three!") and spent his "life traveling the world trying to break eighty or get a hole in one!"

After the cancer came, he lost 40 percent of his body weight and dreaded getting up in the morning. Nine months of treatment later, he was preparing for a major operation that would remove his esophagus and rebuild it, possibly leaving him unable to swallow, eat, or worse.

DeeDee and I visited Brian last year. He and his wife, Renee, stayed in a friend's house in Plymouth while Brian recovered from his surgery. Dee and I sat with them, Brian and Renee taught us more about the meaning of *faith and friends* than we had ever owned or ever earned.

For five days after surgery, Brian was nourished only by a feeding tube up his nose that did little more than keep him alive, cause constant irritation, and inflict plenty of pain.

"The nurses kept asking me how much pain I was in," Brian remembered. "On a scale of one to ten, the dozens of incisions taken together added up to a two or three," he figured.

"During the operation, the surgeons had to separate my ribs to get the camera in during the operation," described Brain. "That was another three or four. Last but not least, that frigging tube in my nose was an eleven all by itself!

By the time we saw him after his surgery, Brian had lost forty-eight more pounds in six weeks!

"Coach," remembered Brian, "picture me having to eat so much of nothing but ice cream that I actually learned to hate it! Things are better now, and I am glad it's over," Brian reported.

"Thank God Renee is not much of a cook!" he kidded. "That way, I didn't really miss all that much good eating during my recovery! It was almost like being at home and having to eat my Irish mother's meals! I'll never forget one Thanksgiving," he recalled. "Ma put out a meal of turkey, ham, and vegetables. 'This is the best cauliflower you ever made!' Brian complimented his mother. 'That's not cauliflower. It's broccoli!' Brian's mom loudly explained. 'Oh Christ, Ma!' Brian countered. 'You must have steamed the broccoli for so long all its colors came off!'"

Even in the face of all he faced, Brian made us laugh…and laugh… and laugh. He recently texted me, "All thumbs up!" Thank God.

Wrestlers

Before I travel any farther into the stories of my friends, let me pause to shed some light on the strongest and most special among them. They are the wrestlers I coached, taught, learned from, and loved.

I have met some of my best *friends* through wrestling.

Our common denominator was always respect. In fact, it was *more* than respect. It was admiration because all wrestlers admire each other.

They know that being a wrestler is like being a Marine, only harder. It is like running a marathon, only longer. It is like going through hell, only hotter!

That is why when one wrestler meets another, there is nothing to earn and nothing to prove. The fact that someone has wrestled is the only fact that matters. Respect is won. Esteem is earned. Admiration is automatic.

I will proudly and loudly tell more stories about "my" wrestlers. But first, I will go to three special friends. They are the friends to whom I have dedicated this conversation and all the stories it contains. None of these friends ever wrestled for me. Still, they have earned my respect, esteem, and admiration as if they had. That makes them even *more special.*

George

I retired eight years ago after a long, long time in school.

Many of my friends and colleagues retired before I did. One of them was the head custodian in the first school I ever served as a teacher.

His name was George, and he worked in that same school for sixty years.

George never taught a subject. He taught much more. He taught about character, courage, and commitment. Everyone who knew George loved him and learned from him. *And everyone knew George!*

George's hours were 6:00 a.m. to 2:00 p.m., but he never worked those hours. He always worked more.

In the words of George's daughter, Kathy, "Although his actual workday did not start until 6:00 a.m., my father was always at work by four thirty." Kathy continued, "That was because my dad wanted his building warm for his teachers and students when they arrived, and making heat from coal for my dad's building was no small or 'tidy' task." By the time George finished prepping boilers, furnaces and pumps to make heat for the school, he needed to change into his clean khaki pants and his perfectly pressed polo shirt.

That is the way he looked for us every day. He looked perfect because he was. He looked professional because he was.

George worked hard all day but never got his pants or polo shirt dirty because he had done his "dirty work" before he changed into those things.

On George's last official day, a small group of his closest friends met in his little basement office beside the boiler room of the school he had served so well for so long. I was the assistant superintendent of schools by then and was invited to be with George. I was honored to join him.

We all toasted George with little plastic glasses of champagne and gave him a cake from Stop and Shop. Then, one by one, everybody left, except George and me. We talked for a while before departing.

As we walked to my car, George said, "Carmen, could you come by my car before you leave? I have something for you."

When we got to George's car, he opened the trunk and gave me something that was round, heavy, and wrapped in a green woolen army blanket.

When I uncovered it, I cried. It was the oak wall clock that hung in my first classroom on my first day as a teacher, almost forty years before.

"We put in a new system years ago," George explained, "and most of the old clocks got thrown away, but I kept this one for you. It was special, and you are special. I knew that then. I know that now."

Friends share many feelings. Some mean more than others. None mean more than George's did to me.

A Place to Pray

For years, DeeDee and I lived across the street from John, Andrea, and their son, Jack, a one-in-a-million young family. Some time ago, John's mother (only sixty-four years old) had a heart attack and went into a coma. She had been healthy and active until then.

One day, as the family agonized over whether or not to take John's mom off life support, Andrea's father, Ronnie, who also lives on our street, took his daily walk. As he passed by our house, he stopped walking. Then as I watched from our kitchen window, Ronnie turned toward John and Andrea's house and knelt at the curb. There, on his knees, Ronnie prayed for John's mother.

The young family was not home. They were all in the hospital with their sick mother. Still, God was home. He must have been. After all, Ronnie was there, praying to Him for John and Andrea's mom.

Love Grows and Love Shows

Ronnie found even more uses for his morning walk! For the children of another daughter, he interrupted his morning constitutional to draw chalk messages to his granddaughters in their driveway.

The girls gleefully watched from their bedroom window as "Grampa Ronnie" performed his daily artistic magic for them.

The message might be "Happy Birthday" with a cartoon of a cake. It might be a simple "I love you!" framed by two hearts or "Have a great day" with a picture of the sun.

In the winter, Grampa would replace his chalk with a mitten and "carve" his messages in the snow. For those little girls, every day started with a Christmas morning and their driveway became a tree full of presents drawn by their biggest fan and loving Santa, Grampa Ronnie!

Come, Sit, Eat!

Despite Ronnie's many prayers, John's mother died at sixty-four. My father passed away shortly after. His wake was long, so Dee and I got home very late.

When we did, we found a big black SUV idling in our driveway.

As we parked and left our car, Andrea's mother, Mary, greeted us and said, "You must be hungry and tired." As she said that, she lifted the tailgate of her big car, turned on the interior lights, and showed us the formal Italian dinner she had prepared.

The meal sat on a white linen tablecloth, fine china, and shining crystal. Every vessel was full of homemade Italian splendor.

"Come! Sit! Eat!" the mother invited. "How long have you been waiting for us?" I asked. "It doesn't matter" came the reply. "Dee and I tried to thank her, but no words worked. So we ate in silence and thought how much of a family our friends had become."

Too Many Cards

A Quincy teacher named Kathy once told me of a story that took place while she was at home recovering from cancer surgery.
"One day, I went out on the porch to get my mail," Kathy said. "There was a beautiful straw basket on the floor under my mailbox.

I didn't know who put it there, so the next day I asked the mailman.

"I did!" he said.

"Thank you," said Kathy, "but why?"

"Because you get so many 'get well' cards every day that they *all* won't *fit* in your mailbox, and I wanted you to have something to put them in!"

Kathy's smile grew as the mailman ended by saying, "You must work in a pretty great place."

"I do," said Kathy.

Friends can be family. Family can be friends.

All That Matters

Some years ago, my uncle died. It was for the best. He had been sick for a long time. Toward the end, he didn't even know us. It got hard to visit him. But my father still did. He visited every day. Once, I asked him why. "Dad," I said, "Uncle Ed doesn't even know you are there. Why do you go?" My father's answer? "It doesn't matter that *he* knows I'm there. It only matters that *I* know I'm there."

My father and uncle were not brothers or even in-laws. They had simply married two sisters. They were not "legally" related, but using the term loosely, you *could* say they were family, and using the term *tightly*, you *could* say they were *friends*!

What follows are a few stories about others whom, using the term *tightly*, you *could* say they were friends!

Family by Another Name

I visited my high school one Saturday morning to support a student car wash.

The wash was taking place behind the school and four students were standing on a traffic island in front with signs that read

"Car wash out back!"

I followed the sign's directions, and after getting my car cleaned, I took a ten-dollar bill and a bag of candy bars from my back seat.

Then I delivered everything to the car washers.

Most of the kids took one bar of candy. A few football players took two. One very little girl took five!

"Wow!" I said to her. "You must be very hungry!"

"Oh, Doctor," she replied, "these are not for me. They are for the kids out front holding the signs."

Related? No, none of those kids were related, but using the term tightly, you could say they were…friends.

New Friends

On my first day of lunch duty in a new school year, I was greeting the students as they entered the cafeteria when four freshman boys walked in and took their place at the back of the serving line.

They stayed close to each other as they entered the line and waited until they had all bought their lunch before they went looking for a table.

Their plan was obviously to sit together, but that plan quickly crashed and burned! Three of the boys got lucky and found empty seats side by side at the same table.

The fourth wasn't so fortunate—at least not at first! He couldn't find a seat at a table that had any other freshmen sitting at it, so he finally opted for a table that was completely empty and began to eat alone.

Not long after, though, two senior cheerleaders noticed the lonely freshman and picked two seats at his table as they left the lunch line. Soon after, two of our other senior cheerleaders joined their teammates and the freshman boy.

Shortly after that, four more cheerleaders filled what seats were still available at the freshman boy's table. By then, all the cheerleaders at the now full table were asking their adopted little freshman about his classes, teachers, schedule, hometown, and more!

By the end of lunch, "a great time was had by all," especially by the little freshman!

As the cafeteria cleared, the freshman strolled by me on his way out. "Doctor," he approached, "can I ask you a question?"

"Sure, son. Shoot!" I replied.

"Can I eat lunch with the seniors *every* day?" the boy ended.

Once again, friends can be family. Family can be friends.

Loose Change

Some years ago, our principal told me of two big jars that our student council had placed in the cafeteria for a sophomore named Palmer. He had woken up with a lump in his throat one morning and needed multiple surgeries at a Boston hospital before returning to school.

"The idea," the principal explained to me, "is to collect loose change from our students that the council can give to Palmer's parents to help pay for parking, pajamas, lunches, and more."

"What a great idea!" I replied. "How has the response been so far?"

"Well," said the principal with her head down, "I must say that so far, there is no change in either jar."

My jaw dropped in disbelief. I told myself that our kids were too generous to let Palmer down.

As I approached the jars, I smiled and understood. The jars had no loose change. Instead, they were *full of bills*! Some were ones. Many were fives. Some were tens. One bill was bigger, much bigger.

Related? No, almost none of those kids were related; to each other, or Palmer. Once again, friends can be family, and family can be friends.

Timing Is Everything

That expression is tired and trite, but true, just ask that little freshman who got to eat lunch with the cheerleaders or ask Palmer, whose classmates "found time" to fill those big jars with so many bills.

Or ask the heroes who fought and died in Vietnam. At that time, they were not even considered soldiers, let alone heroes. They were thought of as pariahs whose country was not proud of the strengths they showed or the sacrifices they made.

Today, in the eyes of vacationers, the shores and sunshine of *Vietnam* are seen as worthy substitutes for Honolulu, Bermuda, Jamaica, or Key West.

Yes. The country has recovered but not all our soldiers have.

What do I mean? Try this true story.

A few years ago, I visited the Quincy District Court House with two of our high school social studies classes and their teachers.

We saw a reenactment of a case that involved a White woman who had married a Black man during the civil war and who was trying to smuggle him into New York from Virginia on the underground railroad. To do this, she disguised herself as a White man and claimed her Black husband to be her slave. It was a wonderful presentation.

At its end, the presiding judge of the district court talked with the students about the case's implications. "The world would not have accepted that Black man as a White woman's husband but did accept him as a White man's slave, even if that White man was a White woman! Timing is everything," ended the judge.

Then he gave a more powerful and personal example of his point. "Thirty years ago," he said, "I fought in the Vietnam War. When I came home, I was assigned to Fort Knox, Kentucky, to finish my tour. On the weekends, I got to leave the fort on pass. The first time I left, I wore my uniform but never again. You see, lots of civilians didn't like the war, so I was spit upon and sworn at during that first weekend. I didn't believe in the war either. Still, I fought for my country when I was asked to because, to me, that was the right thing to do. When I fought the war and left the service, my country didn't see things my way, so people spit and swore instead of saying thanks. Timing is everything."

Yes, timing *is* everything. Today, Normandy Beach is God's way of describing true beauty and defining real peace. No cemetery is more serene. No graveyard is more gorgeous.

In 1941, God used that same beach to give life (and death) to a nightmare.

The invasion of Normandy was a bloodbath. It was anything but serene. It was anything but gorgeous. Same place. Different time. Timing is everything.

Yes, the timing of a *country's* life is everything. So, too, is the timing of a *person's* life. *When* a person dies and *how long* a person *lives* determine *who* that person becomes *and how* that person is remembered.

What do I mean? David's story will tell you.

David

He was a *friend* and long-time high school classmate who died almost two years ago.

For most of that time, David was someone I enjoyed and had fun with. We went to high school together and stayed close after that.

David had a "radio voice," a great sense of humor, and a never-ending appetite! We shared many memories and more lunches! I valued him and saw him as funny, hungry, happy, and healthy.

If you asked me for a story of David, I would tell you about the time my father saw him bending into the refrigerator in dad's kitchen after midnight.

David and I had a sleepover that night, and I was in the attic on a cot. David was hungry (again!), so he took the attic stairs to my parents' second-floor apartment for a snack. My father heard him on the stairs and got up to investigate.

All I could hear (while still in the attic) was my dad's voice asking, "Whose jockey shorts were sticking out of his refrigerator, and what David's fat ass was doing in them?"

Yes, I saw David as funny, hungry, happy, and healthy—that is, until two years ago. It was then that he woke up one morning with a swollen foot and cancer.

After months of treatment and weeks of remission, David went into hospice care.

"My nurse said I am the strongest patient she has ever had," David told me with a marked sense of pride in his voice. And I want to *stay that strong*!"

David *did* stay strong, and David did *die* strong. That is how I will remember him—sick and strong instead of funny, hungry, happy, and healthy. I will remember David as being more than any of those things because he lived long enough to show me *all* that he was.

Timing *is* everything.

The Best Is Yet to Come

Recently, I heard a story that reminded me of David. It is about a nun who loved to eat like David! Her name was Sister Angela. She was big and always smiling, especially in the kitchen! She did not cook but loved to be around people who did!

In her eighties, Sister Angela got sick and started to fail. While in the hospital, she asked to see her Mother Superior.

The Mother visited Sister Angela and asked how she could help.

"Mother, I need a favor," Sister Angela explained.

"Anything for you, Sister," replied the Mother Superior. "What can I do?"

"Could you put something in my casket with me when I am gone?" asked Sister Angela.

"Of course," said the Mother Superior. "What is it?"

"A spoon," replied the sister.

"Why a spoon?" asked the Mother.

"Because at dinner every night in the convent," explained Sister Angela, "when we sat down to eat, there was always a plate, a fork, and a knife at each place at the table. Sometimes, there was also a spoon. I always looked for the spoon," said the Sister. "I always *hoped* for the spoon."

"Why?" asked the Mother Superior.

"Because," Sister Angela went on, "if there was a spoon at our places, it meant there would be ice cream for dessert! That spoon," ended Sister Angela, "meant no matter how good dinner was, *the best was yet to come!*"

"And that is why you want a spoon in your coffin?" queried the confused Mother Superior.

"Yes," replied Sister A. "The spoon in my coffin will remind everyone who comes to my wake that they should be happy for me because no matter how good my life on earth has been when I die, *the best is yet to come* in heaven!"

I bet that, like Sister Angela, my friend David is hoping for a spoon every night at supper too!

So much for friends, now let's tell some stories that give meaning to *feelings*.

Feelings

Feelings are another word of wonder, and the *feelings* that people give to their *families* are forever. (They turn into the *magic of memories!*)

What *are* feelings?

Let's see if we can find out by reading some *more stories!*

Happiness Is a Victory

First, do me a favor. Take a minute and think of the worst thing that happened to you today. Maybe you had to drink cold coffee this morning, put on underwear that had a hole in it, brush your teeth with no toothpaste, or maybe you had to do something even worse!

Think of it now, then try this.

On your way home tonight, stop at a newsstand and pick up a few papers, or check out the front pages of some websites. Now read all the headlines you see!

Then tell me if a story about your underwear, cold coffee, or toothpaste is in any of those headlines. Then turn on the radio. Listen to the news. See if any of those stories about your day make the newscasts you listen to.

If your troubles *didn't* make the news, think about which ones *did*!

I bet they involve COVID-19 or an awful fire or world hunger or flood, a war, or worse, then ask yourself how bad *your* day was compared to what you just read in the paper, heard on the radio, or saw over the internet. If your day was not *that* bad, be happy because it could have been *worse*!

Happiness is not a gift. It is a victory. It is a *feeling*, and happiness is *a great feeling*! So if you end your day (*any* day!) feeling happy, you *earned* a victory! You earned your feeling!

DeeDee's Bag

After twenty-five years of marriage, DeeDee and I earned the victory of happiness, but first, we got a scare. Dee found a lump on the front of her neck that her doctor was afraid might be cancer.

"Let's take it out and do a biopsy," the doctor suggested.

Two sleepless nights later, Dee and I were in the preop ward of the Brigham and Women's Hospital waiting for Dee to be called into surgery.

She had changed into her johnny and slippers and put all her street clothes in a canvas bag that sat on the floor at my feet. "Take care of that bag for me," Dee said, pointing.

I smiled and said, "You can count on me!"

"Not always!" Dee replied, half in fun.

"What do you mean?" I challenged, still partly in fun.

"Let's face it," she retorted, "sometimes you get distracted and sometimes you lose things! Don't get distracted today. Keep an eye on my bag because without that bag, I have nothing with me but my panties, and I don't want to drive home in just them!"

I nodded and smiled again. I thought that would reassure her but soon found out it did not.

We sat together on the edge of Dee's bed while waiting for a nurse to bring the preop medications. The wait was several minutes long and seemed much longer. During that time, my mind wandered, just as Dee had warned it *not* to!

By the time the nurse came, I was deep in memories, thoughts, emotions, and prayers.

Dee was also deep in thought but in another direction. "Okay, do your kissing now!" the nurse cheerfully said as she suddenly came through the curtain that surrounded Dee's bed.

We did, and the nurse helped DeeDee onto the gurney that was being wheeled beside her bed.

As two orderlies pushed Dee across the very large open area that was the preop ward, Dee looked back and gave me a wave. I returned the favor and said, "I love you!" loud enough for every ear in the ward to hear!

Dee kept waving and replied with a softer version of my words. Then she pointed to the floor near my feet and said in her loudest voice, "Don't lose that frigging bag!" More *feelings* from DeeDee to me!

More Victories

After the surgery, Dee's doctor came by to tell us she did not have cancer. I replied with "And she *does* have her bag!" That made me and Dee feel *very happy*!

The doctor smiled, nodded, and said, "I guess you really lucked out, didn't you?" Yes, we really did luck out. DeeDee had her bag, and I had DeeDee!

We felt happy. We felt lucky. We felt grateful. We felt *victorious!* What a great feeling!

Always Mine

Some years ago, my father was in a car accident. He was run over while walking home after visiting my mother's grave. After being hit, Dad lay in the street. He had four broken bones and bruises everywhere.

The woman who hit him backed up her car, opened the door, and ran to Dad. As she stood over him in the street, she kept sobbing, "Oh my god! Oh my god!"

My father listened for a minute, then he looked at her, and said, "Lady, stop your sniveling and call 911, will ya?"

She did, and Dad was rushed to the hospital. It took him a year to recover. In the meantime, he got a check from that woman's insurance company. I happened to visit Dad on the day the check arrived. When I sat down, he gave it to me. "Here," he said. "This is for you and your sister."

I replied "Thanks, but we would much rather have you."

Dad replied, "Don't worry, you will *always* have me." My dad was right.

He died eleven years ago, and I *still* have him! I will *always* have him.

That makes me feel happy. It makes me feel grateful.

It makes us feel *victorious!* What a great feeling!

Always Hers

My mother was very sick at home for two years before she died. My dad was by her side every minute.

When any visiting nurse would come and see the level of care Dad gave to Mom, the nurse would invariably ask how Dad did it.

"My god, Luigi," one nurse asked often, "it must be so hard to do so much for your wife."

Dad answered like this, "It is not hard at all. You see, over sixty years ago, I took a vow to love her 'for better or worse, richer or poorer, in sickness and in health.' That vow makes all this easy."

My mother died almost twenty years ago, and she will always have my father.

The *feelings* that people give to their families are forever.

In their most romantic of moments, my father called my mother "wifie."

In their least romantic of moments, he called her the *same thing*!

When he sent my mother a card or a present, he always addressed it that way, and I mean *just that* way! I mean just like this:

Wifie
19 Woodward Ave.
Quincy, MA, 02169

I never heard him *say* "I love you" to my mom. Still, I saw my father *show* "I love you" to my mom all the time.

He *showed* her his feelings more than he *said* them. Showing made Dad's feelings stronger. They made his feelings louder!

Still More Victories

Years after Dee's operation, it was my turn to have one. I developed double vision thanks to a fold in my retina, so I needed laser surgery. Shortly before the surgery, Dee sat on my bed in the preop ward, just as I had done for her years before.

While we waited for the nurse, we agreed that we would both be *happy* if my operation turned out as well as DeeDee's had.

In the middle of our agreement, a male nurse burst through the curtain with a gurney. It was time for our kiss!

But first, Dee and the nurse had to talk! They had worked together for years at the Brigham and were close friends, so they had to "catch up on all the dirt" while they had a chance!

"Why are you here?" the nurse asked Dee. "My husband"— pointing to me—"is having eye surgery today," replied Dee.

"Is this him?" the nurse asked while he took a turn pointing.

"Yes," said Dee. Immediately, the male nurse, who was much younger and better looking than I am, looked at me, then at DeeDee, then back at me.

He obviously thought much more highly of DeeDee (both physically and otherwise) than he did of me, so he finally squinted at me and asked how long we had been married. "Over forty years!" I announced proudly.

"Boy," the nurse ended with a long pause, "you really lucked out, didn't you?"

Those words again. True again. Yes, I have truly felt lucky, grateful, happy, and victorious thanks to DeeDee. I have really lucked out thanks to DeeDee. What a victory! What a feeling!

Aida

I once read the storyline of Verdi's *Aida.* As best I can recall, it tells of a young couple who were in love but buried alive and about to die together in a grave that was running out of air.

In the grave's darkness, the couple begins to sing words of love to each other, despite knowing that their singing would use more air and end their lives more quickly than if they said and sang nothing. Still, the lovers' singing does not stop until their breathing does. They would rather die sooner than leave their feelings unsung.

I *cannot* sing. But if placed in a moment like that young couple was, I would have tried. I would have tried to sing, and sing, and sing.

I cannot sing, but I would have *felt like singing*!

What a *feeling*!

Favorite Pastime

A Canadian poet named Margaret Atwood once said, "Eskimos use fifty-two different words to say *snow* because snow is so special to them."

We should have that many words for *love*! It is such a special *feeling* just as snow is such a special word. My mother did not have that many *words for* love, but she had that many *ways to* love, and she showed all those ways to Natalie and me.

That reminds me of a survey that was done among thousands of Americans asking them what was their favorite pastime.

The most popular answer to that question was "spending money!" When the researchers followed up by asking "spending money on what?" the most popular response was "*on other people!*"

My mother's favorite pastime was spending money on her children—just like *your* mother's was!

That was how my mother showed me that she loved me more than she loved herself every time we went to the Bargain Center. That was how my mother showed me her *feelings*.

Irregulars

When I was young, my family lived in Downtown Quincy, near a big outlet store called *The Bargain Center*.

My mother and I shopped there for the first twenty years of my life. In fact, we shopped *only* there for the first twenty years of my life! Now shopping at the "Bargie" was an adventure, and shopping for shoes at the Bargie was the *biggest* adventure! The good news was, Bargie shoes were always on sale for five dollars per pair. The bad news was, there were *never any pairs*!

Instead, there were large bins full of single shoes. Customers like me and my mom had to stand at each bin and make pairs by matching the single shoes to each other!

I would stand on one side of a bin, and my mother would stand on the other. When I found a shoe that was my size, I would yell out the color of the shoe I found. If my mother found one of the same color, we were almost home—all we needed was to match the style!

It took time, but sooner or later, we always found at least one pair of five-dollar shoes that fit me and matched!

Then we did the same for my mother, except for one thing. We looked for my mother's shoes in a different bin. Every shoe in that bin had a word stamped on it.

Yes, one word was stamped on every shoe we bought for my mother at the Bargain Center. That word was "irregular." In fact, it was stamped on *everything* my mother ever bought for herself in that store. *But it was stamped on nothing she ever bought for me.*

My mother *sacrificed* what *she* wore for what *I* wore. She did that because she loved me more than she loved herself.

Wonderful love. Wonderful mother. Wonderful *feeling*!

Each of us has our own unique flaws. We are all like the *irregulars* for sale in the Bargain Center! But if we give our strengths a chance to shine, they will! If we give ourselves a chance to *feel* proud, we can.

When darkness and light meet, light prevails, and when strength and weakness meet, strength prevails. So let your *strengths prevail*! Know what you do best and show what you do best. Psychologists say that we all have a *signature strength* that allows us to excel at certain skills and in certain subjects. Find that strength and sign that strength. Most of all, feel proud of that strength.

Feelings Forever

Maya Angelou once wrote that *"I have learned people will forget what you said and forget what you did, but people will never forget how you made them feel."*

So true. *Feelings* are almost as important to people as their *family* and their *friends*!

Better Wheels

Last fall, I saw a college student riding his beat-up old bicycle home from class. He was wearing a backpack that had a bumper sticker on it. The sticker read, "Someday, I will be a doctor!"

The student's bicycle had a bumper sticker on it too.

That one read, "And someday, I will be a Harley-Davidson!"

Thanks to you, right now, *this* "beat-up old bicycle" (in other words, me!) *feels like a Harley-Davidson*!

Why? Because you are spending a part of your life reading my stories! *That* makes *me feel* important. It makes me feel proud. It makes me feel like a Harley-Davidson!

Thanks for that feeling. I owe you for that feeling. I owe you more than I can pay, and I owe you more than I can *say*.

Infected

Some years ago, I attended a testimonial luncheon at the Brigham and Women's Hospital for Dr. Thomas O'Brien. He was not retiring yet but was planning to, in his words, "canter toward medicine's finish line for a while!"

Dr. O'Brien has been at the Brigham for more than fifty years. He is brilliant. He is also funny. So is his tall redheaded son. You may have heard of him. His name is Conan!

Conan couldn't be at the luncheon, but lots of other people were. I was there because DeeDee has worked with Dr. O'Brien throughout her professional lifetime, so DeeDee helped plan the party and made it very clear that she wanted me to be there!

I am glad she did. It was a great day. The best part of it was Dr. O'Brien's speech.

He spoke about his profession and his specialty—infectious disease. Then he said this, "Diseases are not the only things that are infectious. Warmth is. Trust is. Goodness is. I thank you all for infecting me with those things every day of my professional life."

Warmth, trust, goodness, and more are *feelings*, and Maya Angelou was right! Dr. O'Brien will never forget how his party and his colleagues made him *feel*.

DeeDee Fagerlund

When I was in the fifth grade and Natalie was in the second, she brought a friend home for lunch one day.

(Nat and I lived close to our school, so we could come home at lunchtime rather than eat in the school attic or our classroom!)

The name of Nat's friend was DeeDee Fagerlund.

Since I was three years older than each of them, I had little use for DeeDee or Natalie, but they got very close to each other.

Before long, DeeDee was coming home for lunch with Nat every day, and I admit, it was driving me crazy! My mother even ordered me to walk them to and from the house at lunchtime "for safety's sake."

That drove me even crazier!

We were having dinner one night, and Natalie could not stop talking about DeeDee. Finally, my elastic snapped, and I yelled, "DeeDee Fagerlund! DeeDee Fagerlund! I am sick of hearing about DeeDee Fagerlund! I never want to hear that name again!"

After that night, I left the room or the house every time DeeDee came over for lunch or anything *else*!

It wasn't until Nat and I went off to a Catholic high school while DeeDee chose a public school that I finally saw the last of DeeDee Fagerlund…or did I?

During my high school summers, I became a lifeguard at a beach near our house. Guess who the swimming instructor at that very same beach was? Yes! DeeDee Fagerlund!

She was a lot older by then, so she looked different—much different!

I loved how she looked, and eventually, I loved who she was.

Yes, eventually, I *fell in love* with DeeDee Fagerlund!

"I thought you hated her!" my dad replied when I finally mustered the courage to tell him how I felt.

"I did!" I confessed. "But I don't anymore! I can't believe it, but my *feelings* have *changed*."

For a long time, I doubted those feelings, but eventually, I trusted them enough to ask DeeDee to marry me. The rest is history!

Grand Canyon

In his moving book called *Swimming in the Sun*, Albert Haase, OFM, tells the story of his first encounter with the Grand Canyon. In much of Albert's words, his story went like this.

"I arrived for my first visit to the Grand Canyon rather late in the evening. It was already dark, but my curiosity and excitement would not keep until morning! I went first to the Sothern Rim of the Canyon to take a look. Sadly, all I saw through the darkness was a big hole. No splendor. No sparkles. No magic. No majesty. I couldn't help but think that the Canyon is was just another of America's tourist traps! I went back to my tent, decided that my disappointment was not going to ruin this vacation, and fell asleep. I got up before dawn on the following morning, and everything had changed. As the sun inched its way into the sky, the 'big hole' started coming alive with highlights and hues of red, purple, blue, and yellow. Despite the company of other onlookers, I could not keep myself from oohing and ahhing over one of God's daily miracles, which was being made over Northern Arizona. It was the same canyon as it was the night before, but in the light of the morning sun, everything looked different. Everything *was* different. Everything *had changed.*"

So remembers Albert Haase, OFM.

Seeing DeeDee at the beach during our high school and collegiate summers made me think of that story. It was as if she entered the black hole of my teenage years as a twelve-year-old pain in the neck and was transformed into a star whose light made all my *feelings... change.*

Yes, feelings can change. They can also grow. Examples?

Try these stories!

Perfect T-Shirt

On the day I graduated with my doctorate from Boston College, Natalie was at the commencement ceremony. After the ceremony, my parents gave me a party. At the party, Nat gave me a present. It was a T-shirt.

"Someone gave this to me when I became a doctor," Nat told me as I opened the present, "and I want you to have it because now you are a doctor too."

The T-shirt was red with white letters. On the front, those letters said, *Trust me. I am a doctor.*

As you know, my mother always called Natalie "the real doctor in the family," and since that day, I have *felt like* a real doctor too. My feelings as a doctor grew, thanks to my sister. She said the perfect thing. So did her T-shirt!

Thanks for that feeling, Dr. Nat!

The Goalie's Father

The year I went back to my high school alma mater as its first president, I attended a girls' hockey game over Christmas vacation. We were playing a very good team who scored six goals against us in the first period and six more in the second.

At the end of those first two difficult periods, the father of our goalie approached me, shook my hand, and wished me a happy holiday.

I returned his good wishes and asked if I could buy him a cup of coffee before the action started again. "No thanks, Doctor," the dad replied. "I want to get down to the other end of the rink. The goalies just changed ends, and I want to keep my daughter company. This is one of those days when she needs to know how much her father loves her."

That father's feelings for his daughter grew because his daughter needed them to. Yes, feelings can change, and feelings can grow.

I Love You Too

Long ago, at a funeral I attended, the eulogist remembered something very special about the woman who had died. "She never left me or any of her friends," the eulogist recalled, "without telling us she loved us."

Then in honor of the deceased, the eulogist asked the congregation not to end this day without telling someone they loved how they felt.

I left the church after the service and visited my father in a rehabilitation hospital. As I told you earlier, he had broken four bones in a car accident and had been in therapy for a long time. I went there to do what the eulogist had asked and to tell my dad I loved him, but I was afraid he would be embarrassed (or that I would be!).

I had planned to visit for ten minutes, and stayed for two hours!

I just couldn't get myself to say "I love you, Dad!"

Finally, in the middle of a meaningless conversation about the Red Sox, I just blurted out, "I love you, Dad!"

Dad was not embarrassed at all. Instead, he quickly replied, "I love you too, Carm!"

My father lived for four years after that day. During that time, his love grew and grew and grew. So did mine. I visited him almost every night, and I never left his house or his side without shaking his hand and saying, "I love you, Dad." He always answered, "I love you too, Carm."

One Father's Day evening after dinner, I rushed out of Dad's house after visiting and forgot to say I loved him. On my way home, my mistake dawned on me, so I returned to his house in the dark and told him how I felt, just as I always did.

Dad answered just as he always did. Then I left for a second time. Very early the next morning, my father died in bed—alone. The last words he ever heard were "I love you," and they were spoken by his only son.

I will be forever grateful for that. So, I believe, will my dad.

Now it's your turn. Don't wait. Think of someone you love but have never told. Then tell them. Do it now. Do it *now*.

Silence Is Golden

On the night of August 12 of last year, DeeDee made me mad.

She left the sliding doors to our dining room open when she went to bed. It got very windy, wet, and cold that night. The dining room rug and furniture got wet, and I was really pissed!

After I saw what had happened, I headed to our bedroom to have a fight with DeeDee. I had reminded her about the sliders earlier that night, and she forgot, so I was ready to remind her again—only *louder* this time!

Then I remembered something. I remembered some of the many (many!) times in our married life DeeDee had been good to me. I also remembered how many times I had regretted starting a fight with DeeDee.

Even when I thought I was right, I remembered how many times I wished I had kept my feelings to myself when I was mad. My fights with Dee never ended well, no matter what. So why go there? Why start a fight, even if I thought I was right?

Why not keep my bad feelings to myself? "What the hell," I thought. "Why not try it? For just this one time?" And I did! It's true, for the first time in my married life or otherwise, I bit my tongue and let my feelings *lie* instead of letting those feelings *fly*! I went to bed and said nothing.

The next morning, I came down for breakfast, and on my placemat at the kitchen table was a greeting card from DeeDee.

It said, "Happy Anniversary to my wonderful husband!"

Yes, August 12 is our anniversary, and I had forgotten!

I was embarrassed. I was also afraid. Most of all, I was *grateful* that I had not said anything about the sliders the night before!

While DeeDee made our coffee that morning, I sneaked out and got her some flowers and a card at the Stop and Shop down the street. I still felt like a loser for forgetting our special day, but I felt a hell of a lot *better* than I *would* have if I had let my feelings fly the night before over the dining room sliders!

Let Feelings Lie

An Alaskan trapper lost his wife and was left to care for his two-year-old daughter. At times, he had to leave the little girl with his faithful dog so he could work in the woods.

While the trapper was away one afternoon, a terrible blizzard came up. The trapper was forced to take shelter in a hollow tree overnight.

At daybreak, he rushed to his cabin and found the door open, and his dog covered with blood. What was more, there was no little girl to be found.

The father was terrified that something awful had happened.

Enraged by the thought that his child had been killed by the dog, the trapper reached for his ax. In one swift move, he smashed the skull of his faithful canine companion.

Like a maniac, the trapper proceeded to tear his cabin apart in search of his daughter. Suddenly came a faint cry from under a bed.

There was his daughter, in tears, but safe and sound.

Looking further, the trapper found the bloody remains of a wolf in the corner.

Then the trapper knew. His dog had saved the trapper's daughter, and the trapper had killed his dog.

The moral?

We all have feelings, and some of those feelings are bad. When they are bad or when they make us mad, we should "let them lie, not let them fly" until they change! Because, as we said pages ago, feelings *do* change. Feelings *will* change.

Feelings Change

There once was a little boy who had a very bad temper. His father decided to hand him a bag of nails and said that every time the boy lost his temper, he had to hammer a nail into a fence in the family's backyard.

On the first day, the boy hammered many nails into that fence. In time, the boy gradually began to control his temper, and the number of nails he hammered into the fence slowly decreased.

Finally, the day came when the boy did not lose his temper at all. He shared the good news with his father, who suggested that the boy pull out a nail from the board every day that he kept his temper under control.

The days passed, and the boy was finally able to tell his father that all the nails were gone. It was then that the father took his son by the hand and led him to the fence.

"You have done well, my son," praised the father, "but look at the holes in the fence. They will never disappear! When you say things in anger," continued the father, "they leave a scar just like the ones you left in the fence. No matter how many times you with-draw the nails from the fence, the scars made by each nail will never depart."

So control your feelings. Let your bad feelings lie; don't let them fly. Let them *change* because *they will!*

Tender and Tough

Several years ago, a man named Tom Peters studied one hundred of the most successful business leaders in America. He wanted to see what they had in common. Tom wrote a book called *In Search of Excellence* about his study. In Tom's own words, this is what he learned about leaders. "The best leaders in America are two things simultaneously. They are very good to their people. They are also as tough as nails when it comes to standards."

Tom called this the "Paradox of Leadership." He said that to lead, you must be *tender* when it comes to people and *tough* when it comes to standards. Tom Peters said, "To lead, you must be nice and not nice at the same time. To lead," Tom repeated, "you must *change your feelings!*"

My Uncles and Others!

My uncles (Ma's brothers) Albert and Leo must have agreed with Tom Peters! They were both very close to their family and each other. They were also very tough when it came to their expectations and their standards.

Uncle Albert was a career NCO in the Navy and Uncle Leo was a Marine. Once, Uncle Albert told his baby brother George that "when it comes to working with people, I agree with Al Capone, 'You can get more with a smile and a gun than you can get with just a smile!'"

Albert was just kidding of course (?!) Still, he *was* tender when it came to his family and he was tough when it came to his standards.

Uncle Leo, the Marine, later became a detective with the Massachusetts State Police for thirty-five years. He once told me how he handled criminals. "Carmen," he said, "I put them in jail as *fast* as I can for as *long* as I can. Then I *visit* them until they get out!"

Uncle Leo was like Uncle Albert. He was nice and not nice.

He was *tender* on people and *tough* on standards. His feelings about people and standards *changed*!

Paul Fornier was the director of Food Services for Brigham and Women's Hospital. For years, Paul led two hundred people who fed two thousand patients every day.

Paul's employees worked very hard for him, *and* they *loved* him! One day, I asked Paul for his secret.

"How can you get people to work so hard and still love you?" I asked.

"It's easy," said Paul. "First, I make them sweat. Then *I* wipe their brow!" Paul Fornier was tough on standards and tender on people.

Pam Hull taught math at Quincy College in Plymouth. Pam gave her students four exams every semester.

Now Pam's exams were tough! They were also long! None of my sixty other teachers gave harder or longer exams than Pam Hull did. Pam *was* tough on standards.

Pam Hull also baked cookies. No one in the world baked better cookies than Pam did. And guess whom she baked those cookies for?

Yes, her students! And guess when Pam *gave* her students those cookies. Right! While they were taking her hard exams! Pam Hull was like Paul Fornier. She was tough on standards, *and* she was tender on people.

I heard a quote that reminded me of Pam Hull, Paul Fornier, Tom Peters, my uncle Albert, and my uncle Leo. It went like this: "A good parent should be made of some peace, some patience, some help, some hugs, and a whole bunch of time on the naughty chair!"

Yes, good parents should be like good leaders. They should be tender on people and tough on standards at the same time!

I am not a parent, but if I was, I hope I would be tender and tough!

John Patterson

Shortly after it was founded, the National Cash Register Company sent a major shipment of cash registers to Great Britain. None of those machines worked when they arrived. To find out why, the company's first president, John Patterson, moved his desk to the factory floor.

For several weeks, he observed the poor conditions that discouraged his workers. To correct the problem, he cleaned the whole plant and installed special washroom facilities.

Then he opened an employee cafeteria and sold food for less than cost. He even installed an indoor toilet! Best of all, his workers thanked Mr. Paterson for making better cash registers! Patterson *was tender* when it came to people.

This same John Patterson had an executive who was continually late coming back from lunch. One day, Patterson got tired of it. When that executive returned from lunch that day, he found his desk and chair parked outside on the curb in front of the factory. He watched Patterson soak his furniture in kerosene and put a match to it. That was Patterson's way of telling the man he was "fired!" John Patterson *was tough* on standards, and he *did change* his feelings!

So much for *feelings*! Now here come more *family* and *friends*!

Crystal Ball

A boy and his dad went to the circus one day. As they walked among the tents, they saw a juggler performing. He was excellent. He was mesmerizing.

He juggled four balls and never dropped one. The most impressive part of his act was that the balls he juggled were all different! One was rubber, another was stone. A third was made of wood, and the last was formed from crystal.

"Why do you use four different balls?" the boy asked the performer.

"They remind me to keep my priorities straight," replied the juggler.

"Explain!" pursued the boy.

"Well, if I drop the wooden ball, it just lands in the dirt with a thud, then stops. No damage. No worry," replied the juggler. "If I drop the stone ball, the same thing happens. If the rubber ball falls, it will bounce, but as long as I watch it closely, I can get it back after it bounces," continued the juggler.

"What about the crystal?" asked the boy.

"That one is the most valuable and fragile ball of all," said the juggler. "If I drop it, it will break, and I could not replace it."

With that, the father and son departed. As they walked away, the boy pondered in silence.

"What's wrong?" asked his father.

The boy paused and asked, "Am I your crystal ball?"

"Yes, son," replied the father, "*You are my crystal, and my crystal counts!*"

More Crystal

As a high school principal in New England, I spend a lot of time dealing with school cancellations and snow removal.

Once at a finance committee meeting, a debate ensued about whether or not we should completely clean the wide sidewalks in front of our school after a snowstorm or just cut a few small access paths from the street to the student walkways.

One advocate for the complete cleanup asked, "What if a student tried to walk on an unplowed sidewalk, fell, and broke his arm? We'd get sued and lose the case! At least if the sidewalks are done, we have a chance of defending ourselves in court!"

"Forget court!" countered a close colleague of the committee member who had just spoken. "We should clean the sidewalks so none of our students fall and break an arm, period. Suit or not, court or not! We should do what is right. Suit or not, court or not!"

The committee then voted unanimously to clear the sidewalks. Good lesson; forget court. Remember kids.

Kids are crystal, and crystal counts! And if kids are crystal, then grandchildren are gold!

Grandchildren Are Different

Kids make fathers and mothers feel alive. Grandchildren make grandfathers and grandmothers feel *more* than alive! They make them *feel young*!

At a high school reunion some time ago, a classmate talked to me about his grandchildren. "I love them, Carmen!" he said. "And I spoil them. It's funny," he went on. "I was very hard on my kids, not so my grandkids." It reminded me of a quote that goes something like this, "Grandchildren are God's way of thanking you for not killing your kids!"

"That's right!" said my classmate that night. Then he told a story of a pole that stood in the center of his two-car garage for years. "It held up the roof," he explained, "but it got in the way. Years ago, my oldest son ran into it after driving home after a date. I yelled at him for a week and grounded him for a month," remembered my friend.

"My second son did the same thing a few years later. I yelled at him for a day and grounded him for a week. Last month," my friend continued, "my grandson got his license and ran into the same pole when he pulled in to show me how well he could drive. I didn't yell at him or ground him at all. Instead, I apologized for not taking down that damn pole years ago!"

It is true. Grandchildren are more than crystal. Grandchildren are gold.

They are *different*!

Cinderella Man

Fathers and grandfathers are different too! A father's love is like no other, so is a grandfather's. Not long ago, I saw a movie about James Braddock. Besides being a father, he also happened to be the World Heavyweight Boxing Champion!

In the midst of the Great Depression, Jim had to struggle to feed his wife and two children and to keep their tiny ground-floor apartment livable. Because age added to his challenges, Jim was finally forced to go back to fighting.

On the morning of a meeting with his trainer to schedule work-outs and matches, Jim's decision to fight again seemed to have fate's blessing. As Jim prepared to leave for the meeting, his wife asked him to walk out to the apartment's porch and pick up the day's milk delivery.

Jim did as asked, but when he arrived at the milk basket that normally contained three full quart bottles, it was empty. Only a note that read "No payment, so no milk" remained.

After taking on a few relatively nameless opponents, Jim beat a couple of contenders and was offered a match with the defending world champion heavyweight, Max Baer. Max was a huge man who had already killed two opponents in the ring.

Jim's wife, Mae, forbade him from fighting Max, but Jim could not resist the money.

As Jim trained for his upcoming fight with Max, concern for Jim's age and injuries spread among the public. One day, Jim was confronted by a sports reporter who questioned his fitness to fight.

"Jim," started the reporter, "you are too old, too injured, and too slow for Max. How can you possibly beat him?"

"Because I know something that Max never will," replied Jim.

"What is that?" the writer persisted.

"I know what I am fighting for," said Jim.

"And what is that?" continued the reporter.

"*Milk*," replied Jim.

Jim Braddock beat Max Bear for the heavyweight championship of the world because he was a loving father and his children needed milk.

A father's love is like no other. So is a grandfather's.

Inflatable Love

Last year, I took one of my high school's alumni to lunch. I had heard this alum had made a lot of money selling tires and wanted to ask him to share some of his leftover profits with our alma mater for some sorely needed renovations.

Now this alum had made *a lot* of money selling tires! That is a very tough business, and he is a very tough man! Still, in his words,

"Successful people must be strong. They must be soft too." So like John Patterson, this very successful alum was both!

We had a long lunch and talked about lots of things. One of those things was love. "When I got married," the alum began, "I loved my wife completely, totally, with every part of my being. Then we had a baby. I loved that baby as much as I loved my wife, but I *didn't* love my wife any *less* because of the love I felt for the baby! We have had three more children, and I love them all as much as I ever loved my wife or my first child, no less. It is amazing," that alum ended, "my love never diminished, no matter how many times I gave it away. Instead, it grew. It got bigger. It got *stronger!*"

Families love the way that alum did. Their love is expandable, flexible, and stretchable. Their love is *inflatable!*

The Love of (Another) Father

For years, my high school employed two deans, one male and one female. Both were expected to manage the "social development" (in other words, the conduct and discipline!) of our students.

Both of our deans performed their roles very well.

One performed his role *better* than very well. He also performed his role as a *father* even better than he performed his role as a *dean*!

How do I know? Try this story.

Our male dean has a daughter. Her name is Mary. Some years ago, she was a freshman at our school. I, as principal, worried that the dad and daughter might have trouble making their coexistence work.

I was afraid it would be hard for the dad to treat his daughter impartially. Might he be strict enough with her? Might he be too strict with her?

My fears were unfounded, and the dad and daughter made it all work. In fact, they made it all look easy!

When Mary became a senior, I had no worries, but the dad did!

"I have been thinking about retirement," the dean shared with a fellow staff member. "You don't mean now, do you?" came the reply.

"If so, I am shocked! You are so young and so good! Besides, I thought you liked it here!"

"I am, and I do!" the dean replied.

"Then what is the problem?" the staff member pushed.

"It's like this," the dean began. "My daughter has had three good years here, but all three have been spent while sharing her school with her dad. That means for all three of those years, Mary has yet to have her own school, her own dean, or her own dad!"

"There were things at school she could not talk with me about at home," her dad continued, "and there were things at home she could not talk with me about at school! I want Mary to have one year in *her* school and one year at *her home* with *her dad!*"

Wow, I thought as I listened. "This man is willing to give up a job he loves because he loves his daughter more than that job!"

That dean has a father's love, just like James Braddock's. They both were fathers, and they were in love with their children. They were *proud* of their children too.

Student of the Week

A few years ago, I read a magazine article about a platoon of American tank commanders stationed in Iraq.

With the story was a picture. It showed all the commanders and crews mounted on their enormous tanks. One of the tanks had a sticker on its huge steel bumper just below the tank's powerful canon.

The sticker read "My son is the *Student of the Week* at the Grover Cleveland Elementary School!"

As you know, I am not a father. If I were, I bet that bumper sticker would make me very proud, and I bet there is no better feeling for a father to have than feeling proud.

A Mother's Love

Now I know what all of you mothers and grandmothers out there are thinking! Yes, you are thinking "so much for fathers and grandfathers. Now what about us? Is our love chopped liver?"

I will answer that question with another story!

Find Your Keys

A man came home late one night after driving through an angry blizzard. As he approached his house, he noticed that all his lights were out. The storm had obviously extinguished his power.

The man also noticed that he was not alone. His neighbor's house was also in darkness and its owner was on his knees under a street light apparently searching for something.

"What are you doing?" the man asked his neighbor.

"I dropped my keys," replied the neighbor, "and am looking for them."

"Where exactly did you drop them?" pursued the man.

"In my kitchen," replied the neighbor. "They slipped out of my hands as I was trying to let myself in."

"Why are you looking for them out here?" asked the man.

"Because there is *more light* out here than inside!" replied the neighbor.

"But if the keys are *inside*," reasoned the man, "there is no sense looking *outside*!"

So true!

No matter how thoroughly, how long, or how hard the neighbor looks, he will never find those keys outside the house because they are not there! They are inside!

Moral of the story? If what you need, want, or treasure is inside, it makes no sense to look *outside*! Mothers know that. Mothers *live* that!

So mothers spend their *lives looking inside their children* for the love, light, smiles, and strength those children need, want, and wish for.

Every breath a mother takes and every sacrifice a mother makes is for her children. Such is the love of a mother.

If a mother observes a full class in session, she sees only one student in that class—*hers*!

If a mother watches a game being played, by two full teams of players, she sees only one team in that game and only one player on that team—*hers*!

If a mother feels a room full of smiles or tastes a room full of tears, she feels one child smiling and tastes one child crying—*hers*!

Such is the love of a mother.

The love of a mother finds a way to be everywhere, feel everything, share every strength, and *find every key*!

The Candle

At my school's induction ceremony for our foreign language honor society last year, one of the inductees spoke of a candle. She compared the candle's life to that of a person.

"When a candle is lit," said the student, "it gives warmth and light, but its flame will eventually melt the candle and leave it to die. If, on the other hand, the candle is never lit, it will not die, but neither will it ever live."

Once lit, a mother's love will never wilt, wane, or weaken. A mother lives to see her children smile. A mother lives to see her children—period!

Such is the love of a mother.

The Best

On one very cold morning last winter, I was welcoming our students into school when one of my favorites got out of his mother's car, shook my hand, said, "Good morning, Doctor!" and headed for the cafeteria door. No sooner had his mom driven off than the student came flying out the same door, yelling, "Mom! Mom! Mom! Please stop!"

Mom didn't hear her son in time and drove up the nearby ramp to the major highway that connects our school with every thoroughfare in Eastern Massachusetts.

"Doctor, quick! May I borrow your cell phone?"

As I said yes, I realized why he had made the request.

"Hello, Ma?" said the son into my cell phone.

"How bad is the traffic this morning?"

"Oh, that bad, huh?"

I couldn't hear the mom's reply but was sure it was "Why do you care about the traffic?"

"Well, it's like this," replied the son, "I think you are sitting on my phone as we speak!

"What?" the mom pursued.

"Remember?" continued the son. "I used it on our way to school this morning, and now since I can't find it in my backpack, I am pretty sure it is on its way to work with you! I hate to ask in all this traffic," the son continued, "but could you bring it back to me here at school?"

Silence reigned after that. The boy shrugged his shoulders, shook his head, looked at me, and whispered, "I messed up, Doctor!" Then he stood beside me, welcoming other students for the next forty-five minutes, to give his mom enough time to fight the traffic all the way back to school!

When the mom's car appeared coming off the outbound ramp of the highway, her son lit up but not too much! I guessed he wanted to make his mom think he was happy but not *too* happy!

After all, the glee he felt when he got his cell phone back still needed to be tempered by the "sadness he suffered" for forcing his mom to face ninety minutes of rush-hour traffic!

Mom parked at the curb in front of me and her son. Then she rolled down her window, leaned toward me, and gave me her son's phone.

"Please give this to You Know Who, Doctor!" was all she could say. That was enough! When I gave the student his phone, he waved, looked toward his mother, and yelled, "Thanks, Ma!"

Then he turned to me and declared, "Doctor, there goes the *best mother in the world!*"

With all due respect, I beg to differ with that student's proclamation about his mother. In truth, his mother's painfully long morning in painfully "stop and go" traffic did not make her "the best mother in the world!"

Instead, it made her normal! It made her ordinary! It made her simply a mother. What she did that morning in traffic was what any mother would do and has done. Such is the love of a mother.

Good Kid

Like a mother's love, a mother's pride is a big deal too! When a child does something that a parent is proud of, you can almost see that parent grow tall enough to need bigger shoes and longer pants before your very eyes!

At my high school spring concert a few years ago, I talked with a mother during intermission. Her daughter was a senior and was applying to several colleges. "She asked me to go over her résumé and make suggestions," said the mom. "I worked on it all week but had trouble!" I asked her why.

The mom replied, "As I read about all the good things my daughter has done since she was a little girl," said the mom, "I started to cry and couldn't stop. I am so proud of her *I can't hide the pride*!"

More of Love

Many years ago, I read a story in *Reader's Digest* about a father who spent an entire summer taking his teenage son to see a game in every American league baseball park in the country!

"Wow!" replied the reporter who was interviewing the father. "You must really love baseball a lot!"

"No, I don't really love *baseball* that much," replied the dad, "but I do really love *my son* that much!"

If you are the parent of a teenager, how many games, shows, plays, conferences, meetings, and more have you attended over your child's high school career?

How many pizza parties have you hosted, essays have you edited, games of catch have you played, prom dates have you driven home, dances have you chaperoned, science experiments have you watched fizzle, algebra problems have you been embarrassed by, unaffordable sneakers have you afforded, or basketball hoops have you hung?

Was it because you really love games, shows, plays, conferences, meetings, pizza parties, essays, dances, sneakers, algebra problems, or science experiments that much? No. It was because you really *love your children* that much!

Yes, love is another word of wonder! In fact, *love* might be the *granddaddy* of *all* words of wonder! We all use it sooo much, we all understand it sooo little and it has sooo much to do with *faith, family, feelings*, and *more*!

What did you say? You need more stories before you will stop "wondering" about the *meaning* of *love*?

No problem. Just keep *reading*!

Good in All Bad

In my first three years as a high school president, I worked closely with our chief financial officer. He had six children who were all healthy. His youngest daughter, however, had been in an awful car accident when she was a teenager.

For months after that tragedy, the CFO traveled daily to a hospital in Boston to visit his daughter.

He was with her throughout months of traction and countless operations.

After hearing his story over coffee one morning, I replied, "Ed, what a horrible experience for you to go through!"

He smiled and offered, "Not really, Carmen. To tell the truth, in many ways, my daughter's accident was a good thing."

"How can you say that?" I asked.

"You see," the CFO explained, "my wife and I had five of our children in six years. Then we thought we were done! But fifteen years later, my youngest daughter surprised us by being born!"

"Before the accident, my youngest and I were never close because our ages were so different," the CFO went on, "but while she was recovering, I spent so much time with her in the hospital that we became closer than I had ever been to any of my other five kids even though I was much closer to them in age."

"It is funny," he concluded, "even something as bad as my daughter's accident had something good hidden inside it."

That "something good" was that father's love.

More Good in All Bad

Jim Kutsch was a senior in high school when he was conducting a science experiment in his backyard. Things went terribly wrong during the experiment, and the compound Jim was preparing exploded while it was being heated in a beaker. Glass fragments from the beaker were embedded into Jim's eyes and badly damaged his right hand.

Jim has been blind ever since that accident. Such a shame. Such a *bad thing*.

How could any good possibly be found in that bad accident?

Just visit Morristown, New Jersey, and ask the hundreds and hundreds of sightless clients of *The Seeing Eye*!

Jim was the president and CEO of this inspirational human service organization since September of 2006.

Before assuming the role of president at The Seeing Eye, he served ten years on the organization's board of trustees. He has lectured nationally on disability awareness, adaptive technology, and advocacy.

Kutsch even designed and developed the first talking computer for blind computer users as part of his doctoral dissertation research.

Jim earned a BA in psychology and an MS in computer science from West Virginia University. He also holds a PhD in computer science from the University of Illinois.

This man of overwhelming talent, soaring intellect, and remarkable courage have led The Seeing Eye to unimaginable heights in every area of sightless service, and he has done so not only *despite* his blindness but *because* of his blindness!

Jim Kutsch's strength and sacrifice have turned something very bad into something *miraculously good*!

It makes me love The Seeing Eye, and it makes me love Jim's story! Love truly *is the granddaddy of all feelings*!

Hal

Robert Louis Stevenson *once wrote, "You can give without loving, but you can never love without giving."*

Three or four Christmases ago, I read about a father named Hal who loved his daughter, Pierce, enough to give and give and give!

Not long before Christmas Day of 2018, Hal got some bad news.

He learned that his daughter Pierce, who is a flight attendant for Delta Airlines, had been scheduled to spend all her holiday in the air due to her busy flight schedule and lack of seniority.

That meant while Pierce helped thousands of Delta passengers make their way home 0for Christmas, she would spend her day far away from her family.

Hal and his love fixed that! He bought a ticket for himself on *every one* of Pierce's Christmas flights and spent his holiday *in the air with her*!

"This was a special time," recalled Pierce. "I had never been away from my parents on Christmas, and it was the first time my dad had flown on one of my flights."

"My mom helped, too," continued Pierce. "She 'took one for the team' and stayed home with our pets so Dad and I could have our holiday in the air together!"

Presents don't have to be under a tree, and Robert Louis Stevenson was right. Just ask Hal. Just ask Pierce.

Food

We do have fun with our families. We can also have fun with our food, like this.

> My favorite machine in the gym is the vending machine. (Caroline Rhea)

> Every part of me, I owe to spaghetti! (Sophia Loren)

> Inside me, there is a skinny person struggling to get out, but I can usually sedate her with four or five meatballs! (Anonymous)

Most Italians like food.

How can they help it? How can anyone help it? Italian food deserves its own vocabulary because no language contains enough complimentary words to do it justice!

Definitely not Italian!

Shortly after I became the principal of my high school alma mater, our director of admissions told me about an "emotional crisis" she had been through. A mother raccoon and her four babies had taken up residence in the cupola of the director's garage!

"My husband called an exterminator," explained the director, "and he came to kill them, but I couldn't let him!"

"Four days went by, and the raccoons kept doing damage. I said we'd have to put them away," admitted the director. "So I asked how they would die."

"We can drown them or shoot them" came the exterminator's matter-of-fact reply, "or we can poison them or trap them."

"Oh no!" replied the director. "I couldn't let you do any of those things. If I did, I could never live with myself!"

After a wink and some thought, the exterminator offered this, "How about if I just feed the little buggers some of my wife's meat loaf? *That* will kill *anything*!"

That exterminator's wife was definitely not Italian! None of the Italian women I know make meat loaf, and if they did, it would be too great to feed to raccoons!

Great Cooks and Great Food

Italian cooks don't make meat loaf, and Italian cooks don't feed raccoons! Their food is too good for that. Their food is the best!

When he was in his twenties, Tadone Carmine married the cook whose food was more than the best. It was the best of the best! Tadone married the best cook in the world! She became my Nonna Pasqualina, and *even my mother* was no match for her in the kitchen.

The Master's Hand

Once upon a time, a young boy was rummaging through the attic of his home. As he did, he came upon an old violin. The boy took the violin to his father.

"May I learn to play?" he asked the father said yes and arranged for the boy to take lessons. A year passed, and the boy practiced every day.

Still, the music he made on the old violin was not very good.

"I need a new violin," said the boy.

"No, you don't," said the dad.

"Yes, I do," insisted the boy. "A better violin would make better music."

"The violin you have will make better music too," said the father. "Come with me, and I will prove it to you."

With that, the boy, his father, and the old violin drove to the dad's father's home. On the way, the father explained, "This violin belonged to your grandfather. I want you to hear him play it."

When they arrived at the grandfather's home, the boy's father gave his father the violin. "Could you play it for us?" asked the boy's dad.

"Of course," said the grandfather, and he did. His music was beautiful. It was magnetic. It was magnificent.

The boy stood in wonder then turned to his dad. "I practiced," he said. "I studied. I tried. Still, I could not make that old violin sound beautiful, but Grandpa did. How did he do it? What made the difference?"

The father paused and looked at his father holding his violin. Then he said, "*The touch of the master's hand* made all the difference."

When it came to food, the touch of my Nonna's hand made all the difference. She was truly the master!

"Oh sure!" you are thinking. "Every middle-aged [and older!] Italian guy in the world raves about his grandmother's or his mother's cooking. Every one of those guys swears 'on his children's eyes' that his mother's cooking is the best in the world. How could they all be right?"

Well, they can't all be! That's right. All old guys can't all be right about their grandmother's or their mother's cooking, but I can, and I am!

Yes, only one middle-aged Italian guy in the world has a grandmother who was the *best cook* in the world, and that guy is me!

Not sure? No problem! Just go to the back of this book and find the appendix. Then look for the recipes (almost all of which came to me from my cousin Bob, who is one of my aunt Gloria Varrasso's sons. Thank you, Bob, and thank you, Auntie Glo!)

When you find them, cook something using any one of those recipes.

What? You can't cook? No problem! Have *someone else* cook one of those recipes *for* you instead! When you choose that cook, be sure to get somebody who normally *stinks* in the kitchen!

I promise you, even *that* person's cooking will be great!

Yes, the recipes in this book's appendix will make even the world's worst cook *great*!

Left Field

Do you remember the rookie who asked his manager for a chance to play left field in the first baseball game of his life?

At first, the manager said no. Then he caved and let the youngster have a shot. Well, the rookie was bad. He was *very bad*!

He dropped the first fly ball that was hit his way. Then he threw the ball over the catcher's head on a play at the plate. Next, he let a line drive hit him in the chest before it dropped to the ground.

Finally, he rushed a pop fly too fast, so it went over his head.

"Get out of there, kid!" yelled the manager. "And let me show you how it's done!"

The embarrassed rookie ran off the field with his head down, and the manager took over the left field but did no better than the rookie had!

The manager dropped two pop flies, overthrew the catcher, lost two balls in the sun, ran into his center fielder, and let a ground ball go through his legs before he began to run off the field!

As the manager left the game, he turned to the rookie and yelled, "Jesus, son, you've got left field so screwed up that nobody can play it!"

Well, not even that rookie left fielder could screw up my Nonna Pasqualina's recipes. They are that good! *She* was *that good*!

That Good!

My Nonna P could make meatballs, pasta, lasagna, ravioli, and gnocchi taste great. To me, that made her a great cook!
But to my father, Luigi, and my grandfather Carmine, I was wrong.

"Your Nonna is not a great cook because she can make *those* things taste great," said Dad and Tadone, "because *anybody* can make *those* things taste great! Your Nonna is a great cook because she can make snails taste great, and she can make squid taste great, and she can make smelts, eels, pigs' feet, and tripe taste great!"

In the world of Italian food, they were right, and I was wrong! If a person is not Italian, that person cannot imagine snails, squid, smelts, eels, pigs' feet, or tripe tasting great, but a truly great Italian cook can make *even those things* taste great!

My Nonna Pasqualina was *that great*!

My mother spent her entire adult life trying to get her hands on Nonna Pasqualina's meatball recipe! Alas, Nonna only gave it to her four daughters.

My mother *offered money* to each of those daughters! Still, they did not give the recipe up until after Nonna died! I get sad every time I think of all the "Nonna Pasqualina Meatballs" I missed out on!

"When they get to heaven, my sisters will all catch hell from my mother for giving up that recipe," my father would say, "but by then, God will be standing in line for a copy too!"

So much for Nonna Pasqualina's cooking! It truly was great! And guess what, my Nonna Pasqualaina's cooking had company! Who was that company? My Nonna Lucia, of course!

Remember, she and Nonna Pasqualina were born and grew up in the same Italian town, and it was a *very small town*! Remember that she and Nonna Pasqualina brought up their big families just four blocks away from each other in Quincy, Massachusetts, and they were *very small blocks*!

That means my Nonnas shared the same pots, pans, rolling pins, and *recipes*. It means if they needed meat, my Nonnas got it from the same butcher. If they needed vegetables, they got them from the same garden, and if they needed eggs, they got them from the same chicken!

So a lot of one Nonna's cooking rubbed off on the other. If one's was *the best*, the other's was *right next* to the best!

Leave Some Beauty Behind

One day while walking a beach in Florida, DeeDee and I noticed a sea-shell in the sand. It was very small and very beautiful. DeeDee picked the shell up, held it between her thumb and forefinger, and admired it. Then she turned to me and said, "We all leave something beautiful behind."

Dee was right. Some little sea creature had died and left that beautiful shell behind. Nonna Pasqualina and Nonna Lucia were like that little creature. They left some beautiful recipes behind. What is more, they left two beautiful families behind!

"Leave something beautiful behind." Good advice.

And I hope I will one day *take* that advice! One day, I hope to leave some beautiful stories behind. Thus, this book. Thus, this conversation.

That Depends

I saw a movie recently where a man walked into a diner and said to the cook, "I hear you make the best apple pie in town."

The cook nodded, smiled, and replied, "That depends."

"On what?" asked the man.

"On the apples!" replied the cook.

It's true; you *get out* what you *put in*.

I never saw Nonna Pasqualina bake an apple pie, but I know she began by *shopping for the best apples*! "The best insides make the best outsides," she would say, and that rule applied to more than pie!

All four of Nonna P's daughters (Jenny, Rose, Donna, and Gloria) learned how to turn a house into a home from "the inside out" while my father and his brothers (Americo and Peter) went to work or in the service. Good things in; good things out!

Good Things

"Nonna Pasqualina," I once asked, "how do you make everything you cook taste so good?"

She answered in Italian. As she did so, Nonna pointed to the garden-grown tomatoes, garlic, basil, and onions on her table and the freshly butchered meat on her cutting board.

Translated into English, my Nona's words were these, "Carmenuzzo," (I have been told that means *little Carmen*!) "if you put good things in, you will get good things out!"

I couldn't help but think how true those words are beyond food. As I said, Nonna turned her family's house into a home "from the inside out!" Yes, if you put good faith, feelings, fun, and (of course!) food into a family, good things will come out of that family, and in my family's case, they have!

My Nonnas and Tadones have left those good things behind. I am proud of those things, so would be my Nonnas and Tadones.

Way back on that beach, Dee had been right. Some little sea creature had died and left a beautiful shell behind. Nonna Pasqualina, and my Tadone Carmine were like that little creature. They helped to leave a beautiful family behind.

My mother helped her mother, father, brothers, and sisters leave a beautiful family behind, as well. Ma's parents (Tadone Raffaele and Nonna Lucia) couldn't match Tadone Carmine's family in size, but they came close!

They had sixteen children and got plenty of practice serving all those hungry "customers" three times a day! My mother helped a lot and learned a lot in the kitchen, just like my dad's sisters did. She was no Nonna Pasqualina, but she wasn't chopped liver either! (In fact, she could even make chopped liver taste good!)

128

Because my mother was born in the middle of her brothers and sisters and she was too young to get a job but old enough to be trusted around the stove, she was often elected to help her mother with the cooking.

Now, remember, that meant cooking for ten boys and more than half that many girls three times a day! That was a lot of cooking! So by the time I was born, my mother's pasta and pastry were *not* second to *none*, but they *were* second to *one*! They were second *only* to Nonna Pasqualina's!

Filled Pizzelle

Of all the pastry my mother had mastered, she liked to make filled pizzelle best. The outer cookies were about the size of a hockey puck and much thinner. And yes, I said *filled*! Ma *always* filled her pizzelle. For years, the recipe was another of Nonna's secrets but not anymore! I know it includes raisins, chocolate, chopped walnuts, grape jelly, and other good stuff. The book's appendix will tell you more!

I also know that lots of those good ingredients have to be cooked for hours in a double boiler then spread on the cookies and covered with wax paper so the filling would seep into the cookies and make them soft!

As she continued to age, Ma had trouble baking alone, so the only way I got to eat her pizzelle was to help her *make* them! I was no pastry chef, so I always had to recruit my father and Natalie to help *me* help *Ma*!

I must admit, the process was never perfect. Even with help, Ma and I *cooked* a few messes and started a few fires!

On one Sunday afternoon, for example, Natalie, Dad, and I decided to make pizzelle with Ma for what we thought might be the last time.

(We just didn't know how much longer she could be trusted around the stove!)

"Okay," Ma said when we asked her, "you three make the cookies, and I will do the hard part" (i.e., cook the filling!).

Ma always made that choice, mostly because she didn't want to give us the recipe for the filling and partly so she could prove to us that she had more "gas in her tank" than we thought!

As Nat, Dad, and I rolled out the cookie dough, Ma mixed the filling and put it in a double boiler. Then she lit the stove.

It was a gas stove, and with the flame on high, Ma began to stir the filling. After a short time, however, Ma lost her concentration and sneaked into the bathroom for a cigarette!

Ma's Secret

That is where my mother always went to relax. She thought we never knew, but for as long as all three of us could remember, if you went into the bathroom after Ma came out, it was always full of smoke even though the window was open!

The window was even open in the winter, no matter how cold it was or how much snow was coming in! If you used the bathroom after my mother in the winter, your fanny stuck to the toilet seat because it was so cold! That gave away her secret!

Now we all *knew* Ma's secret, but on this particular "Pizzelle Making Day," the rest of us didn't notice that Ma had *left* the kitchen until her filling had burst into flames!

Just as smoke filled the apartment, Ma came out of the bathroom.

"How is everything going out here?" she asked through the smoke.

"Fine on our end," I replied, "but it looks like you might need some help on yours!"

"Carmen, you do your job, and I will do mine!" Ma replied sternly.

Then she calmly but quickly shut off the gas and put the pot of flaming filling in the sink. Next, she poured water on it, spooned it into a bowl, and said, "Okay, this batch is ready to go into the cookies!"

We began filling the cookies right away and then tasted the first batch without letting them sit on wax paper. The filling was black instead of its usual brown, but somehow, it was delicious!

The three of us stared at my mother in amazement as we enjoyed the miraculous cookies. She winked at us, smiled, and said, "Your mother hasn't lost her touch, has she?"

As we shook our heads and smiled, Ma went back into the bathroom to light another cigarette!

Fussy Fathers

Like *his* father, *my* father refused to eat Italian food in any restaurant because his mother and his wife had both *spoiled* him by their cooking!

In fact, one Friday night, I asked my father if we could go to a pizzeria for supper, and he said that he would "never go to one of those places."

"Why not?" I asked.

"*Pizzeria* is the *diarrhea* you get when you eat *pizza* in a *restaurant!*" Dad responded.

Kind of gross but understandable. Dad's mother and my mother were in another world when it came to cooking, so why would anyone miss even one of their meals to eat somewhere else?

My Tadone Carmine was especially spoiled when it came to food and drink, and he knew it. "Why should I buy wine in a store?" he would ask.

"I can make it better and cheaper at home!" and "Why would I eat pasta in a restaurant? My wife can make it better and cheaper at home!"

Jay's Grandpa

To Tadone Carmine, if you came from a certain country, you should *do* certain things and *eat* certain things. Jay Leno tells a story of his grandfather that reminds me a lot of my Tadone Carmine.

"He loved to eat," Jay recalled, "but only Italian food. In fact," Jay continued, "my grandfather had a problem when he saw people of one nationality eating food that was usually associated with a different nationality."

"Oh my god," Jay's grandpa would say, "look at the Chinese guy eating corned beef and cabbage!" or "Can you believe that Mexican woman is eating a bagel?" or "What the hell is that Greek guy doing with a burrito?" or "Oh Jesus, what is that Irishman doing eating a calzone!" and "Why is that Jewish guy eating a pizza?"

And if Jay's grandpa ever saw an Italian person eating anything that was not Italian, he was convinced that person was not really Italian either!

"As far as my grandpa was concerned," Jay remembered, "it was all Italian all the time!"

Yes, my Tadone Carmine and Jay's grandpa would have gotten along very well! They *loved* to eat, and they *lived* to eat, as long as what they ate was Italian! That meant they would have both loved my Nonna Pasqualina, *and* they would have *loved* my Mother Helena!

No matter how good their *last* meal was, their *next* meal would be better. No matter how great their last meal was, their best was yet to come, which reminds me of *another story*!

Nonna's Polenta

Every once in a while, my Nonna Pasqualina reminded all her grandchildren that when it came to her cooking, *the best was yet to come*, and she did it with *polenta*!

Do you know what polenta is? It is just plain old cornmeal, but Nonna Pasqualina's polenta was so good we all loved it and looked forward to it. ("The touch of the master's hand," remember?)

How did she make it so good? For starters, she poured her polenta into a circle on a big wooden board. It looked like a big yellow pizza. Then she cut one slice for each of her grandchildren who were seated at the table.

Every slice of polenta was shaped like a big triangle that ran from the middle of the pie to each grandchild's place at the table.

After that, Nonna Pasqualina worked her magic! She cut a hole in the middle of the polenta pie and filled it with a big pile of her meatballs.

Now, as I have explained, like everything Nonna P made, her meatballs were to die for, and every one of Nonna's grandchildren got to have a meatball after they ate their way to the middle of her polenta!

The first one to finish even got an extra meatball! That was Nonna Pasqualina's way of reminding her grandchildren that (just like Sister Angela's spoon!) "the best is yet to come" in life and polenta!

The Kitchen Table

Whether or not you are Italian, your family's kitchen table is for more than just meals! Lots of things happen there, only some of which have anything to do with food!

Sure, families eat and prepare meals at the kitchen table, but they also play games, have arguments, model clothes, pick bridesmaids, and make friends there.

Families plan trips and funerals around that table. They decide whether or not to buy a new house or paint their old one. They sit around the kitchen table whether they are hungry or happy, lonely, or in need of a loan. They name babies and *tell stories*!

Remember when we were talking about the meaning of the word *family* and said that "there is no such thing as a one-person family!" and "The word *family* is *always* plural."

Well, decisions made at the kitchen table should be made with those words in mind.

Families make their *best* decisions when the *whole family* makes them! Families have the most *fun* when the whole family has it too! Let's tell some stories about families having *fun*!

Fun

When it comes to fun, Mark Twain outdid himself with this quote:

> Against the assault of laughter *nothing can stand.*

Yes, Mr. Twain said *nothing*! That means no death, no disease, no despair, no tears, no troubles, or even no traffic can stand against the assault of laughter. As this conversation continues, I hope to bring you Twain's kind of laughter.

I hope these stories will help you change the meaning of work to fun and of labor to leisure.

One Man's Work

A friend of mine claimed that he once knew a professional fisherman who spent his weekends growing tomatoes. He said it helped him relax and made him feel good.

My friend also knew a professional tomato farmer who spent *his* weekends *fishing*! He said it helped him relax and made him feel good! Yes, the meaning of work can be fun, and the meaning of labor can be leisure.

People look at relaxing differently. They look at *fun* differently, and people *can* change work into fun, or the other way around!

Dinner with a Hero

Even stories about war can be turned into fun. Last year, DeeDee and I went to dinner. We brought a very good man with us.

It was the eve of this man's ninetieth birthday, and his family had big plans for him. We wanted to snatch him away from those big plans before they began!

This very good man was not loud. He is not quiet either. He told many stories to us at dinner. Many were about World War II.

"I was a navigator on a B-17," he explained early in his first story. "We flew over thirty missions from England and bombed all parts of Germany. We even bombed Berlin, our squadron was the first one to do so."

Yes, that night, DeeDee and I were in the presence of *a hero*!

He, of course, denied it. The facts proved him wrong. Still, he had *fun* with the facts.

"It was a long trip to Berlin," he quipped, "so we had to lighten the plane. We threw out everything that wasn't nailed down. In fact, on the way home, one of our engines died, so we told our radio operator to send out a distress signal. 'I can't!' the operator replied. 'Why not?' the storyteller asked.

"'Because we threw the *radio* out of the plane over the English Channel!' he ended. As the navigator," explained our guest, "I sat next to one of the machine guns. I had to use it when we were attacked, but I wasn't much of a shot, thank God!"

"What do you mean by that?" I asked.

"Well," he replied, "we were approached by four fighters, and I started shooting at them but didn't come close to any. As I reloaded my gun, the pilot said, 'Stop shooting! Those fighters are our escort home!' As I said"—smiled our guest—"I was not a good shot, thank God!"

"Did you have any close calls?" I pursued.

"Well," he remembered, "one of our engines caught fire once shortly after we took off on a bombing run. So we had to drop all our bombs and then crash land."

"Where did you drop them?" I asked.

"Over the channel," he replied.

"That must have been dangerous with an engine on fire," I reflected.

"It was," he agreed. "Especially because we had thrown our *fire extinguishers* out of the plane to lighten the load as well!"

War is not fun, but a sense of humor can ease the pain of some horrifying times.

Big Buttons?

One morning, three of my closest friends in the Quincy Public Schools met to prepare a presentation for our school committee. As the others arrived, I had my back to them while pouring myself a cup of coffee. So I could hear them but couldn't see them as they entered my office.

Colleen, the only woman among us, opened the discussion by saying, "Okay, you guys, whatever you do, don't make me laugh today. This jacket is very tight, and if I laugh, I might pop a button!"

Now when I heard the word "button," I pictured a little one—like the ones on the vest of the three-piece suit I was wearing at the time.

But when I turned from my coffeepot and looked at Colleen, I realized I was wrong. The buttons that were sewn across the top half of her jacket were really larger than those on the front of my vest.

So I looked at the top half of Colleen's vest and said, "Wow, you really have big buttons!"

With that, she looked down at her vest, smiled, looked at me, and said, "Oh, thank you, Carmen, but I have never heard them called *buttons* before!"

Yes, against the assault of laughter, nothing can stand.

On another occasion, Colleen and I were having lunch during a principal's meeting. Colleen took three or four bites from a fruit salad. Then she stopped chewing, held her hand to her mouth, and said, "Oh god, I think I have fruit in my teeth!"

An older principal sitting nearby smiled and replied, "That's nothing! When you are my age, you'll have teeth in your fruit!"

Yes, my friends have made me laugh!

Susan

Some friends make us remember. Other friends make us smile. They make us have *fun*! Susan is one of those friends who does both.

She was also another of the principals (and friends) I worked with for many years and a very spiritual woman.

Susan attends mass and receives the sacraments on a regular basis. She gets ashes every year too. One year, she got a lot of ashes!

I saw Susan at a meeting after school on *that* Ash Wednesday and noticed that "her cup of ashes runneth over!" When I commented on how "blessed" her forehead had become with ashes, she replied, "Yes, the priest must have had an extra big thumb!" Then she continued, "When I got to school after morning mass that day, lots of kids and teachers checked out my forehead. At first, I think they were just looking to see if I got ashes or not! When they saw that I had been blessed with more than my share, lots of them commented.

The best comment came from a boy who had no clue about why I looked the way I did."

"What did he say?" I asked Susan.

"He said, 'Hey, Ms. Troy, that's a *cool tattoo*! I want one. Where did you get it?'"

Yes, friends make us remember, *and* they make us smile and have fun.

Nice Sweater

Another one of my favorite principals made me laugh.

It was Christmastime, and I visited his school to wish him and all his teachers a happy holiday.

I got there early, so we waited in the school lobby for the teachers to arrive.

"Is your shopping all done?" I asked my friend.

"Absolutely!" he proudly announced.

(Now the truth be told, my friend deserved to be a little less proud than he was. He, like me, only had to shop for his wife while she shopped for everyone else! Still, he did his job, as small as it was, and took pleasure in boasting about it!)

"Did you buy her anything nice?" I ventured.

"Most of the stuff was boring but needed," he quipped. "Then there was this sweater!" He went on, "It was perfect! I loved it and was sure she would too."

"In fact, he rambled, I liked it so much I made her open it before Christmas! I was sure she would love it and want to wear it to church on the holiday! I even nagged her until she caved and agreed to open it ahead of time!" my friend continued.

"How did it go?" I asked.

"Not well," my friend admitted after a long pause.

"What happened? Didn't she like it?" I pursued.

"Well," confessed my friend, "she opened the box, looked at me, and shook her head. Then she rolled her eyes and said, 'It is nice, but you bought me the *same sweater* for Christmas last year!'"

The assault on laughter continues!

On the Road

Some time ago, I went to mass on Sunday night in a church that I seldom attend. I had heard that its pastor had a great sense of humor, and I was in the mood for some fun!

It was Advent, so the church's choir lined up in front of the altar before the organ began to play the first Christmas carol of the evening.

As the organist sounded its first note of the first hymn, the choir paraded in single file down both side aisles then turned and walked across the back of the church. Next, they turned one more time, merged, and proceeded up the center aisle toward the tabernacle.

Throughout all this activity, the organ played, and the choir sang (admittedly, not well!).

As the leaders of both lines approached the front of the church via the center aisle, they turned to face the pastor before they stopped singing.

As I hinted a few sentences ago, the quality of the music that night left a lot to be desired but far be it from me or anyone else in attendance to comment in that direction, except, of course, for the pastor!

He waited until the organ and the singing stopped. Then he leaned forward, smiled softly, looked in both directions, and addressed the following remarks to the choir, "Well, ladies and gentlemen, it certainly sounds like we'll be needing a lot more practice before we take ourselves on the road this year, doesn't it?"

It is true. Against the assault of laughter, nothing can stand, and I *will* visit that pastor's church again!

Short Meeting

At a principals' meeting last year, one of my colleagues was commiserating over the small parental attendance at one of his PTO meetings.

"I was the *only one* who showed up!" the colleague complained.

"Wow, that is really sparse!" I agreed.

"Yeah, and it *still* took me *two hours* to get through the agenda!" ended my friend.

Yes, my friends do have fun.

Old Speaker, Older Audience

A few autumns ago, I was invited to make a presentation entitled "Life Is How You Look at It" to a group of retired teachers before their biannual luncheon. All went well. They were a magnificent audience, laughing at all my funny stories and even at some of my serious ones!

As I packed my bags after the presentation was over, a very "senior" retiree shuffled from her table to see me. Her table was close. Still, her shuffle was long!

When she reached me, she tugged on my suit coat to get my attention.

I turned and said, "Hi!"

She smiled and asked, "Dr. Mariano, may I ask you something?"

"Sure!" I replied. "Anything at all!"

My little visitor then gave me a wink and said, "Are you married?"

I laughed then said, "Yes, but you could make me an offer I can't refuse!"

She laughed with me and replied, "We would have given you a standing ovation tonight if you had waited long enough, but at our age, we just don't change positions as fast as we used to!"

Another assault of laughter!

Aunt Sadie

One of my oldest aunts was named Pasadea. Her nickname was "Sadie," and it fit her perfectly.

Her sisters always described Aunt Sadie as being "full-figured." I have often wondered what that means. Does it mean that Aunt Sadie filled up her figure with no room to spare? If so, Aunt Sadie *was definitely* full-figured because there were never *any* empty spaces *anywhere* in her figure!

My Aunt Sadie *was* a big, shapely woman, who *lived* to dress! In fact, she made a career out of clothes! She sold women's clothes at Bell Shops and Lee Shops in Quincy Square and R. H. Stearns in the South Shore Plaza. She *sold* a lot of clothes and *bought* even more!

She never met a color she didn't like as long as it was purple! She liked clothes more than food, and she *loved* food!

Like my aunt Mary, "Auntie Sade" worked a lot and gave money to her family to help make ends meet, so she seldom had the time or energy to cook or do housework.

"My sister could find Filenes Basement blindfolded," said Uncle Mike one day, "but she needs a map to find her way from the sink to the refrigerator! I gave her an apron for Christmas one year," Mike continued, "and she said, 'Oh, Mike, I love the dress you gave me, but it has a big hole where the back should be!'"

My family had fun, especially with Aunt Sadie!

Aunt Mary

My mother's oldest sibling was her sister Mary. She worked for years for the city of Quincy.

Aunt Mary never married, and some people thought it was because she took such charge of everything she did.

Aunt Mary was Quincy's *assistant treasurer* for years, and according to one of her brothers, "*To Mary, that meant she was the treasurer's boss*! In fact, to Mary, it meant she was *everybody's* boss!"

One day, my mother defended my aunt when my uncle said that about her. "She is a fine woman and one of Quincy's best employees," insisted my mother.

"She is too pushy!" insisted my uncle. "When she dies," my uncle continued, "every time someone on earth prays the Hail Mary, my sister will think they are talking to *her*!"

As I said, my mother defended my aunt Mary. She respected her, and she was close to her. Their closeness was tested one year just before Christmas many years ago.

My father wanted to go shopping for Ma's present but had no idea what to get her.

Dad's Christmas shopping trips were always an adventure. Even after twenty-five or so years of marriage, Dad knew nothing about Ma's sizes or taste. To be safe, every year, he asked for advice. One year, he visited Aunt Sadie at the Lee shops.

"Sadie," began Dad when he found my aunt in the store, "my wife said she wants a winter coat for Christmas. Can you pick one out for me?"

"Absolutely, Luigi!" replied my aunt in her usual flamboyant tone. "I will find Helena something she will love!"

In no time, Auntie Sade slipped a coat off a rack and gave it to someone to wrap.

"How much?" Dad asked.

Auntie Sade replied with the price. Dad paid, took the present, and left the store.

All went well until Christmas morning. Ma opened Dad's gift and loved the coat. "I can't wait to wear it to mass!" Ma squealed.

There was a problem at mass, however.

As my parents, Natalie, and I said our prayers in our pew before mass, Aunt Mary came down the church's center aisle and took a seat three or four rows in front of us. My mother noticed first, then we all did. Aunt Mary was wearing *the exact same coat* my aunt Sadie had *sold* to my *father* for my *mother*!

At twelve or thirteen years old, I had no idea what the impact of that was, but I quickly found out! My mother's eyes spent the first half of mass *burning* a *hole* into the back of Aunt Mary's head!

During the collection, Ma asked Dad where he had gotten the coat.

"From your sister Sadie!" Dad replied. "Where else!"

My mother's eyes spent the second half of mass burning a hole into the back of *Aunt Sadie's* head, and I spent the next hour saying prayers of thanks that I was *not* Aunt Sadie!

Uncle Albert

No part of our family (or *any* family!) has *ever* been perfect. One of my mother's brothers was a little less perfect than the others! His name was Albert, and he was many things. He was my father's best friend and the "official" best man at my parents' wedding.

Uncle Albert was also my godfather and a chief petty officer in the Navy.

"None of us dared to give our father any shit," recalled one of my oldest uncles, "except for Albert! He was always in trouble and he argued with everyone!"

"One weekend in the 1930s while in his early teens," remembered a younger brother, "Albert stole a car! He drove it home and sneaked up to bed just before the police knocked on our porch door.

"Pa got up to see who it was, and he looked through the door to see the cops standing outside. Before he even asked the cops who they were looking for, Tadone yelled, 'Albert get down here!'"

As the story goes, when Albert appeared at the foot of the bedroom stairs, Tadone grabbed him by the scruff of his neck and dragged him into the kitchen—Navy uniform and all!

Then in front of the police, Tadone gave Albert so much hell Aunt Minnie could hear it from a block away (and Aunt Minnie *couldn't hear!*)

"I think the cops even felt sorry for Albert," reflected my older uncle, and all this happen before the police had a chance to explain why they were there and who they were looking for!

The next day, Albert (apparently unaffected by the entire experience) told Tadone Raffaele, "Pa, I don't understand how the cops found out about that car so fast!"

Tadone replied in Italian, "Albert, there are only ten cars registered in our whole goddamned city. If one is missing, people notice!"

Uncle Mike

My uncle Mike was another of Mom's family who (along with Mary and Sadie) never married. He spent his life caring for a huge tomato garden, which was located beside my grandparents' house next to the Point Webster School.

Uncle Mike was always experimenting with new ways of fertilizing his tomato plants. He tried seaweed, chicken manure, pigeon manure, cow manure, horse manure, synthetic manure, sand, and more!

One day, I visited Uncle Mike in his garden and asked him what he was using for fertilizer this time.

"Your plants look great!" I said to him. "What secret are you putting in their soil today?"

"I am experimenting with Viagra!" my uncle kidded me.

"How is it working?" I played along.

"Not great," he admitted.

"What's wrong?" I continued.

"The plants grow very quickly," replied my uncle, "but when they are fully grown, they all have very long stems with just two little tomatoes growing way down at the bottom!"

After I stopped laughing, Uncle Mike shared a news flash with me that spoke of the same medication and another.

"Carmen, did you know," he asked, "that there is more money being spent on breast implants and Viagra today than on Alzheimer's disease research? That means in thirty years, all the world's old people will have perfectly working sexual parts but absolutely no recollection of what to do with them!"

Yes, my family had fun. They made me laugh…and laugh… and laugh!

Uncle Romey

I wish you knew my uncle Romaio. He, like most of my uncles, is funny. In fact, of all my uncles, he is the *funniest*!

He retired from a machine shop in North Quincy many years ago. When he did, everyone asked Uncle Romey what he would do with his spare time.

"I will become a brain surgeon!" he joked. "But only part-time. I will only operate on Thursday nights! That way," Uncle Romey explained, "I can still bowl, take Cupcake" (Uncle Romey's pet name for his wife, my aunt Jenny!) "to the movies and take up golf if I want!"

Of course, Uncle Romey was kidding! He did not become a part-time brain surgeon! Instead, in retirement, he became a part-time custodian.

Uncle Romey never admitted to that title, however. Instead, he called himself an "environmental engineer," who swept the corridors and parking lots for a local branch of Eastern Bank!

When he was eighty-nine, Uncle Romey got laid off because the bank contracted with a large cleaning company to take care of all their branches. "My funniest uncle" rebounded well, however!

"They paid me my full salary for the next fifty-two weeks as a severance," Uncle Romey announced. "I guess good things really do happen to good people like me!" When his severance ran out, Uncle Romey visited the unemployment office to sign up for benefits ("Why not?" he reasoned. "After all, I *did* get laid off, didn't I?")

When his unemployment counselor asked him what kind of job he would like, my uncle put his tongue in his cheek and replied, "I have been in the banking industry for the last twenty-six years and am looking for something compatible to my experience. How about making me an environmental engineer or brain surgeon?" (Remember, my uncle was over ninety years old at the time, and he is ninety-six now!)

The counselor paused a minute, decided to play along, and pointed to a pile of forms on a nearby table.

After the counselor showed him the pile of forms, Romey replied, "Now what?"

"Oh hell," the counselor said, "just fill out the forms and leave them with me!"

Uncle Romey did so, and abracadabra, he collected unemployment benefits for the next thirty-six weeks!

Yes, my uncle Romey *is* my funniest uncle!

Uncle Romey Again!

My uncle Romaio is more than funny.

He is brave. In August 1944, he and the Eighty-Second Infantry Division marched down the Champs-Élysées to liberate Paris.

Two days later, they left Paris and marched across Belgium, where they became part of the bloodiest encounter of World War II, the Battle of the Bulge.

My uncle and his valiant unit would finish the war marching deep into Germany, encountering many bloody battles along the way. For those two days in Paris, the French treated Romey and his fellow soldiers like the heroes they were.

Yes. My uncle Romey is funny, and he *is brave.*

For his part in the war, he was awarded a Bronze Star and two Purple Hearts. Thanks for your service, my uncle!

Help Me!

As you know, I have many cousins. The funniest are both named John. The older one is Uncle Romey's son and himself a decorated Vietnam War hero, whom I admire beyond words and has the biggest smile in the family. My younger cousin John is a plumber with his own business.

He, like his three brothers, works hard and always finds time to laugh. When he does, lots of people laugh with him, including me!

John always makes me laugh and never more than he did on his wedding day.

It all began when he and his bride named Laura walked down the aisle during their marriage ceremony. All went well until John and Laura knelt in front of the altar after their procession.

They, of course, faced the priest, which put their backs on the congregation. This meant that the soles of their shoes were pointed to the congregation, as well.

No one could see Laura's soles because her wedding gown covered them, but John's tuxedo trousers did no such thing to his shoes, so the world could see his soles.

John had written one word in chalk on each sole. The words were "Help me!"

Neither the priest nor Laura was aware of John's message, but when the congregation saw it, we all laughed like hell!

It is true. "Against the assault of laughter, nothing can stand!"

During the garter ceremony, John struck again. Laura sat in a chair with her legs crossed, and John knelt on the floor in front of her. The bridesmaid who caught the bouquet stood next to Laura, and all the single men at the wedding lined up behind John.

When everyone was in formation, John reached into Laura's dress to (we assumed) retrieve her garter.

Alas, he retrieved more than any of us bargained for, except John. He knew what was coming! Seconds later, he pulled his hand quickly from under Laura's dress and came back with a very large pair of bright red bloomers peppered with a bunch of white hearts and "I love John" printed on them!

Once again, John made me and everyone else at his wedding laugh and laugh and laugh.

The Blindfold Experiment

A very good friend named Ed retired from Quincy High School after teaching English there magnificently for thirty-six years. In that time, Ed's courses covered virtually every significant angle of communication, interpersonal relations, values clarification behavioral modification, and more!

As complex as Ed's courses were, he somehow made them *fun* for him and his students! "For example," Ed once offered, "I would challenge my students by requiring them to watch television shows without the benefit of sound. Then I would quiz them by asking if they could still follow the gist of a situation comedy without hearing a word or if body language and facial expressions could replace meaningful dialogue!"

"In another exercise," continues Ed, "I would have volunteers eat pieces of apples with slices of peeled onions shoved under their twitching noses. Did they taste apples or onions?"

"On another occasion," Ed expanded, "I might invite kids to take a 'taste test' of the contents of a Coke or Pepsi bottle without letting them see the bottle or guess the flavor of some Life Savers without being able to see what colors they were!"

In a more complicated exercise, Ed would blindfold half a class and assign a "guide" to each half for protection. Ed would not only bring his kids through the school's corridors and stairways; he might even head outdoors!

The procession would enter the school playground then take a ride down the slide. After each half of the class had experienced the adventure, Ed would lead a discussion. Did his students gain insights into how to trust each other? Did their sense of hearing and smell become more powerful in their sightless environment?

"The students almost always learned," reflected Ed, "how difficult it was to put their trust in the hands of another person. That revelation was as valuable to them, in my mind, as any lesson I could have given in vocabulary or grammar."

"As one might imagine," Ed reflected, "all the students babbled away at the 'weirdness' of the day's experience, but one year, a young man, who rarely participated in class, raised his hand and solemnly said, 'I have something to say.' The class hushed immediately.

"He said, 'My sister is blind, and I have resented her all my life because my parents have always put her needs first. I felt unloved and unappreciated. Today, having been blind for a half hour, I realize how horrible blindness is. I am ashamed of myself. I owe my family an apology.'"

"That class sat in silence," Ed expanded, "and every year after that day, I retold the story to see the impact of his words on every kid. Not surprisingly, they all felt genuine empathy for those less fortunate than themselves."

"I have always defined," Ed ended, "a teacher as one who takes his students on an experience that they could not have taken themselves. On that special day, that student became the teacher for me and his peers."

"Decades later, while I was speaking to a JFK assassination conference," Ed related, "I noticed one of the attendees was blind, so I told him the Blind Walk Story. He smiled and said that he recognized my voice. 'I know you,' he said, 'Thanks for pursuing the truth about Kennedy.'"

"I was truly amazed that he recognized my voice and appreciated my efforts," reflected Ed. "In fact, I was honored and astounded."

Great story. Great teacher.

Reflection

Recently, my mother's youngest sister, Gloria, called me with some kind words about Ed's stories. She had just finished reading them and wanted to share her feelings. "Reading the second one," she reflected, "made me think of how different my brothers and sisters all were and the many different ways our mother found to show her love for us.

"She did not treat us all the same, and I wanted to challenge her on that," continued my aunt.

"It's true," replied Nonna to Gloria. "It was harder to love some of you than it was others, but the ones who were *hardest* to love were the ones who *needed* my love most."

Nonna was an expert in cooking, in giving, and in *loving*.

Number 12?

My mother liked to share. She also liked to shop, but she liked to *talk* even more than she liked to share or shop! *And she talked to anyone*!

That caused a problem for my father when he drove her to the market every Friday to buy the weekly groceries.

One day, Ma needed some cold cuts, so she led Dad to the deli counter at Roxie's and took a number.

As they waited, Ma saw someone she knew, who had also taken a number and was waiting to be served. Ma and her friend talked for a long time. Dad just waited and watched.

All the while, the man behind the counter called out numbers. He did so until he got to the number 12. Then there was a problem. Number 12 didn't answer. "Number 12?" called the man. "Number 12? Is Number 12 here?" As he called, Dad walked closer to Ma, who was still talking!

He took the number from Ma's hand and looked at it just as the man yelled, "Does anyone know where Number 12 is?"

"Yes," answered my father just as loudly. "Number 12 is over here *shooting the sh—t with Number 16!*"

Number 12 would shoot the sh—t with anyone, and my family made me laugh.

Pardon the Interruption

As I just noted, my mother (a.k.a. Number 12!) would shoot the sh—t with anyone, especially her sister Millie! One afternoon, I visited Ma at home and found her and Auntie Mill "shooting" on the phone for an amount of time that appeared to be approaching the world's record!

While I waited for the call to end, I had a beer (and more!) with my father. As Dad poured…and poured…and poured, I asked him how Ma was getting along.

Dad winked and replied, "You know, Carmen, I can't say. I haven't spoken with your mother in three days!"

"Oh my god!" I replied. "Why not?"

"Because I don't want to interrupt her phone conversation with your aunt!" Dad answered. Now was he kidding or not? I honestly cannot answer! ("I wonder!")

Our talk about fun has been fun!

Now let me end that conversation with one of my favorite stories about my father.

Dad's Pills

When my dad had stomach cancer, he got some very bad stomachaches.

The doctor gave him some pills for the pain, but they upset his stomach more than the cancer did.

The doctor gave Dad something for that too. They were suppositories that Dad called "torpedoes." Dad used both pills and did fine. One killed the pain, the other settled his stomach.

One night, I went to visit Dad after I had been to my dentist. The dentist had done some drilling and filling, so my mouth was a little sore. I complained about it a lot.

Finally, my dad, who was in much more pain than I was, said, "Carmen, stop your whining." Then he reached for two of his pills. "Take these," he said. "Swallow one and sit on the other. When they meet in the middle, you will feel like a million dollars!"

I laughed—and stopped whining—then I promised myself never to whine again, thanks to my father.

My family and friends have made me laugh.

For me, they have led the assault of laughter! Mark Twain would be proud.

Strength, Success, and Sacrifice

So far, so good!

So far, we have talked about how blessed we are by our *faith, friends, family, feelings, fun, food,* and much, much more!

So as we canter toward our finish line of "Meaning," let's "wonder" about three more words. Let's start with *strength*. Yes, *strength* is a word of wonder.

Do you know what it means? If you think you do, try answering the following question, Who is the strongest person you know? My answer would be easy.

My answer would be the person we have talked about more than any other. My answer would be my father.

Why? Try this story!

Dad's Shopping List

One night, a few months before my father died, I was driving him home from the hospital after we met with his two doctors. His kidney doctor said Dad needed to go on dialysis right away or suffer renal failure. Then, alas, Dad's heart doctor said the dialysis would make him feel better, but it would eventually cause his heart to fail.

"It sounds like I am going to die," said my dad. "It's just a question of how, right?"

The two doctors dropped their eyes to the floor and nodded.

"Let's try the dialysis," my dad said.

As I drove my dad home that day, I fought back the tears of a son who was about to lose his father. Dad, on the other hand, was in good spirits.

He sat with a smile on his face listening to the radio. (Howie Carr was on, and Dad always *loved* Howie Carr!)

Finally, I spoke, "Do you need anything at the market?"

Dad said he did, so I asked him to make a list.

After writing for a minute, Dad gave me his list. I put it in my pocket as I drove without looking at it. Soon after, I dropped him at his house and went shopping.

As I pushed the cart up the market's first isle, I pulled Dad's list from my pocket. It read,

> Dad's shopping list:
> *Eggs*
> *Milk*
> *Onions*
> *Pears*
> *Apple juice*
> *One new heart*
> *Two new kidneys*

I laughed. Then I cried. Then I did both at the same time.

When I got back to Dad's house, he asked me what I thought of his list. "It was...good," I replied.

"I just thought you might need something to help you smile today," Dad said.

Yes, my father was not only *strong* enough to smile through that day's bad news; he was strong enough to help *me* smile through it, as well.

He was strong enough to help me smile in the face of sadness and to feel safe in the face of fear. How strong did that make my father? Do you wonder...?

My dad wore glasses for as long as I could remember. Still, glasses or not, he always had perfect vision.

How could that be?

Sounds crazy, doesn't it?

Not at all because glasses or not, my dad was always able to *see the best* in anyone and everything. That made his vision *perfect*. It made him more than strong!

More Perfect Vision

While Nat and I were growing up, my family suffered through many financially difficult times. During one of those times, my dad told us a story at dinner.

None of us thought Dad's story could be true. Still, we all *wanted* it to be because it reminded us of Dad's perfect vision. He really *could* see the good in everyone and everything!

Dad's story went like this.

One day, a poor little girl wrote a letter to God. It reached the postmaster general instead. The letter read:

Dear God,

Please send my mother one hundred dollars
to help her feed our very poor family.

The postmaster general was so touched by this plea he took a twenty-dollar bill from his pocket and forwarded it to the little girl!

A few days later, another letter from the same little girl arrived in the postmaster general's office. It read,

Dear God,

Thanks for the one hundred dollars, but please send another donation, and this time, don't send it through Washington. The government people got a hold of the first one and deducted eighty dollars in taxes!

We all worried a little less about money that night, thanks to my father's strength, his smile, his story, *and his sight*! He really *could see* the good in everyone and everything!

Speaking of strength, let's talk about Patrick!

Patrick

I once visited an elementary school to congratulate a fifth-grade teacher for a math project her students had just completed.

They had written letters to sailors on the USS *Enterprise*, an aircraft carrier that was in combat in the Middle East.

The students told of how much they appreciated the sailors' bravery and sacrifices. Then they asked the sailors some math questions like "How long is your ship?" and "How tall is it?" and "How much does it weigh?"

When the sailors wrote back (yes, they really did write back!), the students had some fun with the answers they got.

One student compared the length of the *Enterprise* to the length of their school. She calculated the ship to be 2.2 times longer than the school! Now *that* is *long*!

Another group of students calculated that if they stacked thirty-four of their school on top of each other, the *Enterprise* would still be taller. Now that is tall!

One student had some real fun. He figured out how many Hershey bars (without nuts!) it would take to weigh as much as the *Enterprise*. His answer was in the millions.

That last fifth grader's name was Patrick. I didn't know Pat then but came to know him well.

A year later, Pat became my hero. By then, I had learned of his troubles. I had learned of his cancer. I had learned of his *strength*.

I saw him thin, I saw him bald, *and* I saw him *happy*. I *always* saw him happy. I *only* saw him happy. That is what made him my hero.

Patrick died in 2005 while he should have been in high school. The world missed most of Pat's life. (Poor world!) Pat was a teenager when he learned he had cancer and spent the rest of his life being strong.

"He played every sport," said his dad while speaking on the radio during a Jimmy Fund event, "even while he was having chemo. Once after a hockey game, I saw him take off his pads. As he did, the skin peeled off his legs. He never complained. He never even noticed.

We were talking one day," Pat's dad continued, "and I told him how badly I felt that he had cancer. Pat replied, 'Dad, don't feel bad. I wouldn't change a thing about my life. Besides, I would rather that I have the cancer than you or mom or one of my sisters'."

What does strength sound like?

It sounds like those words.

It sounds like that young man. It also sounds like the strong young man whose story follows.

His name is Palmer.

Palmer

Remember him? Yes, Palmer is the special student for whom his classmates collected a jar full of bills instead of loose change! I visited Palmer at home during his illness to bring dinner to him and his family.

"How is he?" I asked his mom as Palmer entered the room. "He's tired. He has had chemo every day this week and starts a month of radiation on Monday, all in Boston. It is so hard."

I shook my head and turned to Palmer, planning to say how sorry I was for all he was going through. He never let me. Before I could speak, he smiled, looked at me, and said, "It's nothing I can't handle."

I put my hand on his shoulder, smiled back, and said nothing. As I stood in silence, I asked myself if I could have *said* and *meant* what this brave, beautiful young man just did.

Palmer and his mother came to visit me at school on Palmer's birthday to thank me for a Red Sox jacket I had given him. They were on their way to Brigham and Women's Hospital, where Palmer was about to begin a month of radiation treatment *in addition* to the chemotherapy he was already receiving.

As they sat at my little office table, I asked Palmer if he wanted something cold to drink. Before responding, he paused, turned to his mother, and asked, "Would *you* like something? When she said, "No thank you," he said the same. The sound of strength speaks again. It speaks in the name of Palmer.

Joe

Patrick, Palmer, Anne Marie, Lucas, David, and more taught me about the wonder in the word *strength*, and they were not alone. Joe kept them company. Joe taught me about strength too. He taught me what it means. He taught me what it cost.

Joe carries strength in his smile and hope in his heart *every day*. That strength and that hope speak to the people who know Joe and who meet Joe.

As he looks up from his wheelchair at them, Joe makes those people want to look *up at him, as well!*

Joe *sits* taller than those who *stand* near him. He is that inspirational. He is that majestic. He is that "tall." He is that *strong*.

No one has given me more strength than Joe has because no one has *shown* me more strength than Joe has. I never thought anyone or anything could teach me more about strength than wrestling has. I was wrong. Joe has.

Barely out of his teens and shortly after his high school career ended with graduation, Joe dove into the wrong end of a swimming pool and broke his neck. That was dozens and dozens of years ago. His legs have not served him well since then nor have his arms.

Still, his strength has.

I saw Joe's strength before his accident when he wrestled for me. I see it today. I will see it tomorrow.

When I wrote of being a wrestler many pages ago, I said it "was like being a Marine, only harder; running a marathon, only longer; and going through hell, only hotter!"

I said that, among wrestlers, "respect is won and esteem is earned immediately, automatically—period."

Those words go double and more for Joe.

Joe's life has rules that make wrestling's hardest rules look easy and wrestling's easiest rules look like no rules at all!

Without the use of his arms and legs, Joe has earned a bachelor's degree and a driver's license. He works part-time and explains that "it would be full-time, but I need the extra hours to keep up with my therapy."

Joe has won the admiration of every friend he has and every person he meets. His injuries may limit his limbs, but they will never overcome his resolve. They will never weaken his spirit. *They will never vanquish his strength.*

I once asked Joe to share the source of his strength with me so I could share it with you, my readers. My request was rewarded with these words from Joe: "I have a strong faith and ask God daily to do for me what I can't do for myself. I have been blessed to have great role models, starting with my parents and supportive siblings who have always had my back and been there to pick me up at times when I've fallen.

When I was newly injured and not dealing with life very well, my older brother Mike (a captain of one of the best wrestling teams Quincy High ever had) came to me and said, "Joe, this injury is like a wrestling match, but it will be the longest and most difficult match you will ever face."

"I've never forgotten that," reflected Joe, "and to the best of my ability, I have applied the Quincy High School 'Men at Work' wrestling mentality to combat my injury every day for the past thirty-one years. I have also drawn strength from coaches. They have been my mentors and heroes."

Yes, Joe's injury is relentless. So is Joe.

"What can I say about the sport of wrestling?" Joe ends. "It taught me so many lessons in life! I found this quote on the internet. It sums up how I feel about wrestling and the strength it has brought me.

"Most…people…will go their entire life and never understand the feeling and the strength that only wrestling can bring."

Joe is the best teacher of strength I ever had.

Thank you, Joe, my teacher and my friend.

Nick

He was born *without limbs and without limits*!

His name is Nick Vujicic, and he is a motivational speaker from Australia.

In his book *Life without Limits*, Nick explains that an avalanche of birth defects left him with no arms, no legs, no hands, and one foot.

He stands at a table when he speaks to an audience just so he can be seen.

Does Nick have strength? Do you wonder? If you do, try these words. They are Nick's.

"If you can't *make* a miracle, *be* one! If I had arms and legs, I would be sad because people would not come to hear me speak. It is because I am *so different* that people come! So my not having what other people have makes me happy. In fact, I love my life as much as I would love theirs!"

Yes. Those are all Nick's words, thoughts, or both.

As I said, *Nick is strong*! In fact, he has so much *strength*, he gives meaning and muscle to that word.

So much for *strength*. Now let's wonder about *success*.

What does it mean? Maybe the sometimes tragic and other times magic story that follows will help us answer that question!

Sylvester Stallone

Sylvester was born in New Your City in July 1946. During his delivery, he suffered a severe facial nerve that resulted in his droopy facial appearance and slurred speech.

Today he is one of this country's most accomplished movie stars. Early in his career, though, Sly struggled. In August 2019, six years after *Rocky* was released, he was sleeping at the Port Authority Bus Station between low-level acting jobs!

He became so desperate that he stole his wife's jewelry and sold it for a place to stay. He eventually became homeless and once again had to "reside" in that New York bus station!

Stallone's eldest son had autism and died at thirty-six from a drug overdose. Sly divorced three wives and lost a half sister who was taking sixty-five OxyContin pills a day when she died.

Despite so many setbacks, today Stallone continues to make movies and has a net worth of four hundred million dollars!

Tell me, is Sly Stallone a *success*? No matter what your answer, are you sure you know the meaning of that word, or do you…wonder?

Need more stories? So do I!

Two Gardeners

Two gardeners from wealthy estates on Long Island met one day at the local hardware store. "I hear you're working for that banker fellow now," said one.

"You've got it all wrong," replied the other. "He gets up at five thirty every morning to get on a dirty, overcrowded train and commute to the hot city so he can keep up his estate, and pay me a good wage.

I spend my day outside in the fresh air, taking care of the beautiful trees, shrubs, lawns, and flowers he pays for. No, *I'm* not working for *him*. *He* is working for *me*!"

Is either of those gardeners a success? Do you wonder?

So do I!

Ronald's Gift?

Ronald Davis worked with special needs students for twenty-five years.

He wrote a book called *The Gift of Dyslexia*.

That's right. Ronald's book is titled *The Gift of Dyslexia*, not the curse, or disease, or burden, but the *gift* of dyslexia.

In his book, Ronald says students with dyslexia *have gifts*. They are highly aware of their environment, think in pictures, have vivid imaginations, and are very intuitive and insightful.

That is why Ronald says, so many famous people have dyslexia.

"What famous people?" you ask.

Well, try Hans Christian Andersen, Alexander Graham Bell, Winston Churchill, Thomas Edison, Walt Disney, Henry Ford, George Patton, Woodrow Wilson, Galileo Galilei, Tom Cruise, Keanu Reeves, Steven Spielberg, Pablo Picasso, Cher Bono, and more!

Yes, Ronald Davis looks at dyslexia as a *gift*.
Does that make Ronald or anyone else with dyslexia "successful?"
I wonder!

John Quincy Adams

At seventy years old, a man once said, "My whole life has been a succession of disappointments. I can scarcely recall a single instance of success in anything I have ever done."

No, that man was not a criminal or a convict. He was not poor or unpopular either. That man distinguished himself as a secretary of state, member of Congress, and president of the United States.

His name was John Quincy Adams. Did President Adams die successful? Do you wonder?

The Last Supper and more

Approaching death, an artist asked forgiveness for what he felt had been his greatest sin. "I have offended God and mankind," he confessed, "because my work never approached the quality it could have." That artist painted *The Last Supper*. He painted the *Mona Lisa*. He set a standard of excellence that others have been trying to match for four hundred years. Still, *Leonardo da Vinci died dissatisfied*.

Did he die successful?
Do you wonder?
So much for *success and for strength*!
Now for our *last* word of wonder!
It is *sacrifice*.
What does it mean? Lots of stories could help here.
Let's try some!

Special Sacrifices

As our country reels in the throes of the coronavirus, countless families are making sacrifices beyond expectation and even beyond inspiration.

A young mother and doctor in Atlanta, for one, describes her family's sacrifice in these terms: "My husband is a physician assigned to a local emergency department and is actively treating virus patients. We just made the painful decision for him to move into our garage for the foreseeable future. We have a three-week-old newborn and two youngsters and just can't risk infection," laments the mother as she wrestles with many mixed emotions and major sacrifice.

"It pains me to wonder how many weeks will go by before my husband will get to hold our baby or see our children," reflects the young mom, "but their safety comes first. Our children come first."

If you were looking for the meaning of the word *sacrifice*, would you look in the dictionary, or would you take a ride to Atlanta and listen to that young doc and her husband tell their story?

Do you wonder?

Safety at Any Cost

A brave epidemiologist who lives in California sleeps in his scrubs and mask in a tent to protect his young family from what he calls his "dangerous presence" while two doctors in St. Louis bought a trailer that they "can't afford!" for one of the docs to live in while he weathers the storm of the pandemic.

That doc travels many miles every day from his hospital to his "new home on wheels" rather than enter the house that holds his elderly parents, wife, and very young child.

Do those *stories* give more *meaning* to *sacrifice* than any words ever could! Do you wonder!

More than His Life

Need one more story about *sacrifice*? Me too!

DeeDee and I visit our parents' graves often. It is the least we can do to honor their memories. One of our recent trips was taken on Veterans Day.

Both of our fathers fought in World War II, so each of their graves, like hundreds of others, was adorned with an American flag.

"Imagine how many of them gave up their lives in battle," whispered Dee as she gazed at so many flags. "Yes," I quietly replied. Then I wondered what those World War II casualties truly *did* sacrifice because none of them were alive in their graves to tell us that day. I borrowed the words of a mother who had lost her twenty-year-old son in the Middle East just months after he graduated from high school—my high school. "When my son was killed," this *Gold Star* mom recalled, "our family lost more than his life. We lost the father he could never be, the grandchildren he could never give us, and the generation we could never look forward to. Losing heroes like my son," his mother continued, "costs their families more than memories, it costs them legacies. Those heroes sacrifice pasts, presents, and futures that cannot be measured, counted, or even imagined.

Yes, families like those and sacrifices like theirs gave meaning to our last word of wonder. So will we if we take the time to *find and tell the stories* of that word.

Chapter 2

Giving Muscle to Our Messages

So much for how *stories* can help give *meaning to words*. Now let's talk about how stories can help give *more* meaning to *more* than *words*!

Let's talk about how stories can give *muscle to our advice and our direction*. Let's talk about how we can give *muscle* to our *messages*!

What do I mean? I will answer with (of course!) another story!

Some years ago, I heard an eloquent and intelligent celebrity give a commencement address to the graduating class of a large and prestigious Midwestern University. In his address, this speaker gave his young audience and their families *lots* of advice and *plenty* of direction!

Like what? Like this:

"Work together…"
"Walk your talk…"
"Never give in…"
"Work hard…"
"Stay positive…"
"Have direction…"
"Be creative…"
"Welcome failure…"
"Believe in yourself…"
And more!

Most of that speaker's audience had heard those "pearls of wisdom" before but never followed, remembered, or even listened to them!

Why? Because the speakers who had given those messages before never gave their audiences a *reason* to follow, remember, or listen to them!

When I was young, my father was sometimes like that speaker. He gave me advice or direction without a reason. *Sometimes* he was serious. *Other times*, he was kidding. *Most* times, he said it right after he told me to do something, and I asked him, "Why?"

If Dad told me to take out the trash or shovel the driveway, I would ask why, and he would answer without a reason. Instead, he would just say, "*Because I said so!*"

If *he* asked me to *wash* the car or if I asked *him* to *use* the car, we both would almost always follow up with a "Why?" and another "Because I said so!"

Last but not least, if I asked him for a bigger allowance and he refused, I would ask him why, and he would say, "Because I said so!"

Now those words worked for my father every time he used them. They had a perfect record. They batted a thousand. They were *undefeated*!

Yes, after he said those words, I did whatever Dad told me to do just *because he said so*!

If only you and I, dear reader, could have the same record and bat the same average with those same words! If only we could tell even one of our friends, family, or followers to do something, remember something, or listen to something "because we said so" and if only one of those people *accepted* those words! Alas, those people never have and never will, nor should they!

What did you say? Did you say "prove it!"? Sure! You want proof? Here comes proof! Just think of the last time *you* attended a graduation speech and the speaker gave you a recipe for success!

How many of that recipe's ingredients did you listen to, follow, or remember since that speech?

Did you say none?

Well, if you *did* say "none," you just got your proof!

Giving audiences or followers advice or direction without a reason or explanation has never worked and never should!

So as speakers or leaders, we have no right to expect unfettered or unfounded attention or obedience from any audience or any followers!

We have no right to expect our friends, families, staff, or supporters to choose our direction, support our agenda, or follow our footsteps *because we said so*!

Instead, we should *earn* the right to be followed, listened to, or remembered. And *how can* we earn that right?

We can strengthen our messages with the muscles that we make from stories! Stories will give muscle to messages that deserve to be stronger.

How *well* will it work? Let's find out! I will tell some stories that are meant to strengthen your advice and direction. After you listen to my stories, ask yourself if any of them bring *muscle to any of your messages*!

The first message we'll make stronger by adding muscle is "work together!"

Work Together

The USS *JFK*

Years ago, I took a tour of the USS *John F. Kennedy*. At the time, this nuclear aircraft carrier was the biggest ship ever built.

As I gazed in awe at the size, scope, and strength of everything I saw, I turned to my tour guide and said, "Imagine, once upon a time, the world's biggest ships were made of wood! I haven't seen any wood on this ship at all."

"That's right," my guide replied. "There isn't any material on this ship that, by itself, can float. Still, as long as those materials hold *on* to each other, they can hold *up* four city blocks of people, planes, and power."

What if after telling my story, I said this to my followers, "Ladies and gentlemen, *you* are like those materials. As long as you hold *on* to each other and work together, you can hold *up* anything. That is the lesson of the USS *JFK*."

Would telling that story give my followers a better chance of "working together" than "because I said so" would? If so, good! And here comes another story!

Shared Light

My high school's National Honor Society induction of a few years ago included, as always, a candle lighting ceremony in which each of the society's four officers lights a candle in honor of the four founding principles of the society.

The president began the ceremony by lighting a match and holding it close to the wick of one of the candles. Despite a valiant effort, however, she could not get the candle to light.

She lit match after match with no luck.

Finally, the candle lit, and the president sat down.

The vice president stood next and tried to light the second candle.

Again, he lit match after match with no luck.

Finally, his candle lit.

The treasurer came next.

She walked to the third candle and reached but not for the match. She reached for the vice president's candle and lit her candle with that candle's flame.

No problem!

Instant success!

What is the moral of that story?

Shared light is the brightest light of all.

So share your light and yourself with the world, with your family, your friends, and with each other.

Would telling that story give my followers or audience a better chance of *working together* than telling them to work together *because I said so*?

If yes, good again!

Never Hurt What Little They Have

As you may know, *My Brother's Keeper* is a Christian ministry located in Easton and Dartmouth, Massachusetts. Like Nonna Lucia, "MBK" comforts and inspires all that it serves.

After some students and I were given a tour of the charity's facility by its founder, he took us outside to see a huge bronze statue of Jesus washing the feet of Peter.

"This statue has a message," explained the founder. "It reminds us that it can be *harder* to *receive* than it is to *give*. Think about it," he continued as we pondered his curious statement, "when Christ began to wash Peter's feet, Peter was embarrassed. He asked the Lord to stop.

"'It is I who should wash *yours*,'" Peter said to Jesus. Still, Jesus continued. His message was that, to give can be hard and to receive can be harder!"

"When our volunteers make deliveries," our special tour guide continued, "we remind them of that. We tell them if they deliver a bed to a home that has none, the people living in that home and sleeping on the floor will be more embarrassed than thankful. They will be more self-conscious than excited."

"Even people who have nothing *have something*," he ended. "They have pride. They have feelings. When we give to them, we must never forget that. We must never hurt what little they have."

Might telling that story help our followers or an audience tune into each other, listen to each other, or work together more than they would if they were simply told to work together without a reason or "because we said so?"

If so, good!

Big Trees

Anyone who has visited the Great American Northwest has been in the awesome presence of the world's oldest and largest living things.

Yes, the redwood trees of the Great American Northwest are the tallest trees in the world. Some of them are as many as three hundred feet high and over 2,500 years old.

You would think trees that large and that old would have a tremendous root system reaching down hundreds of feet under the ground just to keep them up! On the contrary!

These enormous redwoods actually have very shallow root systems. Still, those shallow systems are unbelievably strong.

Why? Because they are *joined to each other*!

As the redwoods grow, the root system of every tree seeks out and finds the system of every neighboring tree in its grove and bonds with it until those trees share the *same system*!

So when storms come or winds blow, the redwoods *stand tall* because they *stand together*.

What if after telling that story, I said this to my followers, "Ladies and gentlemen, we are all like redwoods. We stand together much better than we stand alone. We work together much better than we work alone. So *work together*!"

Would telling that story give my audience or followers a better chance of taking my advice to *work together* than saying nothing or giving a better reason than *because I said so*?

If so, good one more time! And let's try another story!

Dixie

On the day after the surrender at Appomattox Courthouse, Abraham Lincoln appeared at a second-floor window of the White House because citizens had requested his presence so they could serenade the president in his moment of victory.

They called for a speech, but Lincoln declined. Instead, he asked the band to play "Dixie."

That song had been the unofficial anthem of the Confederacy during forty-eight bloody months of Civil War, and on that night, from that window, Lincoln chose to honor it.

"I have always thought 'Dixie' to be one of the best tunes I have ever heard," the president reflected. Many close to him believed the gesture to be Lincoln's way of encouraging a nation that had ripped itself apart in the Civil War to begin knitting itself back together in peace. Maybe it was.

In any case, might the playing of "Dixie" stand a better chance of convincing our nation's North and South to follow Lincoln's *work together* message than *because I said so*?

If so, good for Mr. Lincoln!

Can I suggest any other stories that might give more muscle to my "Because I Said So" message?

Try these!

Courage as a Coach?

It all started with seventh-grade football. The junior high school in Quincy, where I first taught, needed a coach, and although I had little talent or knowledge that applied to that sport, I was good with seventh graders, so I gave it a shot.

I leaned hard on my first team and harder on myself. In my second year of coaching football (like my first year), we never lost. In that year, however, we did have two ties. One of our ties came late in the season, and I didn't like it. In that game, we had made too many mistakes for what was by then an experienced team.

By the time we got back to school after that game, it was dark, and I was pissed. I overcame my anger just as our team bus stopped and asked myself where the teachable moment was in the day's outcome.

I left the kids on the bus, ran into the school, and asked the custodian (not George) what time he was locking up. "At six o'clock," he replied. That gave me twenty minutes—not enough time to make the point I had planned.

So I went back to the team, who by now was standing in a cold dark parking lot, and told them to go into the locker room and get their street clothes out of their lockers. (They had changed at the school and bussed to the away game in their uniforms.)

Then we marched to the field behind our school and *corrected our "mistakes"* for an hour by the headlights of my 1967 GTO convertible. After that, I left my team to walk home carrying all their gear, books, and heavy coats.

Over the Top

Win, lose, or tie, what I did was over the top. Those kids were no more than thirteen years old, and I sent them walking home alone in the dark with no dinner after seven that night. There was no courage in that. There was no strength in that.

I have always hated to lose. Still, that night as my seventh graders walked home alone in the dark, I decided to hate losing less and to love my athletes more.

I decided to be good enough to win and to be strong enough to lose.

I decided to take the high road *and* the hard road.

That night, as my seventh graders walked home alone in the dark, I decided to make their mistakes their teachers, not their undertakers.

Most of all, I decided to never send my seventh graders *anywhere alone in the dark again.*

It was a good decision for me and them. It served us all well in football, in wrestling, and in life.

The next day before practice, I explained how I felt and apologized to my team. It seemed to matter. It seemed to bring us closer together.

And oh yes, I never told my kids to do anything "because I said so" again!

The next time I told my kids to "work together," they did it better than ever before. More muscle in my message? I think so. I hope so.

The more I coached wrestling, the more I loved what the sport stood for, and the more I stood for what the sport did. I was driven. I was dedicated. I was passionate. I was committed, and most of all, I was indebted to my athletes. I gave my wrestlers more than I asked from them, and I asked a *lot* from them!

Most of my wrestlers were in their teens when I coached them. Today, many of them are over sixty. (Time does fly!) I still see them from time to time, and we talk about "the good old days!"

"Almost everything we remember happened to us as a team," says more than one of "my kids" when we reminisce. "I don't remember what we did, but I do remember how we did it," they go on. "Whatever we did, we did it together."

Work together! Forget being number one. Remember being one.

More muscle in my message? I think so. I hope so.

The Meaning of T-E-A-M

When it comes to coaching, there is one word of wonder that makes all the others seem worthless and weak. It is the foundation of every coach's career and the font of every leader's legacy. That word is *team*.

Yes, you know how to spell *team*, but do you know what the word *team* spells? It spells Together Everyone Achieves More. Lame? Yes, True? Yes, yes, yes!

Helen Keller once said that *we can do things together that we could never do alone. Helen was right, so good coaches bring athletes together. Good coaches make athletes one with each other. Good coaches make athletes one with their coach*! And making athletes one with their coach can be hard!

Special Sneakers

You have all heard about the two men who were on a camping trip. One morning, they woke up to find a huge bear racing toward them from across a clearing. The first man who saw the bear frantically began to put on his sneakers—the second man saw the bear a minute later, jumped up, and began to run away from the bear with nothing on his feet.

As he did, he looked back at the first man and yelled, "What are you doing?"

"I'm putting on my sneakers," came the reply.

"And I suppose your sneakers are going to let you outrun that giant bear!" said the second man. "I don't have to outrun *the bear*," said man number 1. "I only have to *outrun you*!"

It's true! Sometimes getting people to work together is hard! Why? Because "this is America!" And in America, we are all independent contractors. We all work for ourselves. We all listen to the same radio station, and it is called WIIFM, otherwise known as "What's in It for Me?"

And Americans are not alone! The English language has over 450,000 words, and I have been told that most of our daily conversations use only four hundred of those words, and by far, the most commonly used of those four hundred are I, *me, my,* and *mine!*

Yes, sometimes people work for themselves! When they do, we need to put muscle in our "Work Together" message!

Not sure? Just ask the landlord in the next story!

I Confess!

Recently, a man went to confession. He started like this, "Father forgive me. During World War II, I hid a refugee in my attic."

"Son, that was a blessing. You saved his life," said the priest.

"But, Father," replied the man, "I made him pay rent."

"That was not so nice," the priest admitted. "But you put yourself at risk, and so you can be forgiven."

"Oh, thank you, Father," said the man. "But I have one more question."

"What is it, my son?" asked the priest.

"Do I have to tell him that the war is over yet?"

It's true. People work for *themselves,* not because they are *selfish* but because they are *human!* So sometimes they need more muscle for their "Work Together" message! What kind of muscle? Try this story about some strong and special horses!

Ben-Hur

A long time ago, I saw a movie called *Ben-Hur.* It was a classic movie that I will never forget. The movie tells the story of a Jewish prince played by Charlton Heston and named Judah Ben-Hur who earned the favor of a Roman general only to fall from that favor when Judah decides to follow Jesus Christ.

The most famous scene in the movie involves a chariot race in which Mr. Heston's character defeats and kills a Roman general.

To prepare for the race, Ben-Hur visits an Arabian chieftain who owns four beautiful white stallions that will become the team that will pull Ben-Hur's chariot.

When Judah first sees these spectacular horses run, their driver loses control and they run off the track and into a tree. Their owner is distraught, but Ben-Hur explains the problem.

"Your horses are magnificent," says Ben-Hur to the Arab owner, "but they are not in the right places. One is older, wiser, slower, and stronger than the others. He must run on the inside to steady the younger and faster ones."

Judah then says that the two horses in the middle of the four should be the tamest because they must stay in formation. They must run in close quarters.

Last, the tallest, youngest, and fastest of the four should run on the outside to give him space and freedom so he can push the others.

Judah's message was not easy, but it was simple. It would not be enough that these magnificent animals were *harnessed* together. They had to be more. They had to be *driven* together. They had to be driven as a TEAM.

They must do more than *be* together. They must *work together*!

Strong Horses

Speaking of horses, once at a county fair, there was a horse-pulling contest in which powerful horses were asked to pull heavy loads up a steep incline. The first-place horse pulled 4,500 pounds.

The second-place finisher pulled 4,000 pounds.

After the contest, the owners of the two horses were curious to see how much weight the two strongest horses could pull together, so they hitched them up and let them pull as a team.

True story.

How much weight do you think the two horses pulled together?

Do you think it was 8,500 pounds?

Do you think it was less? Do you think it was more?

That's right, it was more than 8,500 pounds (otherwise, I would not be telling you this story!).

In fact, together, those two horses pulled *12,000 pounds*!

They did that by working together. They did that by becoming a TEAM because T-ogether E-veryone A-chieved M-ore.

More Strong Horses?

As I drove along a country road years ago, I passed a farmer trying to remove a large tree trunk from the road's apron.

The stump was old and very good sized, so the farmer had recruited some help! He harnessed an old plow horse, who was himself very good sized, to the stump and urged him on as the farmer pulled alongside.

As the horse gave the task his all, the farmer cheered him on like this, "Come on, Brownie!" "Pull, Blackie!" "Go, Barnie!" "Harder, Bobby!" "Work, Bailey!"

As I passed the scene, I double-checked my first impression that only one horse was working with the farmer.

When I was sure of that, I stopped my car and walked back to the busy farmer and his helper.

"Pardon me, sir," I interrupted. "But where are the other horses you are calling for?"

"Oh, this is the only horse I own!" explained the farmer.

"Then why are you calling so many names?"

"Well," shrugged the farmer, "Brownie seems to do a lot better when he thinks he has company!"

Take it from that farmer and Brownie. T-E-A-M!

And muscle for our "Work Together" message, here we come!

Expensive Sandwich

Some time ago, I read a story in this month's *Reader's Digest*. It was about a man who decided to make a sandwich from scratch, and I mean *from scratch*! That means by himself. With no help. With no team.

The man planted and cultivated the lettuce and tomato. He distilled salt from sea water, weaned and milked a cow, then made the cheese. He planted and harvested the wheat then milled the grain he needed to make his bread. Then he kneaded the dough and baked the bread. He helped to birth a baby pig then farmed and slaughtered it. Then he cut and cured the meat.

That sandwich cost this man four years of his life and fifteen hundred dollars!

Using a team would have been cheaper. Using a team would have been better! So much for that expensive meal. Now let's talk about the dessert! Now let's talk about the cake!

Baking a What?

Believe it or not, a cake is a perfect example of a team! Think about it. Every cake is made by mixing a lot of ingredients together.

Most cakes include flour, sugar, butter, milk, eggs, flavoring, baking powder, baking soda, and more. Before the cake is made, each of those ingredients *does* "exist in isolation!" Each ingredient is "an island entirely unto itself."

When the cake is baked, however, every ingredient becomes "a part of the mainland; a piece of the whole."

Every ingredient actually *gives up its identity* to become part of the cake!

Without any one of its ingredients, the cake would not be a cake just like without any one of its members a team is no longer a TEAM!

How about it? Would that story give muscle to my "Work Together" message? If so, good again and again!

T-E-A-M and the Real Doctor

I hope you have gathered by now that my sister Natalie (a.k.a. The Real Doctor!") is amazing!

After retiring from a forty-year career in medicine on the Cape, Nat decided to take violin lessons. Three years of lessons later (at sixty-eight years old and out of nowhere!), she took a seat with the second violins of the Cape Cod Community Orchestra!

I have heard the full orchestra play several times and have loved their music every time. Their work gives me goose bumps. On occasion, it even makes me cry.

Nat and her "music mates" practice often. When they do, as I understand it, they work alone or in sections and anyone who listens to them feels no bumps and sheds no tears!

"If you heard us practice," Nat explains, "you would not like or even recognize the sound we make. In fact," Nat goes on, "even something as famous and familiar as the William Tell Overture rings no bells for me if it is played by sections of the orchestra instead of the whole company!"

"Why?" you ask.

"Because," Nat continues, "during practice, every section of the orchestra plays its own instruments *and its own music!* The cellos play the cello's music, the bass play the bass' music, the brass section plays the brass section's music, and so on! And *none* of that music," Nat crescendos, "is the same!"

True! None of the CCCO's sectional music carries the sound of the entire piece, so none of that music sounds the same or is familiar to most of their audiences or even to most of their members!

"But when all the instruments and their music are played together," Nat ends, "get ready for those goose bumps and tears because they will find you! When all those different pieces are played by all those different instruments at *the same time*, the volume, vibration, and depth of the full score are born, and 'the whole is worth much more than the sum of its parts.'"

So much for T-E-A-M!

Where would Natalie, her orchestra, and their music be without it?

Would telling that story give muscle to my *work together* direction?

If so, good again!

We are almost done with our first message. Before we move on, I know what you are thinking! It is this, "Carmen, those were all good stories! But, in case you haven't noticed, getting people to do anything together *is hard*."

(Remember the "Special Sneakers" story and "WIIFM"?)

Gonna Die!

Even couples who have been married for a long time have trouble doing things together. They even have trouble *being* together and *staying* together.

Take the woman who took her husband to the doctor, for example. After examining the husband, the doctor spoke privately to the woman in his waiting room.

"I am sorry," said the doctor, "but your husband is gravely ill. There is only one way you can keep him alive."

"What can I do?" asked the woman.

"First, fix him three delightful meals every day," answered the doctor. "Next, protect him from all stress and exertion. That means *you* will have to mow the lawn and take out the trash and wash the cars. It also means you will have to give in every time you argue!"

"Is there anything else?" asked the woman.

"Yes," said the doctor. "You must make passionate love to your husband every night! If you do all those things, your husband will live a long life. But if you miss even one thing, your poor husband will…die!"

The wife thanked the doctor for his diagnosis then walked to her car to meet her husband.

On the ride home, the husband asked his wife what the doctor had told her.

"He said *you* are gonna *die*!" replied the woman. It's true, getting people to do anything together is hard.

Watch Out!

While out for dinner one night, a man's wife suffered a heart attack and died. Her funeral was held a few days later. As the pallbearers left the church carrying the casket, they had to make a sharp turn at the rear doors and banged the casket against the church's back wall by mistake.

Soon after making that contact, the pallbearers heard a noise. It continued to get louder, so the bearers put the casket down, opened the top, and beheld the man's "dead" wife lying in the casket with her eyes open!

"It's a miracle!" heralded everyone in the church.

The husband remained silent while taking in the whole scene with disbelief and reflection.

A few years later, while eating at the same restaurant, the man's wife had another heart attack and was pronounced dead again!

At the funeral, as the pallbearers again approached the church's back wall, they heard the same noise! Immediately, the man left his place at the front of the procession and ran to the lead pallbearer.

"Whatever you do," he whispered, "watch out for that frigging wall!" warned the husband!

It's true. Even couples who have been married for a long time have trouble being together and staying together!

Still, Helen Keller was right. "We can do things together that we could ever do alone." So use stories to help your followers *work together*!

Want more? Just one!

Twinkies and Broccoli

One of the world's most thorough research projects on relationships tracked the lives of seven thousand people over nine years. In that study, researchers found that people who did not have many friends were three times more likely to have health problems than people who *made* friends and *kept* friends.

Even people who had bad eating habits or who smoked or drank but had strong social ties lived significantly longer than people who had great health habits but kept to themselves.

In the words of the study's leader, and I quote, "Our data has shown unequivocally that *it is healthier to eat Twinkies together than it is to eat broccoli alone!*"

So much for giving muscle to our "Work Together" message!

Now let's bring on more messages, more direction, more advice, *and more muscle*!

Walk Your Talk

The next message that deserves getting some muscle from some stories is "Walk Your Talk" because *actions speak louder than words*!

The right stories can give those messages *muscle*! What stories might be right? Try these!

Our Anthem

For me, *motivation* is a word of wonder. I have spent my life *wondering* how people *are motivated*. I have become convinced that the most powerful way to motivate is *without words* because we say much more with actions than we do with anything else!

Francis Scott Key wrote the words to our national anthem, but he did *not* write the anthem! John Stafford Smith, an English organist, wrote the anthem's melody for a social club he belonged to in London.

According to Mr. Smith, "The club wanted a drinking song that would mark its founding and celebrate the virtues of wine and friendship!"

The melody of John Stafford Smith's drinking song became our anthem with or without Mr. Key's words!

What do I mean? Think about it. How many times have you watched with goose bumps as an American athlete bent over to receive an Olympic gold medal while our anthem is being played? How many words were sung by the band as you watched?

How often have you stood to recognize the anthem being played before a sporting event? Did you hear notes, words, or both?

Sometimes you heard words. *All times*, you heard notes!

The music is our anthem, not the words. Words don't make music. Words don't make much. Actions make more. Actions speak louder than words.

Ralph Waldo Emerson says it best, "What you do speaks so loudly, I cannot hear what you say." Listen to Emerson. Do more than you say. Walk more than you talk.

We are all bilingual. We all speak two languages. We speak one language with our words and another with our actions. People understand, follow, and remember the language we speak with our actions much better than the language we speak with our words.

So speak with your actions more than with your words!

No More Sugar

A mother once met with Gandhi and asked him to get her son to stop eating sugar. Gandhi said nothing then told the mother and the boy to return in two weeks for another meeting.

Two weeks later, the mother brought the child back. Gandhi then told the boy to "stop eating sugar;" and the boy obeyed!

Puzzled by Gandhi's approach and her son's compliance, the mother replied, "Thank you, but I must ask, why didn't you tell him to do that two weeks ago?"

How do you think Gandhi answered that mother's question?

Yes! Gandhi's answer was "Because two weeks ago, *I was eating sugar!*"

Be like Gandhi. Walk your talk.

Telling stories like that and the many that follow might give muscle to my "Walk Your Talk" message. Try another!

St. Francis's Words

Saint Francis of Assisi used different words to stress the "loudness" of actions. His words to fellow priests and preachers were these: "Preach the Gospel always. If necessary, use words!"

Listen to St Francis. Know that actions speak louder than words.

St. Paul

St. Paul had something to say about actions too.

He was talking about prayer to a group of disciples when he reminded his audience that "if a man is starving to death, do not pray for him to find food. Instead, bring him some bread!

Take it from St. Francis. Take it from St. Paul.

Actions speak louder than words!

Cousin Chuck

Many years ago, my father had a cousin named Chuck. He was my dad's life insurance salesman. Every year, Chuck sold my dad a bigger new policy, telling Dad that if anything happened to him, the bigger policy would take care of my mother, my sister, and me "extra well" for a long time.

"It is awfully expensive," my dad would say to Chuck every year before he agreed to the new policy.

"Lou," Chuck would always reply to my father, "you are getting this great coverage at a rock bottom rate. I make almost nothing in commission on this policy at this price."

After Chuck said that, my dad always bought the bigger policy until one year! That was the year when Chuck drove up to our house driving a new car.

In fact, Chuck's car was not only new, but it was also big! It was not only big, but it was also a convertible. It was not only a convertible, but it was also a *Cadillac*! My dad happened to be looking out the window of our apartment and saw Chuck getting out of his big new Cadillac convertible and walking our front steps.

That year, Chuck's visit was a short one. He did not even get into our house! He did not sell my dad a new and bigger policy either. In fact, Dad bought a *smaller* one!

Why? I bet you can answer!

Why didn't my dad let Chuck into our house after he saw Chuck's new car? Because "actions speak louder than words," and so do Cadillacs!

Five Frogs

Five frogs were sitting on a log. Four decided to jump off. How many frogs were still sitting on the log?

Yes! Five! Why? Because until they *decide* to jump and *do jump*, all those frogs are *still sitting* on that log! Actions speak louder than decisions. Actions speak louder than words. So speak with your actions. Walk your talk.

Moneymaking Priest

My parents wintered in Florida for years. DeeDee and I visited them for a week in March. They stayed in a condominium development that was home to many senior citizens. For years, their condo was very close to the ocean but not very close to a church. So my parents had to drive a long way to attend mass on Sunday morning.

Then one year, a new church was built across the street from my parents' condo. They loved being able to walk to church, and they loved the church's pastor. He is an amazing man. He raised enough money to pay off the new church's mortgage in just two years!

He went on to lead a drive to expand the church and build a school. I went to mass one Sunday with my parents because I wanted to see this man in action.

Now it is not easy to get money from retired people. They worked hard for what they have, and they are on fixed incomes. Yet this priest has senior citizens *standing in line* to give him money! I wanted to see how he does it.

For starters, he seems very sincere. He is not pushy, but he *is* committed. He does stand for something, and everyone in his parish knows what that is. It is raising money!

There is one more thing. When it comes time for the collection in the middle of mass, this priest stops all the ushers before they take the collection plates down the aisles. He reaches into *his* pocket and puts a donation into every plate.

He does that at every mass, on every Sunday. Then he lets the ushers pass the plates to the congregation. Might that action put more money in that priest's collection plate? If so, good. Might that story put more muscle in that priest's message of "Walk Your Talk"? If so, good!

Gas Men

Two men from the gas company were checking the meter at a woman's home. When they finished, one man challenged the other to a foot race back to the truck.

As they came tearing around a corner, they realized that the lady of the house they had just visited was huffing and puffing right behind them. They stopped immediately and asked what she was doing, "When I saw *two gas* men running as fast as they could away from *my house*," she replied, "I figured I'd better run too!"

Actions speak louder than words. So walk your talk.

More muscle in my message? If so, good!

Giving Thanks

When Dee and I go for a beer at a restaurant near our house, we make sure to notice the name that is always pinned to our server's uniform. After finishing our beer, DeeDee or I always writes "Great job" or "Thanks so much!" on the check, followed by the name we had noticed.

Getting our note and seeing her name seems to matter even more to the server than her tip! One day, the restaurant's manager explained that like this, "Carmen and DeeDee, every customer *says* thanks, but you do more. You *give* thanks." Your notes *do* something. Doing *says more* than saying. Actions speak louder than words."

When I stick a Post-it note to the kitchen faucet after we finish dinner and DeeDee goes to bed, I often write "I love you" or "Thanks for dinner!" on it.

Dee lights up the next morning when she sees my note. It really seems to matter. Again, *doing* says more than *saying*! Actions speak louder than words.

My Day

Most of the time, DeeDee asks me what I want for my birthday. Last year, she never did. I wondered why and hoped I hadn't done anything wrong!

When *the day* (or should I say *my day*?) came, Dee remained in bed while I got up for church, as I always do. (Dee is not Catholic, so I go to church every morning on my own, except for an occasional Christmas or Easter. I can't lie. I am lonely when I worship alone. But that loneliness is a small price to pay for having DeeDee as a wife.)

On that birthday morning, I kissed Dee goodbye and headed off to church. As usual, I arrived before the custodian, so I began my prayers in my car. When the first few church lights went on, I knew I could enter!

I took my usual seat in the second pew and continued to pray. Twenty minutes later, I felt a tap on my shoulder. I turned to find DeeDee waiting for me to move over so she could sit next to me and *surprise* me *at mass* for my birthday!

I moved, Dee sat, and mass began. We shared no cake and no candles. We shared no words either. We simply sat in silence and celebration throughout the mass. Dee's present needed no wrapping or ribbon, and her gift will never stop giving.

Actions speak louder than words. So learn from DeeDee. Walk your talk.

Would that story give muscle to our "Walk Your Talk" message? If so, good!

Still not sure? Try another story!

Kendrick

He was eighteen years old and scheduled to graduate from high school in a week, but God and Kendrick Castillo's courage had other plans. This friendly, unassuming, heroic young man was in literature class when two shooters entered his school and began firing at Kendrick's classmates.

183

Kendrick leaped from his desk and charged the two attackers, sacrificing his life to buy classmates time to escape.

Kendrick's swift action gave the rest of his class time to crawl under their desks and later run across their classroom safely.

"To find he went down as a hero does not surprise me," said Kendrick's supervisor at his part-time job.

Another student who was soon to graduate from Kendrick's high school helped to restrain the shooters. When asked what part Kendrick played in the saving of lives, Kendrick's classmate replied, "He showed complete disregard for his own safety in an attempt to save us. He was friendly, modest, and excited to help people."

(That last adjective struck me. Kendrick was more than *willing* to help people. He was *excited* to help people. His actions proved those words to be true.)

"Thanks to Kendrick", the student continued, "we all refused to be victims!" No brag—just brave. No words—just action.

Did Kendrick's story give more muscle to our "Walk Your Talk"? I hope so!

Trying Is Lying

Many years ago, I met a fellow wrestling coach at an instructional summer camp. We became instant and eternal friends.

As we parted after sweating all over each other for a week, my new friend said, "Let's get together next year, same time, same place, and same purpose!"

"I think it's going to be a busy year," I offered, "but I will try to make it."

"Wrong answer!" came my friend's retort.

"What do you mean?" I asked.

"Trying is lying," answered my friend.

"What do you mean?" I repeated.

"Carmen," he began, "it's like this. When I am not coaching, I teach history for a community college in New Jersey. I give two exams to every class every semester. One is the midterm, and the other is the final. On the night before one or both of those exams, I get a voice mail from at least one of my students. That voice mail always begins like this, 'Hi Professor, I am sorry to bother you, but something has come up, and I might not be able to make it to your exam tomorrow. *I will try* to be there but might have to miss and make it up!'

"Of all the legions of students who leave me that message," continued my friend, "*none* of them have ever made it to their exam! They all reschedule it, lose some points, and move on after their makeup is corrected!

"As I said, Carmen," continued my friend, "trying is lying!"

Listen to my friend and fellow coach. Don't try. In Yoda's (of *Star Wars* fame!) wise words, "There is no try!" So don't try. Don't offer words.

Instead, offer action because "actions speak louder than words."

Would telling that "Trying Is Lying" story gives my followers or my audience a better chance of *walking their talk* than *because I said so* would?

If so, good! And here comes another message that needs muscle!

Yes, here come some stories that will add muscle to the message that says "never give in!"

Never Give In

Winston Churchill's Words

Those words were part of a twenty-minute speech Winston Churchill gave at his alma mater, the Harrow School.

Among those words were these: "Never give in. Never give in. Never give in. In all things large or small, great or petty, never, never, never give in."

Good advice, and Mr. Churchill knew what he was talking about!

After leaving Harrow, he applied for the Royal Military Academy at Sandhurst, England.

It took him three tries to pass the entrance exam, but he never gave in. It took Churchill three years to get through the fourth grade because he had trouble learning (of all things!) English, but he never gave in.

On his path to being prime minister, "Winnie" lost more elections than he won. But he never gave in, and Churchill was not alone.

I will prove that to you with more stories. As I do, see if any of my stories give Churchill's message more muscle!

George Steinbrenner

Shortly after George Steinbrenner died, I watched a special about *The Boss* on ESPN. The most powerful few minutes I saw was a taped interview between Mr. S and Roy Firestone. Part of it went like this:

> Roy: What do you want to be remembered for?
> George: I want people to say, "George wasn't always the best owner, but he never stopped wanting to be."

George Steinbrenner never gave in either. As the owner of the Yankees, he changed managers twenty times in twenty-three years and became a laughing stock among baseball purists, but he never gave in.

After all that looking, George *finally found* the *right* manager! He found Joe Torre. George stuck with Joe for twelve years, and together, they won six American League Pennants and four world championships. Never give in.

Michael Jordan

Legend has it, Michael Jordan was cut from his high school basketball team. When the coach told Michael that he had not made the team, Michael pressed the coach for a reason.

The coach explained that Michael was not a good free throw shooter and needed to improve before he could try out for the team again.

So what did Michael do? Michael *practiced* his free throws! In fact, Michael practiced so much that he *made five hundred free throws* every day for a whole season!

No, I didn't say Michael *took* five hundred free throws every day. I said he successfully *made* five hundred free throws every day for a whole season!

Taking free throws was not Michael's job. His job was *making* free throws, so before Michael left the gym every night, he *made* five hundred free throws!

Eventually, Michael made his high school team. Then he made the team at the University of North Carolina, and finally, he made the team in Chicago called the Bulls.

He made free throws on all those teams.

In fact, while playing for the Bulls, Michael Jordan made five hundred free throws *every day for ten years!*

Michael Jordan never gave in. Be like Michael. Never give in.

Who Am I?

I was born to lose. I was fired from my first job when I was twenty-three years old. I ran for public office that same year and lost.

I failed in business one year later. My sweetheart died two years after that. Then I suffered a nervous breakdown.

When I was twenty-eight, I ran for office again and lost. I lost a nomination to congress at thirty-four and again at thirty-seven. I applied to be a land officer when I was thirty-eight but was rejected.

When I was forty-five, I made an unsuccessful bid for the Senate. Two years later, I failed in an attempt to be nominated for vice president.

I was defeated in my second run for Senate two years after that.

Who was this expert in failure?

That's right. It was Abraham Lincoln—a man called by many one of the greatest leaders and successes our country has ever produced.

What made Lincoln great? He certainly wasn't born great. Lincoln was great because he never gave in until he *became* great!

Become great yourself. Never, never, never give in.

Formula 409

Why did the Clorox Company name it Formula 409?

Because the first 408 formulas *didn't clean anything!*

It is true! Formula 409 is a brand of home and industrial cleaning products whose name is actually a tribute to the tenacity of two young Detroit scientists who were committed to formulating the most effective all-purpose cleaner available!

Those young scientists were hell-bent on producing the greatest grease-cutting, dirt-destroying cleaner on the planet. The thing is, creating "the ultimate cleaner" doesn't just happen on the first try. It didn't happen on the 101st or the 301st try, either. In fact, it didn't even happen on the 408th try! It wasn't until batch number 409 that the young scientists were finally satisfied.

So the name stuck, and so much for Formula 409's true story!

Be like those scientists. Never give in!

Victor's Uncle

"Don't be like my uncle," once warned Victor Borge. "He tried to market a variety of soft drinks. He gave them names from 1-up to 6-up. Then he quit. Some other guy kept going with my uncle's idea. He just added one more *up* and did great!"

Old Rock

I once knew a teacher who kept a big rock on the corner of her desk—all the time.

One day, I got up the nerve to ask her why.

"I use this rock to teach my students something about faith," the teacher said. "On the first day of school every year, I point to it, look at my students, and say, 'This rock is two hundred million years old. That is how long it will take **me** to lose faith in **you**. And that is how long it should take *you* to lose *faith* in yourself."

Listen to that teacher. Never, never, never give in.

The English Channel

The English Channel is twenty-two miles wide. Its waters are angry and cold. Thousands of athletes have tried to swim the channel. Most have failed.

In 1961, a forty-two-year-old man from Argentina swam the English Channel. His name was Antonio Albertondo. It took Antonio nineteen hours to make his swim. When he came ashore in France, his friends congratulated Antonio for accomplishing what they thought was impossible at his age.

Antonio paused for a few minutes to sip a hot drink. Then he told his friends they had not seen the impossible yet but were about to.

With that, Antonio dove *back into the water* and swam for *twenty-two more hours* all the way back to England!

Antonio never gave in. Be like him. Never, never, never give in.

Leonardo da Vinci

Remember him? It took Leonardo Da Vinci ten years to paint *The Last Supper*. One painting—ten years. But he never gave in.

Lucy

Lucille Ball's parents once received a letter from her acting school. It explained that "Lucy has no talent" and recommended that her parents "not waste any more money on her theatrical training." As a young actress, Lucy failed hundreds of auditions. She was forty years old before she landed her first noteworthy role. But Lucy never gave in.

Consider these findings from the National Sales Executives Association:

> Eighty percent of all new sales are made
> after the *fifth call to the same prospect*!

Never give in. Never give in. Never, never, never give in.

A person's life should not be measured by its bricks but by its mortar. We should not be judged by our possessions or titles but by how tightly we hold our goals and how strongly we embrace our dreams.

All you need to succeed is the belief in yourself and a big pot of glue. Smear some on you and some on your dream. Then *stick* to that dream until it is *done*!

So much for another message and a lot more *muscle* that was given to that message by *more stories*! What follows is another message and still more stories!

Work Hard

Now I know what you are thinking again! You are thinking, "The coming message 'Work Hard!' is even more tired and trite than 'Work Together!'" I agree. Every person you know and most of the people you don't know deserve to roll their eyes, smile, and wag their heads every time you or anyone else tells them to "work hard!"

Would you follow such advice just because my father, your father, your boss, my boss, or anyone else said so?

Do you…wonder? If so, let's try giving that message some muscle with more stories!

The Butterfly

One day, a Boy Scout was walking along a stream in the woods. As he looked down, the Scout noticed a cocoon on the ground. He picked up the cocoon, and when he did, he noticed a small opening in it.

The boy held the cocoon and sat for hours as the butterfly inside struggled to force its body through that little opening.

Eventually, the exhausted butterfly seemed to stop making any progress.

It appeared as if the butterfly had gotten as far as it could and it would not go any further.

So the Scout decided to help the butterfly. He took a small stick and made the hole in the cocoon much larger.

The butterfly then emerged without any trouble at all.

But when it did, the boy noticed that the butterfly had a withered body and tiny, shriveled wings.

The boy continued to watch because he expected that, at any moment, the wings would open and expand enough to support the butterfly's body.

But that never happened!

Instead, the butterfly could only crawl among the leaves with its still-withered body and still-shriveled wings. It was not able to fly, nor would it ever be.

What that Scout, in his kindness, did not understand was that the small hole in the cocoon and the struggle required for the butterfly to get through that tiny opening were nature's way of forcing fluid from the body of the butterfly into its wings so that it would be ready for flight once it achieved its freedom from the cocoon.

In fact, nature had intended to make the butterfly work for its freedom, knowing that such work would make the butterfly strong and successful. That is what work does. Work makes us strong. Work makes us successful. You know that. You live that.

So you would rather work at something than do nothing. That is why you (and I!) *complained* so much about having nothin' to do during the pandemic!

What is more, I know you will find this hard to believe, but people not only want to work, but they also want to work hard! It's true! Everyone works hard at something! Think about it; you work hard at doing your job, caring for your family, finding time to relax, and more.

Not all people work hard at the same things you do, but all people work hard at something!

Some people work hard at making money. Whether or not those people do a good job along the way is gravy. What they really work hard at is making money!

Other people work hard at mowing their lawn, growing their garden, keeping their house clean, losing weight, bringing up their children, or playing golf. They work harder away from their job than they do at it, but they *do* work hard *at something*!

Other people work hard at looking young. Elizabeth Taylor is one of those people, so are Barbara Walters, Jane Fonda, and Nancy Pelosi! Other people work hard at having a successful marriage. Liz Taylor isn't one of those people. She is too busy working hard at looking young!

There are even *some* people who work hard *at not working hard!* I had a friend in graduate school like that. He conducted a nation-wide computer search trying to find a research paper on a certain topic so he could copy the paper and turn it in for one of his courses. The search took him two months and cost $300. It would have been faster and cheaper to write the paper himself.

But my friend was too busy. He was busy working hard at not working hard!

Don't be like my friend, but *do* be like most people! Find something at home or at work that you love, like, or are good at. Then make it your *signature strength* by working hard at it!

Join the club. Be like everybody else. *Work hard!*

Michelangelo

When Michelangelo was in his early thirties, he was summoned to Rome by the pope to sculpt a magnificent papal tomb. When he arrived, he was asked to work on a painting project instead.

At first, Michelangelo wanted to refuse. He had no desire to paint a dozen figures on the ceiling of a small chapel in the Vatican. Even though, as a boy, he had been trained to paint, his true passion was sculpture. Still, the pope asked, so the artist answered! He reluctantly accepted the assignment.

It was a difficult decision, but once Michelangelo *made* it, he acted on it. He *worked* at it.

He expanded the project from a simple drawing of the twelve apostles to include more than four hundred figures and nine scenes from the book of Genesis.

For four years, the artist lay on his back painting the ceiling of the Sistine Chapel. By the time he finished, he was virtually blind from the paint that had dripped into his eyes.

Michelangelo's commitment was complete, and his work was wondrous. His masterpiece set a standard of excellence that changed the meaning of the word *beauty*. Be like Michelangelo. *Work hard*!

His First Words

I once heard a United States Senator tell a story about his father, who had immigrated to our country from Cuba.

The senator used that story to applaud the work ethic of so many Cuban immigrants who, like his father, came to America unable to speak English but were still willing to earn their own living and make their own way.

"My father was in this country for many months," recalled the senator, "and in all that time, he only learned how to ask one question in English. That question was 'Can I have a job?'"

As Mark Twain once said, "The only place where *success* comes before *work* is in the dictionary." There truly is a wonder in work. Just ask that senator. Just ask his father.

Beautiful Plumbing

While working in Quincy, I was asked to interview a lot of teaching candidates. Many were good. Many were great. Some were beyond great. One of the "beyond greats" had been a plumber for twenty years and wanted to teach in our technical school. I asked him why.

"Mostly for the kids," he said. "I just want to give back a little of what life has given me." Good start, and he got better. "But a part of my reason for being here is selfish," he went on. "It's because I take pride in my work. When I fit pipe, I do it perfectly, as well as it can be done. My work is beautiful. It makes me proud. But when I'm done," this special candidate continued, "the carpenter and plasterer come in and cover my work. By the time they finish building walls, no one can see or will ever know how beautiful my work really is. It kills me. I wish they could put up glass walls, so when company comes to the house I worked on, they could see how well I did my job! If I teach," this special candidate ended, "at least my students will see my work. I will be able to show them how truly beautiful plumbing can be."

I hired that man as a teacher and as *my plumber*! There is wonder in work.

Cousins and Teachers

One summer, when I was in high school, I worked with one of my many uncles on a construction project. We were building some condominiums, and I signed on with no idea how hard the work would be or how much of it my uncle would expect me to do!

They were all big condos with big foundations. My uncle gave me a small shovel, pointed to one of the big foundations, and said, "Level this off. I will be back at noon with your lunch."

I said, "Fine."

Then as my uncle left, I leaned on my small shovel to wait for the big backhoe or bulldozer that I was *sure* would be coming soon to help me complete this big job in just four hours!

Well, instead of a backhoe or bulldozer, my uncle sent me one of his sons and one of his nephews. Yes, they both were my cousins and had small shovels like mine, but they were *not small cousins*!

In four hours, thanks to those two cousins, we were done with our big project!

I say "we," but I mean "they" because my two cousins did almost all the work. I did what I could, but they did the most. It reminded me of a professional basketball player named B. J. Armstrong. He spent several years playing basketball for the Chicago Bulls with Michael Jordan.

Once a reporter asked B. J. to describe his fondest memory of playing with Michael. "I remember one game" recalled BJ, "when the two of us combined to score 72 points in just one game." Then he paused for a second, smiled, and confessed, "Michael scored 69, and I scored the other three!"

On the day I worked with my two cousins on the condo foundations, I felt like B. J. Armstrong. They scored 69 points, and I scored three!"

I didn't *do* a lot that day, but I did *learn* a lot that day. In fact, those two cousins with their small shovels were the best teachers I ever had. Why? Because they taught me *how to work*.

After that summer, I never leveled a foundation again, but I never stopped working…and working…and working as hard as I could at whatever I did.

That day, I would not have traded either of my cousins for a backhoe or a bulldozer. Those cousins knew how to work. Thanks to them, so do I.

Work and Pride

My father worked as a machinist at the Fore River Shipyard in Quincy for twenty-five years. At the end of every day, he looked at the floor as he left his machine shop.

"I just wanted to see what I made that day," he told me years later.

"Some days, there was a piece of a ship's guidance system on that floor," recalled my dad. "On another day, part of some hydraulic unit might be there. On other days, there might be more. If it wasn't for me," said my dad, "there would have just been an empty floor. That is why I worked."

"I worked," Dad went on, "to fill that floor. *I worked to be paid,* and *I worked to be proud.* I worked to get something done."

That is what the best of workers do. They work to be paid *and* to be proud. They work to get something done.

Work helps us be strong. Work helps us be successful.

Calluses and Collateral

Most of the people who came to the United States when my grandparents did know what work felt like and what work could do. They came from many countries. They found jobs from New York City to San Francisco. In all those jobs, they worked so hard that their hands became their signature.

Every hand was gnarled and calloused. Every hand showed the signs and sacrifices of hard work. In fact, as the story goes, one bank president in San Francisco shook the hand of all his loan applicants before reviewing their request. If the president felt calluses, those applicants were approved automatically. No questions. No problems.

"Congratulations," the bank president would say to his new applicants "*your calluses are your collateral*, and your application is approved."

As I said, work makes us strong and work makes us successful, so *work hard*!

What do you think, dear reader? Would those stories add more muscle to our message of "Work Hard," or should we go with "Because I Said So"? Do you wonder?

Now, on to the next messages that need more muscle!

Stay Positive

What is your most treasured gift?

Would you say money? I hope not. Money can be stolen. Might you say love? Nope. Love can turn to hate. How about faith or hope? Sorry, faith can be lost. So can hope. Health? Again, no. Health can flee in the face of disease. Youth? No. Time flies and takes youth with it.

So life's greatest gift is not money, love, faith, hope, health, or youth. It is not even *you*! It is not even *me*!

Happiness

There is only one gift that you can always win back after it has been lost and only one gift that can find you, no matter how hard you hide from it. That gift is *happiness*!

So let's read some stories about happiness. Let's read some stories that put some muscle into the message "Stay Positive!"

Hamilton

For starters, let's read some advice from one of the world's most popular plays. The play is called *Hamilton*, and the advice goes like this, "Smile more. Talk less."

Obey Hamilton's advice. Be positive. Stay positive.

Father Bob

Once upon a time, there was a priest named Father Bob who was famous for his long sermons. During one of those sermons, Father noticed that a young male parishioner rose from his pew and left the church.

The parishioner returned to the service quite a bit later. When he did, Father Bob was still talking. After mass, Father Bob approached the parishioner as he left the church.

"Excuse me," Father said, "but why did you leave my sermon for such a long time?"

"I am sorry," replied the young man, "but I went to get a haircut."

"Why didn't you do that before I started speaking?" challenged the priest.

"Well, Father, it's like this," replied the lad, "*before* you started speaking, I *didn't need* a haircut!"

Don't be like Father Bob. Smile more. Talk less. Be positive.

From the Ashes

I visited Brazil some years ago to teach a graduate course to teachers in an American school there. It was a two-week course, and we "played" a little on the Sunday in between.

My students took me to a fair. It was in a big green space in the city's center. Tents were everywhere. Some were full of clothes for sale; others sold food. Still, others displayed crafts and original artwork.

One such tent was full of statues and sculptures made from ashes. The ashes had been glued together into blocks, and the artist carved beautiful bodies, faces, flowers, and more from them.

I bought one of those pieces—not because I liked the piece so much but because I liked why the artist said he made it.

"For years, I made carvings from wood," he said. "But nothing sold. So I burned what work I had left and sculpted the ashes. Now I cannot keep up with the business.

"We all experienced fire in our lives," continued the artist. "Things burn. Hopes are lost. Dreams are destroyed. But we can build more from the ashes if we try. So try. Be positive. *Stay positive!*"

Would that story make muscle for your message of "Stay Positive"? If so, that is good. If so, that is great!

No Less Beautiful

On another weekend while I was in Brazil, my students rented a jeep and took me to the outskirts of the rain forest. We traveled for many miles on a dirt road until we entered a clearing.

As we picnicked there, I noticed some flowers at the clearing's edge, far from our blanket. As I approached the flowers, I commented on their beauty.

"I have never seen anything like these," I exclaimed. "I am overwhelmed!"

I ended by lamenting that "it is a shame the world will never see the beauty of these flowers as we do now."

"Yes, Doctor," one student replied, "but that *makes* those flowers *no less beautiful*."

How often have we mourned not being recognized for a special accomplishment or worthy deed? Forget the recognition. Remember the accomplishment. Remember the deed. Remember those flowers.

Their beauty, like your accomplishment, will be no less beautiful forever. So stay positive.

Would any of those stories put more muscle in our "Stay Positive" message? I wonder! Let's try another story!

No Waves

While kayaking in Falmouth Harbor a few years ago, DeeDee and I found no waves. No, I don't mean the water was calm because it wasn't. Truth be told, the weather and the water in the harbor that day were as "uncalm" as we had ever seen them outside winter! Still, we "found no waves!"

What do I mean? The answer was on the Island Queen.

As all good Falmouthites know, *The Queen* is a ferry that runs back and forth from Falmouth Harbor to Martha's Vineyard, from Memorial Day to Columbus Day. On this particular Sunday before *The Queen* retired for the season, she was *anything but* packed each time it left Falmouth Harbor!

The underattended *Queen* passed by Dee and me in our kayaks a few times that day. Each time she did, we waved to each of the handfuls of people in attendance! In return, we got *no waves*. That's right, not even one person returned even one of our greetings all day.

Why? I wonder!

Can we change things?

Absolutely. How?

One wave at a time!

Wave to someone today, even if they are not on the Island Queen. Be happy. Stay positive!

In Charge

A little boy once wrote a letter to God. It read,

> Dear God,
>
> If I were in charge, life would be different!

God wrote back to that little boy.

Guess what he wrote?

He wrote,

> Dear little boy,
>
> You *are* in charge!

And ladies and gentlemen, so are *you*! So are we. We are in charge of our happiness. Because we are in charge of our perspective.

Always Good

I had a drink with an old friend last week. We had made the date months ago. Since then, his mother had taken very ill. "I just came from her side," he said when we met. "I have to go back soon."

I told him how sorry I was.

He thanked me and said, "It is just all coming at such a bad time." So true, my friend is a city councilor and has been part of some very difficult budget cuts recently. "I am sick about it all," he said, "and my mother is sick, as well."

"Be strong," I said, "and remember this. There is good in all bad. I promise. You will find it, even now, I promise."

"Not this time," he said. "My mother will die. My city is being destroyed. There is no good to be found in that."

"Who is with your mom right now?" I asked with no idea of the answer.

"My brother is in town," my friend replied.

"Where's he from?" I asked.

"The West Coast," he replied.

"Wow! He came a long way," I noted.

"Yes, it really is a miracle," continued my friend. "He has been out of touch for years, but Mom's illness brought him back. It brought him home. I never thought I would see him again and am glad I was wrong."

With that, I looked at my friend and smiled. He looked at me and smiled too. We both knew why we smiled. My friend put the reason into words.

He said, "Yes, it's true. My mother's being sick is a good thing because it brought my brother home. There *is good*, even in all this bad."

My friend was right. There *is* good in all bad. Look for it. Find it. Celebrate it! Be positive. Stay positive.

God Will Provide

A man stood in his front yard during a torrential downpour. The water came down so fast all the storm drains were clogged. It reached his knees in no time. A rowboat came by and offered the man a ride to safety. The man shook his head and said, "Don't worry about me, God will provide."

Two hours later, the water had risen to the man's waist. A motorboat came by and offered him a lift.

Again, the man declined, saying, "God will provide."

The rains continued. Three hours later, water had reached the man's chest. A helicopter flew overhead and dropped him a line. The man waved it off, again insisting that "God will provide."

By nightfall, the water in the man's front yard had reached his chin. He turned his eyes to heaven and screamed, "What happened, God? I placed my trust in you and you let me down!"

A booming voice answered back, "Let you down? I sent you two boats and a helicopter! What do you want from me?"

God *will* provide! So be positive. Stay positive!

Mourn or Celebrate?

Last year, I had lunch with two of the best teachers I have ever known. One is retired. The other *was taught* by the one who had retired! ("No wonder he turned out so good!")

One taught English. The other teaches Art. At lunch, we talked about both subjects; and much more.

Many years ago, the English teacher taught the art teacher a course in "comedy, tragedy, and satire."

"There is a fine line between comedy and tragedy," said the course's teacher. Then he gave many examples to support his claim. Here is one of those examples.

Pearl Harbor

Was Pearl Harbor a tragedy? Of course! Think of the thousands of lost lives. Think of the hundreds of lost ships.

In fact, history will forever remember the Japanese attack on the United States Pacific Fleet on December 7, 1941, as "A Day of

Infamy" and the most devastating defeat ever suffered by our country's Armed Forces.

Now if that is true (and it is!), why did Winston Churchill, the prime minister of England at the time, openly celebrate that devastating attack. Why did Churchill *publicly thank God* for that ruthless, destructive, deadly massacre?

Yes! Because it is universally believed by the most notable of the world's historians that the Allied Forces would have lost World War II, had the US not entered that conflict when we did, and what *made* the US enter the war at such an important and necessary time? Yes! Pearl Harbor!

Tragedy? Comedy? Mourn? Celebrate? Fine lines, all.

Find a comedy in your next tragedy. Be positive. Stay positive. You can.

The Bright Side

Recently, I watched a science fiction movie about a comet that threatened to collide with the earth unless our planet's most brilliant astrologists could alter the comet's course before the collision.

The movie's heroes launched a rocket ship into space in the hopes of hitting the comet with nuclear explosives to reduce its size and alter its course.

Problems ensued rapidly, and the heroes were forced to remain on the rocket beyond their planned time of departure.

"If we don't exit this craft in a very short time," warned the ship's pilot to all on board, "we will explode with the craft!"

The project's commanding officer replied with a wink and smile.

"Well, look at the bright side!" the pilot quipped. "If that happens, all of us will get our name put on the front of a high school!"

Look on the bright side. Stay positive!

Medical Mastermind

My father-in-law was in the hospital for abdominal surgery. At ninety-one years old, he did not recover well from the anesthesia. As he fought to regain consciousness, a team of health-care assistants was at his bedside twenty-four hours a day.

One of the assistants was a young woman from Brazil with an infectious smile and a magnetic love for life and her patients.

While giving my father-in-law some water one day, she said, "I love water! It tastes so good, even when it's warm. I can't get enough of it!"

Imagine getting that excited about warm water!

During another of my visits, my father-in-law's incision was causing him a lot of pain, especially when he coughed.

"He needs a pillow to press against his incision so it won't hurt so much when he coughs," said the same assistant. She came back with a blanket and roll of tape. "There are no pillows right now, so I'll make him one." She folded the blanket and wrapped the tape around it.

Then she found a magic marker and wrote, "Hug me!" with two smiley faces on the tape for my father-in-law to see. He smiled. So did I. So did his special helper from Brazil.

She was positive. She *stayed positive*!

Gotta Be a Pony!

Once upon a time, there was a family with twins. The girl twin was positive, and the boy twin was negative. One year, when the twins' birthday came, their parents decided to conduct an experiment. For his birthday, the boy twin was given a shiny new bicycle, a tool kit, and an electric train. The girl twin was given a room full of horse manure and a small shovel.

Shortly after the twins got their presents, their parents went into the boy's room and asked him how he liked what he got. The boy was sulking. He shook his head and said, "The train might electrocute me. The hammer and nails might make me puncture my finger and get lockjaw. I might fall riding the bike and fracture my skull. These presents are awful!"

Then the parents went into the girl's room and asked her how she liked her gifts. The little girl was busy and excited. She was shoveling manure as fast as she could with her new little shovel. She had a big smile on her face.

As she shoveled, she exclaimed, "You are the best parents in the world. Thank you so much for these wonderful presents! It's a lot of work, but I know it will be worth it. With all this manure around, I know there has gotta be a pony in here somewhere!"

Be like that little twin girl. Stay positive!

Tree Tragedy?

Last Christmas, DeeDee asked me to buy our tree. It was cold and dark on the day that she asked me, so I didn't want to go. Still, I said yes and did my best to pick a good one.

I went to four places and looked at every tree. I stood them up. I measured. I agonized. I asked for help. Finally, I picked one and brought it home.

DeeDee helped me get my tree in the house and put it in its stand. Then I asked her what she thought. She said, "Carmen, I have some bad news and some good news."

"What is the bad news? I asked.

"This tree is too tall, too wide, and too dry," DeeDee replied. "We will have to cut it and trim it and water it constantly. We will be *lucky if it lasts* until Christmas! *That* is the bad news!" finished DeeDee.

"After all that," I countered, "what good news could you possibly have for me?"

"*You* won't have to *buy* the tree *next year*!" Dee answered.

DeeDee was right; that *was good news*! Be like DeeDee. Find the good news! Find a comedy in your next tragedy.

Well, dear reader, what do you think so far? Are any of my stories putting muscle into our "Stay Positive" message?

If not, would you rather give some stories about "The Kids Today" a try?

The Kids Today

We hear that expression a lot. It is often followed by criticism like "The kids today are lazy" or "The kids today are crazy!" or "The kids today are losers!" or "The kids today are loafers!"

Other times, that same expression is followed by a compliment.

I like to hear our kids complimented much more than criticized because our kids *deserve compliments*! Why? Read some stories about "The Kids Today" and find out!

In Good Hands

Like most high school principals, I attend many athletic events and love doing so.

Often, more than one of our teams plays at the same time but in different locations, so I must miss one game to attend another. When that happens, I see our away teams off on their buses then attend one of the games being played at home.

One snowy afternoon, our boys' hockey team was traveling to Springfield while our girls were playing hockey at home. As I arrived to say goodbye to the boys, half the team had already stowed their gear and boarded the bus.

I stood on the pavement at the bus door and shook the hands of the remaining athletes as they lined up to board.

As the last of them boarded, the twelve or so athletes who were already seated on the bus when I arrived, saw me, stood in unison, filed off the bus *into the snow*, and lined up to allow me to shake their hands before *reboarding* the bus!

We *do* hear concerns about "the kids today" and their impact on our future. Trust me. Our future is in good hands; so, stay positive and celebrate the kids today!

It has been said that "youth is a gift of nature while age is a work of art." In truth, youth is *also* a work of art! As our conversation shares more and more stories about what good friends, givers, fans, partners, and people "the kids today" can be. Celebrate the compliments those kids deserve and why I appreciate the good hands God has put our future in.

More Good Kids

A few years ago, on a hot September afternoon, our varsity girls' soccer team hosted a game against a much smaller and younger team from the North Shore.

The visitors only had eleven players and were losing badly by the second half even though by then our coach was using a lot of junior varsity players. With five minutes left in the ninety-minute game, we had a nine-goal lead. At that point, our coach called one last time out.

"They are completely exhausted," he said to our team. "Remember, you have had rest and replacements while each of them has played the whole game with no breaks, and it is hot out there. So don't lay down," the coach continued, "but don't embarrass them either." The coach then began to review a few plays that he wanted our girls to run as the game wound down.

As the coach spoke, a number of our team members started taking water bottles from a big cooler next to our bench. The activity distracted our other players and it aggravated our coach.

"Ladies," he said, "you can get your water when I finish talking. For now, pay attention!"

"Oh, Coach," responded our players in unison, "we are not getting water for us. We are getting it for the other team! They need it more than we do."

Yes, our future is in good hands. It belongs to the *kids today*!

So be positive! Stay positive!

Last Gasp

Last fall, I attended a cross country meet.

At the time, twelve of our student-athletes (mostly freshmen) were competing against a rival high school from Arlington on our home course by running two miles as fast as they could; most of it through the woods of Braintree.

The runners began with a one-fourth-mile lap around a field then went into the woods for a mile and a half then came out of the woods to face another quarter mile around the field to the finish line.

Now when I call those students *runners*, I *mean runners*, not *joggers* or *walkers* or *pacers* or *trotters*. They were *runners*, and they *ran* for two miles!

One of our best runners finished fourth and was totally exhausted as he crossed the line. He stopped abruptly and hunched low with his hands on his knees. He gasped for air over and over. I thought he might faint or get sick or both. I know I would have!

As he struggled to recover, I walked over to him, patted his back, and said, "Nice job." He immediately looked up and found a way to smile. Then still struggling to breathe, he said, "Dr. Mariano, it really means a lot that you came!"

It was a very short speech to a very small audience. That audience was me, and I will never forget that speech. I have no idea where that athlete found the class, respect, strength, or oxygen to *think* of his words, let alone *say* them.

No speech has made me happier. No speech has made me prouder of the kids today, and, yes, I celebrate the good hands God has put our future in!

Good Grace

Soon after that race, I watched our kids run again. This time, they were competing on our beautiful new track that is part of our seven-sport stadium. The first race was the two-mile. Two of our boys competed in that race. They placed first and second. Two of our girls did the same. Great day. Great work. Great kids!

One of our female finishers has one of my favorite *names* and one of my favorite *words*! That name *and* word is "Grace!" As a two-miler, Grace had to run eight laps around our four-hundred-meter track. It was a test. It was a trial. It was torture!

I stood in the track's infield and cheered Grace every time she passed. One cheer was "Great work!" Another was "Well done!" then came "So far, so good!"

And every time I cheered, Grace *thanked* me! Yes, every time she ran by me and I offered a cheer that was meant for her, Grace looked at me and said, "Thank you, Doctor!"

Her words were softer than they were strong. (After all, she *was* *tired*!) Still, she thanked me and thanked me *and thanked me*!

Grace is one of the kids today. They hold our future in their good hands. That makes me positive. That will make me *stay positive*!

A Reason to Smile

Recently, I was sent a beautiful little book called *Generous Faith* written by Sister Bridget Haase, OSU. It contains many wonderful and true stories!

One tells of a sticky summer day during which Sister was "wearing civilian clothes" as she boarded a bus to a retreat center. As she settled into her seat, she noticed a street person staring at her. The stranger slid over and said hi, then he extended his unwashed hand, and offered Sister an unwrapped peppermint.

"Want a peppermint?" he kindly asked.

"Thanks, sir," Sister replied, "but I've given up sugar for the summer, so I would like *you* to enjoy it *for* me!"

When the bus approached Sister's stop, she stood up. As she did, the voice of the street person called out. "Miss, that 'no sugar' diet is really working. You're lookin' very good!"

"Life changed in a flash," Sister reflected. "I got off the bus with a dance in my step and a song in my heart. I don't know what made the difference. The offer of an unwrapped peppermint or the sweetness of my diet being noticed. But one thing I do know, God always offers us a reason to smile."

Be like Sister. Find a reason to smile. Then smile! Be positive. *Stay* positive!

And if you ever *forget* to stay positive, just *remember the kids today*! Because besides being considerate, generous, creative, and courageous, the kids today *can* be *positive*. The kids today can make you laugh!

How? Like this!

Young President

One night shortly after I became our school's first president, I was in my office trying to catch up on a bunch of e-mails.

One of those e-mails was from a mother and went like this.

> Dear Dr. Mariano,
>
> You have only been our president for two weeks, and I thought you might like to hear a review of your performance so far!
>
> Your name came up at our dinner table last night, so I asked my daughter what she thought of you.
>
> "He's okay, I guess," she replied. "He has a lot of energy and is always smiling. He's kind of like a *fifteen-year-old kid* trapped in a *sixty-five-year-old body!*"

Today's kids have helped that "fifteen-year-old kid" *remain* fifteen years old! How? I will show you more stories!

Classmates?

When I introduced myself to a class of freshmen on their first day at our high school, I said, "Ladies and gentlemen, I am proud to be your president and prouder to be a graduate. That's right. I went to this school. I sat in those seats, and I walked on this stage just as you are and just as you will. This school changed my life, and I am here to help it change yours."

After a polite applause, we left the auditorium together. One of the freshmen tugged on my suit coat as we exited. I turned to face him and he asked, "Dr. Mariano, did you say you went to this school?"

"Yes, I did" I replied.

"*Wow!*" he exclaimed. "What year did you graduate?" he asked.

I answered, "1964."

He yelped, "1964! God! Then after a pause to reflect, he asked in all sincerity, "Was Archbishop Williams in any of your classes?"

"No," I answered him. "He died in 1908. I just missed him!"

Yes, today's kids have made me laugh, and they were not alone! What do I mean?" Keep reading!

Smart Smile

The root of all humor is intelligence. The most intelligent (and there-fore funniest) man I know is Dr. Thomas O'Brien.

As I mentioned earlier, he is a world-renowned medical author-ity in the area of infectious disease. He is also Conan O'Brien's dad and a riot! Years ago, I was with Dr. O'Brien in the lobby of the Brigham and Women's Hospital where he worked with my wife DeeDee for over thirty years.

"How is your family?" I asked Dr. O'Brien (he has a wife and eight children besides Conan)

"No better!" kidded Dr. O'Brien. "I keep hoping that obedi-ence and reason will one day overtake them, but so far, no luck!"

After laughing, I scanned the large lobby of the hospital and noted how many doctors walked by with their most common piece of equipment around their necks or bulging from one of their pock-ets. "Boy," I said, "I have never seen so many stethoscopes in one place!"

"Yes," said the doctor, "to some of their owners, they are *instru-ments.* To others, they are *ornaments*, but in any case, they beat wear-ing a tie!"

Are you hearing any stories that might make muscle for my "Stay Positive" message? I hope so. I think so!

Life Is Difficult

The Road Less Traveled by M. Scott Peck begins with one of the most profound truths and notable sentences ever written. It ranks with "Call me Ishmael," "They were the best of times," "Let there be light, and "You're gonna need a bigger boat!"

That sentence says this: *Life is difficult.*

Life *is* difficult. According to Peck, once we know that, accept it, and expect it, life becomes *no longer difficult*!

Still, according to Peck, most of us do not fully accept that fact. Instead, we moan about life's difficulties as if those difficulties and life itself *should be easy*!

Too bad and too true.

The more we expect life to be easier, the harder life is.

The more we expect life to be hard, the easier life will be!

So expect life to be hard and know that your expectation will make life easier.

Stay positive!

Beauty Is…

One summer, a colleague went to Maine on vacation. When she got back, I asked her how it was.

"It was amazing," she said. "I got up early every morning and sat on a porch overlooking the ocean. I could see the waves and feel the wind. I could hear the birds and smell the flowers. It was breathtaking. It was beautiful."

Then my colleague went on. "One morning," she said, "I fell asleep on the porch. When I woke up, it was much later. Instead of seeing the waves, I saw crowds of people. Instead of hearing the birds, I heard trucks and traffic. Instead of smelling the flowers, I smelled exhaust and dust. At first," she continued, "it seemed like someone had taken away all the beauty and replaced it with something less. But that had not happened. The waves were still there. I could see them if I looked. The birds were still there too. I could hear them if I listened. The flowers were with me, as well, and I could smell them if I tried."

"Beauty," she ended, "is always there, and it is everywhere. We need only to find it, and *we can*!" So find the beauty. Find the good news. Stay positive.

Possessions or Privileges?

A rich man visited an orphanage one day. He was looking for a child to adopt. He met many children but chose none of them. They all seemed too happy. They all seemed too comfortable. They all seemed too cared for to need the old man's help.

Months later, the man returned. This time, he found a boy who was different. He seemed lost, angry, and in need of help.

"I have a big house, lots of land, and lots of money," said the man to the boy. "I can give you anything you want. I can make you happy."

"I don't want your money, your house, or your land," said the boy. "I don't want your possessions. Instead, I just want your privileges."

"What do you mean?" asked the old man.

"I want your family, and I want your friends," said the boy. "I want your faith, and I want your future. I don't want your *possessions*. I want your *privileges*! Those are not things you have *earned*," the boy went on, "they are things you were *given*, and those things have been given to you by God. So if you give me those things, I will thank God instead of you, and I will be happy with or without your money, your land, or your house."

Be like that boy. Thank God for your privileges. Use your privileges to stay positive!

Win Some, Lose Some

A minister's wife was suffering from a bad cold and stayed home one Sunday morning instead of going to church. When the minister came home, his wife asked him about the morning service.

"What did you preach about his morning?" asked the wife.

"I talked about charity," the minister said. "I told the congregation that it was a duty of the rich to give to the poor."

"How did it go over?" his wife asked.

"About fifty-fifty," the minister replied. "I convinced the poor!"

Be like that minister. Stay positive!

Dinner

Years ago, DeeDee, Natalie, her partner Shelley, Dad, and I took my mother to a new restaurant for dinner. She just had a birthday, and my family wanted to celebrate with her, but the hostess took an hour to seat us!

The cook took forever as well—and the meal was only fair.

By the time we were seated, many of the specials were no longer available.

Still, we had a great time! Why? Because our waiter *made* it great! He apologized. He smiled. *He shined!*

He complimented us on how nice we looked. He brought us a free drink!

Our waiter cared! He made us feel important. That *waiter made* a difference and he made our night. *People* make a difference. *People* make *all* the difference. Of that, I am *positive!*

Happy Anniversary!

Last summer, I went to the mall to buy DeeDee an anniversary present. It was after work, and it was late, but I went. I spent an hour looking and found nothing to buy. If I found the right *color*, the *size* was wrong. If I found the right *size*, the *color* was wrong. If I found the right *color* and *size*, the *style* was wrong. *Everything* was wrong! But I still had a great night. Why?

Because the person who waited on me *made* it great! She smiled. She cared. *She shined!* She made me feel important. She even told me I looked like Paul Simon!!

She brought out dress after dress and sweater after sweater. Somehow, she knew as much about clothes as my aunt Sadie did! She never gave up. She never got mad.

Finally, I bought something. I gave it to DeeDee on our anniversary. DeeDee didn't like it. She took it back the next day. But that was okay! I still had a great night shopping because of that salesperson! *People* make a difference. *People* make *all* the difference. Of that, I am *positive!*

Flat Tire

Last fall, I got a flat tire. It happened right in front of my house, so I drove into my driveway on the rim and called Triple A. A truck came by shortly after my call. The man who came never rang my bell or said a word. He took the tools out of my trunk, changed my tire, and left. *He did not shine!*

I found my tools the next day. They were in the driveway under my car. My flat tire was easier to find. It was in the middle of my front lawn on top of some grass seed DeeDee had just planted.

Now let me tell you something. *I would have given anything to have that waiter from that new restaurant change my tire!*

I would have given anything to have that salesperson from the mall change it too!

Why? Because people make a difference. People make all the difference.

Of that I am *positive*.

Be positive. *Stay positive!*

Aunt Gloria

My aunt Gloria (Dad's sister) stayed positive! She spent a lot of her time smiling just like my father did, and she spent a little of her time yelling just like my father did! She loved her children just like my father did, and she worshiped her spouse just like my father did!

Long after my father's older brothers and sisters left Tadone's house and went on their own, Aunt Gloria remained.

"My mother and father needed my company, and I needed theirs," Auntie Glo explained. "So until I got married, I stayed with them. In fact, long *after* I got married, I stayed with them!"

That's all true! When she finally did marry, Gloria became a Varasso! Her husband (and my uncle) John owned a construction company with his brothers. No one in any of my families worked more or talked less than he did!

I envied Uncle John from the day he got married because I was sure he had landed the world's best cook in the making! After all, Auntie Glo learned from "the master," right? I mean, she lived with Nonna Pasqualina for almost thirty years, and at least some of that talent must have rubbed off during all that time!

No such luck! "She can't even scramble an egg!" Uncle John confessed to me after being married to Aunt Gloria for a few years. "And you could paper the walls with her homemade pasta! It stuck to everything!"

"Didn't she learn from Nonna?" I asked Uncle John one day.

"I expected so," he kidded in response. "But after her first dozen disastrous dinners, I began to wonder if she was adopted!"

Then two things happened.

First, Nonna Pasqualina had a heart attack on the eve of her fiftieth wedding anniversary and died. Then Tadone Carmine stopped eating!

He had to! Aunt Gloria's cooking was just too much for him to bear! After a trip to the doctor with Tadone, Auntie Glo came home with an announcement. "Pa needs to eat, so I will learn to cook for him!"

No one believed her, *except her*! By the time she died, my Auntie Glo had become one of the best Italian cooks in any of my families.

She could do it all! Sauce, meatballs, ravioli, lasagna, gnocchi, pastry, soup, biscotti, pizzellas—all as good as the north end's best. In fact, all *better* than the North end's best!

She could even make the *bad* stuff taste good! People raved about her tripe, pigs' feet, squid, and snails just like they had about Nonna's, and Nonna never taught her how to make them!

One day, I told her she was not a cook—she was an artist! In fact, I told her that her married name was perfect because it was *Varasso*, so it rhymed with *Picasso*!

I said, "Auntie, that guy was an artist, and so are you!" So true! So true!

When she wasn't cooking, Auntie Glo was with her children, taking a ride on one of her sons' motorcycles, driving one of their trucks, or working in her garden.

"I never asked her to name her favorite crop," said Natalie while giving Aunt Glo's eulogy at her funeral. "If I did, I bet she would have said 'hope!' Auntie always hoped. She always looked ahead. She never whined or complained."

In fact, that was what she and my dad shared the most. When it came to strengths and smiles, my father and his "baby sister" were a perfect match. They could have been twins.

According to Professor Terry Deal of Harvard, there are two kinds of people in the world—plums and prunes. Plums are positive. They are full of juice. Prunes are negative. They have no juice of their own, so they spend all their time sucking the juice from the plums!

My father was like his baby sister. They *both were plums*! Sometimes Dad and Aunt Gloria were even sick at the *same* time! At other times, they took turns being sick.

When either of them was healthy, that one would visit the other in the afternoon with pastry. (They both loved pastry with their afternoon tea!) So you never had to ask how Dad or Auntie Glo was feeling. All you had to do was see who brought the pastry and who brewed the tea!

Auntie Glo had cancer for eight years. She never whimpered. She never whined. She was always positive. She always stayed positive.

Dad's Blood Test

My father's cancer got a head start on Auntie Glo's. (After all, he was much older than she was!)

Dad's cancer was aggressive, so his doctor wanted to make up treatment with some "muscle" to fight back with.

His choice was a powerful form of chemotherapy. "I want to mix up something strong for you!" the doc announced.

"Go for it," Dad said. "I have an industrial-size blender at home that I can bring you!"

The blender and the chemo worked, but when the cancer left, Dad's kidneys failed so he had to go on dialysis for a year.

He went to the hospital between his chemotherapy treatments to have his blood tested.

The blood test was always an adventure. Over time, Dad's veins had been poked by a lot of needles, so poking them again and again was never easy.

After one of his blood tests, Dad rolled down the sleeve of his white dress shirt that he always wore to the doctors and began to leave the hospital. As he walked down the corridor toward the parking lot, one sleeve of the shirt turned red. His vein had opened, and blood was pouring from the puncture site.

We rushed Dad back into the phlebotomy lab and laid him down as a doctor was paged. The doctor came and redressed Dad's arm. We all began breathing again, except Dad.

He had never stopped! He had never missed a breath.

The doctor made Dad lay still for ten minutes. He didn't like that. Then we left with Dad in a wheelchair just to be safe. Dad didn't like that either. As I wheeled him to the car, I said, "That was scary."

Dad said, "Yeah, and I will be sure not to scare you again."

I had no idea what he meant by that but soon found out. The next time I picked Dad up for his blood test, guess what he was wearing?

Yes, a *red shirt*!

"If I bleed the next time," Dad reasoned, "no one will notice. It will be camouflaged!"

Like my aunt Gloria, my dad was positive!

Be like them both. Be positive. Stay positive.

Might my stories about my aunt Gloria Varrasso help make muscles for my "Stay Positive" message? I wonder!

Will they make better muscles than "Because I Said So?"

I think so!

Different Sisters

As I said, from the inside out, my dad and his baby sister *could* have been twins. They *should* have been twins.

Two *other* sisters should *not* have been twins! They *could not* have been twins! Thanks to God, they *were not* twins!

It's true. My wife, DeeDee, and her sister Martha were different. They were *very* different! They were not twins!

How different were they? Do you remember Terry Deal's plums and prunes? Just to help you recall, plums are positive. They are full of juice.

Prunes are negative. They have no juice of their own, so they spend all their time sucking the juice from the plums!

Now that you remember the difference between plums and prunes, DeeDee and her sister, Martha, were *that different*!

DeeDee is a plum. She is a magnet with a smile! People are attracted to DeeDee. They bathe in her presence just as they bathe in the sunlight on a crisp winter day.

DeeDee makes people smile. She makes them laugh. She makes them happy. She *is a plum*!

For years, DeeDee's sister Martha was not a plum. She had no juice. She made no smiles. Even Martha's daughter Kristen seemed to have trouble finding Martha's juice.

Then something changed. Martha got sick and spent time in the hospital. While she was there, Martha found her smile. She got some juice! She made people laugh. Kristen was one of those people. So was DeeDee. So was I!

In the hospital, Martha became more like DeeDee. She became more like a plum!

Martha had always complained about people. Sometimes she even teased them. In the hospital, she did it for fun—*their* fun!

No one got embarrassed. No one got upset. No one got hurt. Instead, the people who Martha teased *teased Martha back*!

Everyone had fun, even Martha!

One day, Kristen read Martha what she called *the senility prayer*. It went like this:

Dear God,

Please grant me the senility to forget the people I never liked, the good fortune to bump into the ones I enjoyed, and the eyesight to tell the difference!

When Kristen finished, Martha replied with "Why did you read that to me?"

Kristen countered (in fun!) with "If you don't know, I picked the right poem!"

Martha replied (still in fun!) with "If I had a gun, I would use it on you!"

Kristen offered, "I am glad you don't have a gun!"

Martha ended with "How can you be sure?"

Martha lived as a prune, and she died as a plum. She lived weakly, and she died strong. I celebrate that. So does DeeDee. So does Kristen.

I hope Martha is celebrating too.

Another John, Another Plum

DeeDee has a brother whose name is John. Like DeeDee, John is a plum, especially when he makes fun of how old we are all getting!

Someone once said, "People don't stop having fun because they get old. They get old because they stop having fun." As he gets old, John *doesn't* stop having fun!

I once told John that my father, at seventy, complained that "the older he gets, two things go first. One is his memory, and he forgets the other one!"

Well, I shared that with John one day, and he replied, "Carmen, I know what you mean! Do you know how I deal with it?"

"How?" I asked. "I just recite a little poem to make sure I am not forgetting anything that I need to take with me when I leave the house."

John answered, "How does the poem go?" I pursued.

"It's just a little checklist of the things, and it goes like this, 'Spectacles, testicles, wallet, and watch!' I would be screwed if I left home without any of those things, especially the testicles!" confessed John.

Yes, John makes a very good plum!

Janet

My uncle Johnny was her father, and my aunt Molly was her mom. Janet and I were close. We went to high school together and shared many friends. After high school, however, we saw less of each other because college called! Mine was in Washington, DC, and hers was in Western Massachusetts.

The Accident

Three months into our senior year of college, I got a call from my mother. She had very bad news. Janet, who was attending UMass Amherst, was driving from there to meet her Navy nurse commander in Springfield.

On the way, she had an accident. It was a bad one. Janet's neck was broken, and her brain was injured. She had surgery right away and was fitted with Crutchfield Tongs and a Stryker frame to immobilize her neck.

The tongs were as scary as they sounded. They consisted of four ice picks that were mounted on springs and screwed into Janet's skull. Each tong was attached to a weight that pulled her skull away from her shoulders.

Janet remained in that painful traction from early November through the following January. On the Stryker Frame, she could be turned to look only at the ceiling or the floor.

Janet's mother (herself a nurse) made things better by mounting a small mirror that allowed Janet to see the door to her room while looking only at the ceiling.

Janet's sister, Lu-Ann, who was a "real doctor" like Natalie also helped. She would lie on her back facing up while Janet was in traction, facing the floor. That allowed the two sisters to chat during one of Lu-Ann's many trips "home" from medical school!

My father "chipped in" as well! He, once again, "went to work" on his lunch hour at the shipyard and fashioned a stainless steel spoon with a hinged cover. This let Janet eat ice cream and soup without spilling!

Still a Smile

When I saw her again at Christmas, Janet's ice picks were still ugly, and her smile was still beautiful. Through everything that happened, she never lost her smile *or* her courage.

Janet explained, "It wasn't courage that kept me strong. It wasn't that I was that brave. Instead, I was just too stubborn to let myself stay paralyzed." Yes, Janet was stubborn. Janet was also brave.

I went to visit Janet during her ordeal and was still in awe of her smile. During one visit, I was especially sensitive to how much pain she seemed to be in, how uncomfortable her position seemed, and how prominent her scars appeared.

"How are you, Jan?" I asked feebly.

"I am okay," she replied with a weak but brave little wink. "Now tell me, how does my hair look today?"

Yes, Janet is brave. She is a plum, and Janet is not alone!

What do I mean? Keep reading!

Shoe Salesmen

A large shoe company sent two salesmen into the Australian out-back to drum up business among the Aborigines. Sometime later, the company received telegrams from both men.

The first one said, "There is no business here. *None* of these people *wear* shoes!"

The second salesman said, "There is a great opportunity here. *All* these people *need* shoes!"

Like Janet, the second salesman was a plum!

Show Business

A man sat next to a stranger in church one day. The stranger smelled awful. After church, the man asked the stranger why he smelled so bad. The stranger blamed it on his job. He explained that he worked for a circus and got paid to clean up after the elephants.

"Oh my god," said the man. "What an awful job! Why don't you quit and find something else to do?"

"What and give up show business?" asked the stranger.

Like Janet and the salesman, the stranger was another plum!

385 Smiles

Research done at the University of Michigan shows that the average American *child* smiles four hundred times a day while the average American *adult* smiles fifteen times a day!

Now tell me, where did those other 385 smiles go?

That's right; they are still inside plums like Janet and you!

So *find* those smiles and *smile* those smiles. And how can you find those 385 smiles a day?

Look for them! Look for reasons to smile!

Look for reasons to *stay positive*!

Look Inside

During a geography lesson about Hawaii, an elementary school teacher asked the class what words came to their minds when they looked at a coconut. Many students immediately raised their hands and offered answers like *dark, dry, dull, hard, hairy,* and *holey*. While closing his eyes and shaking his head, the teacher replied, "That's funny because when I see a coconut, I see words like *sweet, soft, juicy, milky* and more." "Teacher!" The kids challenged, "How can you see words like those?" "*By looking inside,*" came the teacher's final response.

When you look for reasons to stay positive, follow that teacher's advice and look inside yourself!Now let's talk about looking!

Reticular Activation System

When we look for something, we use our eyes. We also use our brains! We use a small system of cells that is called our reticular activation system or our "RAS" for short.

Nothing gets to your brain unless your RAS lets it!

Let's say I asked you to find everything in your bedroom that is blue. If you tried, your RAS would help you.

As your eyes scanned the room, your RAS would let the blue images into your brain and filter all the other images out.

Not long ago, Dee's brother, John (the plum!), bought a new car. It is a Jeep. For weeks after he bought it, John would not stop saying, "You know, Carmen, I never noticed how many Jeeps are on the road until I bought mine!"

Now tell me, did Jeep just happen to have a *huge boom* in sales on the *exact day* John bought his new car?

No! That was just his RAS at work, letting every Jeep in and keeping everything else out!

Did the same thing ever happen to you?

If so, good! Your RAS is working! Yes, your RAS works on *colors*, and it works on *cars*. Your RAS works on *happiness* too!

If you let it, your RAS will look for and find reasons for you to be happy. It will filter and find things in life that will make you happy—every day, every minute—if you let it. *So let it*!

Let your RAS find you reasons to smile!

Look for reasons to smile every minute of every day.

Let your brain find those 385 smiles every day!

Stay positive!

Are you ready to find some of those smiles? Are you ready to let your RAS help you find them? Great! Start by thinking of all the stories about married couples and their fights or funerals that have made you laugh!

Did you say you have never heard any such stories? Did you say stories about fights or funerals have never made you laugh? Did you say finding them would be too hard? Impossible?

Not at all! Try these.

Small Tools

It's like the couple whose lawn mower was broken. The wife kept hinting to her husband that he should get it fixed, but somehow, the message never sank in. Finally, she thought of a clever way to make her point. When her husband arrived home one day, he found his wife seated in the tall grass, busily snipping away with a tiny pair of scissors. He watched silently for a short time and then went into the house.

He was gone for only a few moments. When he returned, he handed her a toothbrush.

"When you finish cutting the grass," he said, "you might as well sweep the sidewalks too!" Did that story about a married couple's fight make you laugh? Let's try another!

Bad Luck

A man was very sick in the hospital with his wife by his side. He slipped into a coma for three days. His wife never left him. When he regained consciousness, the man motioned to his wife to come close.

He whispered, "You have been by my side through all this suffering, haven't you?"

"Yes," she said. "I have."

The husband when on, "And you were by my side when I lost my job. You were with me when the house burned down. You were by my side when I wrecked our car."

His wife nodded and smiled, "Yes," she said. "I was."

"Do you know what?" asked the man.

"No, what?" the wife asked back.

"I think *you* are *bad luck*!" replied the man.

Another fight! Another laugh?

Sleeping In

A man was informed by his doctor that he had only twelve hours to live. He rushed home and told his wife, who collapsed in a flood of tears. Eventually, she pulled herself together, took her husband's hand, and said, "Then I am going to make tonight the best night of your life." Then she went out and bought all his favorite foods. Opened a bottle of fine wine, served him dinner, dressed in a sexy nightgown, and led him up to bed, where she made passionate love to him.

Just as they were about to fall asleep, the husband tapped her on the shoulder, "Honey, could we make love again?"

"Sure, sweetheart," she said sleepily and obliged.

"Once more, baby?" he asked afterward. "It's our last night together."

"Mmmhmm," she mumbled, getting tired, and they made love a third time.

Then the persistent husband asked, "One last time, darling?" He begged a little later, shaking her by the shoulder. Exhausted and no longer "in the mood," the wife sneered, "Sure. After all, what do you care? You don't have to get up in the morning!"

Keep looking for fights. Keep looking for fun!

Not Yet!

An elderly man was at home dying in bed. He smelled the aroma of his favorite chocolate chip cookies baking. He wanted one last cookie before he died. He fell out of bed and crawled to the stairs. He rolled down both flights and crawled to the kitchen where his wife was busily baking the cookies he had smelled.

With waning strength, he crawled to the table and was barely able to lift his withered arm to the cookie sheet. As he grasped a warm moist cookie, his wife *whacked* his hand with a spatula.

"Why did you do that?" he whispered.

"These are for *after* the funeral!" she responded.

Fight, funeral and fun? Yes!

Good Business!

When a woman got married many years ago, she put a shoebox in her closet and told her husband not to ever open it. After over fifty years of marriage, however, the woman took very ill and told her husband to open her box.

When the husband obeyed, he found two doilies and twenty-five thousand dollars in the box. He then took the box to his wife and asked her to explain the contents of the box.

She replied, "When I got married my, mother told me to crochet a doily every time I got mad at you and put it in this box."

Hearing this, the husband smiled, thinking of all the years of their marriage, his wife was only mad at him twice!

Then he asked the wife what the twenty-five thousand dollars were for. She explained, "That's the money I got from selling the doilies!"

Are you finished? If so, good!

Well, how did you do? Did you find any "fun" inside any of those fights or *fun*erals?

If you did, that is great! You looked for that fun, and you found it with the help of your RAS!

Grandma Moses

Yes, "*Life is what you* (and your RAS!) *make it. Always has been always will be.*" Grandma Moses said that. Grandma Moses produced fifteen hundred paintings in her life, and she didn't *start* painting until she was almost *eighty* years *old!* She completed *most* of her *best* work after she turned *one hundred!*

Listen to Grandma Moses! Life *is* what you make it. Life can be *kind* if you *make* it kind. Life can be *beautiful* if you *make* it beautiful. Life can be positive if you *make* it positive.

So make life positive. *Stay positive!*

Most of us miss out on life's *big* prizes—the Pulitzer, the Nobel, Oscar, Tony, Emmy. But we are all eligible for life's *real* prizes—a pat on the back, a fist bump, a sunrise, an empty parking space, hot soup, cold beer.

We can all win enough of *those* prizes to be happy and to be successful. It is all a matter of looking. It is all a matter of staying positive!

So what do you think? Over the last bunch of pages, have I told you enough stories to put muscle in your *stay positive* message?

If so, good! Now use them the next time that message needs that muscle!

Have Direction

Way back in our dedication, I quoted Yogi Berra like this, "If you don't know where you're going, you might never get there!"

Very true! Direction, goals, objectives, purpose, intent, and more are important!

Energy without direction is wasteful. Energy with direction is powerful.

Steam coming from a teapot comes at a cost and offers no value unless it is confined and directed. When it is, that steam can make electricity, power a locomotive, heat a building, and more.

Thus, "Have direction!" is good advice. But how can we *give* that advice *muscle*?

Try these stories!

Dan

One of the cousins who taught me how to work taught me something else. He taught me how to focus. His name is Dan and is the youngest son of my aunt Rosie and uncle Freddie. (He was also Amazing Grace's younger brother!)

Dan is a year younger than me. Still, he is wiser, smarter, and stronger. Why? Because from the minute I knew him, Dan knew where he was going. For as long as I can remember, *Dan had goals!*

When we were in junior high school, Dan lived in a cramped, modest, two-family house just like I did. There was a basketball court near Dan's house, and we played there often with just about every kid in the neighborhood.

On the way to that court from my uncle Freddie's two-family, we passed a doctor's house. It was one of the biggest, nicest, and most expensive houses in our city. It even had an office attached to it!

Dan looked at that house every time we passed it on our way to and from the basketball courts. As he looked, Dan always pointed to the house and said, "That is Dr. Chiminello's house, and it will be mine someday. That office will be mine too," Dan would say, "because I will be a lawyer instead of a doctor, and my wife will be my secretary."

Dan even knew who his (beautiful!) wife and secretary would be! Yes, when he was in junior high school, my cousin Dan knew where he was going, and he got there! He had goals. He had direction. I have always admired him for that. I learned from him, as well.

The Reverend Billy Graham tells a story that happened early in his ministry when he was driving through a small Southern town late one Saturday night.

He needed to mail some letters back to his parish, so he asked a young boy who was standing on a corner where the post office was. The boy gave Reverend Graham directions, and Billy thanked him.

Then Billy told the boy, "If you come to the Baptist Church tomorrow morning, I will be glad to tell you and all the other people in the church how to get to heaven."

"Heaven?" retorted the boy. "How can you tell us the way to heaven? You don't even know the way to the post office!"

My cousin Dan knew the way to the post office. He still does! He *had direction*. He still does!

Lost Knight

There was once a knight who, after many months away, returned to his king's castle in a state of total disarray. His armor was dented. His helmet was falling off. His face was bloody. Even his horse was limping.

"What hath befallen you, Sir Knight?" asked the king.

"Oh, sire," answered the knight, "I have been laboring in your service, robbing and plundering and pillaging your enemies in the West."

"You what?" cried the king. "I don't *have* any enemies in the West."

"Oh," hesitated the knight. "You do now!"

That king may have had direction, but he never gave it to his knight!

Would any of those stories put any muscle into the message "Have Direction"? If so, that is good! Keep reading!

Lost Company

A consultant to a major aerospace company once asked the president of that company what business he was in. The president answered, and the consultant asked if he could pose the same question to the company's seven vice presidents. The president said the exercise would be a waste of time but agreed to allow it.

When the vice presidents were given the question, they claimed to be insulted, but the consultant persisted. He asked the vice presidents to describe their company's business in a single sentence. When they handed in their papers, all seven vice presidents had *very different* answers, and *none* of them matched the president's answer!

Like the king from the previous story, that president may have had direction, but he never gave it to anybody! Don't *you* be like that president!

Have direction and give direction! Put muscle in your direction message.

Wrong Way?

You heard about the woman who was driving home from her job in Boston when her cell phone rang. Answering, she heard her husband's voice urgently warning her, "Honey, be careful! I just heard on the news that some crazy woman driver is going the wrong way on Route 128!"

"God," replied the wife in a voice filled with panic. "I am *on* Route 128 right now, and it's not just one car that's going the wrong way. There are hundreds of them!"

That woman needs some direction soon!

Walt Disney

When Disney World first opened in Florida, Mrs. Walt Disney was asked to speak at the grand opening in her deceased husband's place. She was introduced by a man who said, "Mrs. Disney, I just wish Walt could have seen this."

She stood up and said, "He did! Walt *saw* this years ago. He just died before it was built."

Walt Disney got where he was going because he knew where that was.

He *had* direction. He knew where he was going, so Disney World got there, even after Walt died.

Burn the Boats!

More than six hundred years ago, a conqueror named Hernando Cortez is said to have invaded a rich South American empire in search of a priceless treasure. He brought hundreds of soldiers and sailors with him.

On the long journey from Spain to the treasure, Cortez's men lost faith. They questioned their leader, his resolve, his mission, and his plan.

Cortez spoke often to his men in an attempt to stiffen their mettle and amplify their courage to little avail. When Cortez's armada reached the empire's shore, however, he gave his army an order. That order was not "Attack!" Nor was it "Be brave." That order was not even "Charge!"

Cortez's only order was this: "Burn the boats!" That's right, in the face of an army that could not be beaten, Cortez gave his men an order that gave them no way home. His men would either conquer the unconquerable foreign army or die on a foreign shore.

So Cortez directed his army *to* those boats, and that direction redoubled their courage, erased their doubt, and saved their lives. It also made muscle for Cortez's message!

My cousin Dan would have done the same. So would Walt Disney!

Run to the Roar

Over many, many years, on the African savanna, lions have developed a hunting technique.

It features the strength and weaknesses of the oldest lion in the pride. This member is often infirmed. He is at times lame with rotten teeth and a shabby coat. This lion cannot hunt. He cannot kill.

But he still has lungs and can still give the deep-throated, primeval roar of the jungle's king.

When the pride spots a herd of antelope, the oldster heads upwind into the tall grass while the rest of the pride spreads out in the bush in the opposite direction.

Then the old lion roars...and roars...and roars.

The antelope instinctively gallop away *from* the roar and slam into the force of younger lions.

They should ignore their instinct and confront their fear. The antelope should run toward the roar.

The most successful coach in college history knows that, and he teaches it to his players. His name is Paul Assaiante, and he coached a sport called squash.

Where does Paul lead his athletes? He leads them to the roar.

Paul teaches his players the importance of confronting "the roar" of challenges, fear, and problems both on and off the squash court. That's right, Paul Assaiante gives his athletes direction. He teaches his athletes to run to the roar.

The Wall, Not the Ball!

As I have proudly told you many times, the athletic program at my high school has enjoyed much success over the years. Our boy's baseball team has contributed significantly to that success! Their coach deserves much of the credit. He knows the game very well and manages his players even better than he knows the game! I love to learn from him and to watch his team play.

He has lots of rules, and his players follow those rules. One of my favorites is this: "Look at the wall, not at the ball!"

What does that rule mean? When an opposing batter hits a pop-up that seems to be drifting foul, the coach tells any one of his players near that pop-up to take their eyes off that ball and look at the foul line, fence, or wall that separates fair territory from foul ground.

As soon as a player sees that line or that wall, the coach tells him to run to that spot. When the player gets there, the coach tells him to look up and find the ball in the air.

From there, the player will be able to tell if the ball is coming down in the fair or foul ground. Easy, right?

If, on the other hand, the fielder ran toward a foul line, fence, or the other boundary while looking up at the ball, he might end up either banging into that boundary, stopping while still in the fairground, or dropping the ball because he fears imminent contact with any number of immobile objects!

Moral of the story? Know where you are going before you try to get there!

Poor Dog!

A man bought a little dog for his children. The kids named it "Stay."

Anytime they wanted the dog to be with them, they would look at it and say, "Come, Stay! Come, Stay! Come, Stay!" The dog just sat there, not knowing whether to come or to stay! After a while, the poor little thing had a nervous breakdown! (Only kidding!)

That little dog needed direction. *So do you! So do we!*

A Matter of Life

Viktor Frankl spent four years in a Nazi concentration camp during World War II. He wrote of his experiences in a book called *Man's Search for Meaning*. While captive, Viktor calculated that only one person in twenty-eight survived the horrors of the camps, and he made a personal study of how the survivors differed from those who perished.

Viktor observed that the survivors were not necessarily the healthiest, strongest, youngest, best-fed, or most intelligent. He found that those who made it had a reason to stay alive. They had a goal. In Frankl's case, it was a burning desire to see his wife's face again. Other survivors had *different* goals, but they all *had a goal*. That goal saved their lives. It defined their lives. Goals will do the same for you. They will do the same for your followers.

It Was the Fog

Florence Chadwick was a great swimmer. Once Florence tackled the twenty-mile swim from Catalina Island to the California coast. But Florence picked a *bad day* for a swim. The currents were strong. The waves were high. The water was cold. Worst of all, a dense fog made it almost impossible to see.

Despite all that, Florence swam for fifteen *hours*. Then just *one-half mile* from shore, she gave up. Later, when asked why she quit so close to her destination, she replied that it was not the current or the waves or the cold. It was the fog. Florence said, "I failed because I couldn't see the shore. I failed because I *lost* my *direction*." Everyone is like Florence Chadwick. Everyone *needs* direction.

Let's take another test.

Another Test

Picture a lion tamer entering a cage full of lions. What would he carry into the cage? That is your test.

Yes, a whip, a gun, and a stool. You know what the whip and gun are for, but why does he take the stool?

Because if he holds the stool by its seat and points the legs of the stool at a lion, the lion will not attack.

Why? Because it *cannot decide* which leg of the stool to go after! The lion freezes because it has no direction.

Don't freeze. Have direction. Have goals.

Loud and Clear

I had a track coach in high school. Every day before practice, he told me and my teammates to "work hard—and run fast!" How was that for direction? Was it loud and clear?

No! I mean, how hard is hard? How fast is fast?

The next year, we got another coach. He never told us to work hard or run fast. He just told us "to run five-quarter miles in under a minute. Then to run five faster than that." That was good direction. It was loud and clear. I knew if they got there and if I didn't.

So did the coach!

Be like that track coach. Give your life direction that is loud and clear. Set goals that are specific and measurable.

Important Days

As I mentioned pages ago, Mark Twain once said that "the two most important days of your life are the day you were born and the day you found out why."

We should all celebrate *both* of those days by giving them direction.

So much for *having direction*! What is our next message in need of muscle?

<u>Be Creative!</u>

As we look for that message's muscle, I have a question.

What are the four favorite subjects of any audience?

Yes! They are *food, fun, money*, and *themselves*.

And which of those four subjects is the most favorite of any audience? Yes, *themselves*!

People like to talk about themselves. They like to read about themselves, write about themselves, hear about themselves, and think about themselves!

People even like to think *for* themselves! It is true; most of the people I know like to think they have the answer to any question and the solution to any problem!

Some of those solutions are better than you would ever think, and others are worse than you could ever imagine! But for every problem, there is a solution. And every solution begins with a box.

What do creative people do with that box? They *think outside* it!

Robert Kennedy once paraphrased a quote from George Bernard and said, "Some people see what is and ask 'why?' I see what has never been and ask 'why not?'"

That quote is a great way to look at creativity. "To be creative is to *see what has never been*, and 'what has never been' can only be seen from outside the box!"

It can only be seen if you think in the right direction.

Now I know what you are thinking! "Didn't we just spend the last chapter talking about direction?"

Yes, we did! We spent the last chapter talking about *moving* in the right direction, and we'll spend *this* chapter talking about *thinking* in the right direction!

Because to be creative, we *must think* in the *right direction*!

What do I mean?

Well, we have the ability to think in two directions: *vertically* and *horizontally*.

When we think *vertically*, we move from one point to another in a logical, predictable fashion. We reject any solutions that don't follow the rules or fit the pattern we have set in our minds. We don't skip steps. We don't leave the beaten path. We fit the mold. We play it safe.

When we think *horizontally* we have no rules! Our mind follows no path. We allow ourselves to be wrong. We take chances. We welcome change.

We don't assume we know where we are going. In fact, we don't assume anything! We ask questions. We don't impose any solutions; we consider them all!

Guess what direction makes you creative and takes you out of the box?

That's right—*horizontal!*

Picky Men

There was to be a big inspection at the microbiology lab of my wife, DeeDee. She knew the inspectors who were coming. They were two very picky men.

DeeDee and her staff worked hard to prepare. They cleaned everything in the lab. On the day of the inspection. Their area shined.

Then just before the inspectors arrived, DeeDee remembered a storeroom in the lab that she had overlooked. She hurried to it and opened the door. It was a mess—too messy to clean before the inspectors came.

So DeeDee thought horizontally. What did she do?

I'll give you a hint. She made a sign and put it on the storeroom door. Mum's the word. What did the sign say?

Yes! *Women*!

Now tell me, would that story give muscle to your message of "Be Creative"? If so, good! Now let's find some more stories and make some more muscle!

Inmates of Imagination

The publisher of JK Rowling's books puts no scenes from any *Harry Potter* movie on the cover of any *Harry Potter* novel.

Why not? Because in the words of that publisher, "The pictures of those scenes could deprive all of Ms. Rowling's young readers of a chance to imagine what the scenes looked like in their version of the story they were reading; thus, 'turning those young readers' into inmates of someone else's imagination!"

Such a sentiment reminds me of how much reading differs from movies or television. How do they differ? Think about it! Ishmael had one face for every reader of *Moby Dick* unless, of course, any of those readers *saw the movie*! In that case, Ishmael had only one face— the one that was in the movie!

The same goes for Scrooge, Tom Sawyer, Davey Crockett, Scarlet O'Hara, Jesus Christ, Ben-Hur, Moses, Luke Skywalker, Yoda, and more. Horizontal thinking strikes again!

Baxter

My cousin Jimmy has a dog named Baxter. Baxter is a very big German shepherd. He is also very smart. "Why just last night," Jimmy told me one afternoon, "it was cold in our bedroom. My wife and I were fine because we were tucked under our nice warm comforter in our nice warm bed, but Baxter was lying on the cold floor. He was not so warm and not so fine. "At about three o'clock in the morning, Baxter changed all that," Jimmy went on. "He went to the kitchen door and began to yip as if he needed to go out. I groaned, got up, and put on my sweat clothes," said Jimmy, "then I walked to the kitchen to let Baxter out. Just as I was about to open the door, Baxter turned, ran back to the bedroom, and jumped onto my nice warm spot on the bed! I chased him, then stopped, and laughed. I looked at Baxter in my bed. He was too comfortable [and too big!] to move, so I let him stay. Yes," Jimmy ended, "Baxter spent the night in my bed, nice and warm. I spent the night on the floor, not so nice and not so warm."

A problem was solved, thanks to horizontal thinking and to a dog named Baxter!

Carry the Scale!

My sister-in-law, Bonnie, is a gracious hostess, dedicated nurse, and wonderful mother.

Among her many talents, Bonnie is very good at horizontal thinking!

A few days before this year's Thanksgiving, her husband, John, brought home a good-sized turkey and asked Bonnie where she kept the bathroom scale.

"What do you need that for?" Bonnie asked.

"I need to weigh the turkey to determine how many hours it will have to stay in the oven on Thursday morning to be sure it is safe to eat," John explained. Bonnie said the scale was in the upstairs bathroom.

John said thanks, took the turkey from the kitchen refrigerator, and started carrying it up the stairs. "Where are you going with that?" Bonnie asked John.

"I am taking the turkey upstairs to weigh it on the bathroom scale!" replied John.

After a moment of thought and a few rolls of her eyes, Bonnie offered John this question, "Instead of carrying that *twenty-pound* turkey *up* the stairs, why don't you carry the *six-pound* scale *down* the stairs?"

Good question. Great horizontal thinking!

Wheaties

In 1921, a man from Minnesota was making some porridge for breakfast one morning. Alas, the man stirred the gruel too vigorously, and it splattered all over the hot stovetop! As the man scraped the splattered porridge from the hot stove, he noticed that it had cooked into crisp flakes.

Rather than waste all the porridge that had splattered, the man put the scrapings in a bowl, put milk over them, and began eating. To the man's surprise, the flakes tasted better than the porridge.

Do you know where this story is going? Right to the *Breakfast of Champions!* Yes, those flakes became a cereal, and that cereal became *Wheaties*!

Stadium Lighting

After many years of waiting, our high school celebrated the completion of a new athletic stadium. It has been the source of lots of enjoyment and lots of pride ever since.

Still, it has not come without its problems.

When the stadium's four very large light poles went up and went *on*, one of those problems "came to light!"

It seems that more than a few neighbors were upset by the lights. One, in particular, complained to the town that the light coming from the new poles was too bright and made sleeping difficult for his young children.

The repetition of such complaints kept us from using the lights (and the stadium) for months!

I was sharing that fact with an alum of our archrival high school one day. "I know what you mean," he said.

"We had the same problem when we put lights on our field! I found a solution, though."

"What did you do?" I asked.

"Well, I knew there was one neighbor who lived closest to the field who was going to complain for sure once the lights went on," revealed the alum, "so I purposely added two extra bulbs to the pole closest to his house. Then I pointed both bulbs at that neighbor's bedroom window. Five minutes after the lights went on for the first time," continued the rival alum, "the neighbor was on the field, complaining. The alum said, 'No problem!' and shut down the two bulbs that were shining into the bedroom [which had nothing to do with the lighting the field, anyway!].

"The neighbor was so happy to have less lighting shining into his bedroom, he never complained a bit about the sixty bulbs that were lighting up the rest of his house like a Christmas tree!"

"Everything in life," the man ended by quoting Albert Einstein, "is relative."

Lots of problems get solved using "behind the lines," "out of the box," and "horizontal thinking" solutions. Lots of muscle gets made for the message "Be Creative" too.

Join the club! Do the same!

Be creative!

Lots of Rocks?

A man attempted to cross the Canadian border on his motorcycle. He carried two saddlebags strapped across his seat. The border guards questioned him. "What is in your saddlebags?" the guards asked.

"Rocks," the man replied.

The guards emptied the bags to inspect them. Finding nothing but rocks, they sent the man on his way.

A few weeks later, the same scene occurred. A few weeks later, it happened again, and again, and again, and so on every two or three weeks for several months.

Finally, the guards could no longer stand it. "We know you are smuggling something across the border, but every time we check your saddlebags, there is nothing in them but rocks. It is driving us crazy. Tell us what you are up to, and we promise not to turn you in."

Write down what the man was up to.

Yes! He was smuggling stolen motorcycles!

More muscle and more stories, here we come!

Sticky Burrs

For centuries, hikers have had burrs in their socks. But it wasn't until 1948 that a Swiss mountaineer got an idea. While peeling burrs from his socks, he realized that nature had provided us with a natural fastener.

He turned that observation into a marvelous product with a million uses worth millions of dollars. Those man-made sticky burrs became known as? *Velcro!*

Rubber Waffles

One morning, Bill Bowerman was eating a waffle his wife had fixed him. As Bill stared at that waffle, he could not stop thinking about what a good running shoe it would make if it was made out of rubber.

It would cushion the foot, give good traction, be waterproof, wear well, and be light. Bill thought as he chewed on his waffle. Finally, he got up from the table, took his wife's waffle iron out to this garage, and poured some melted rubber into it!

That ruined the waffle iron, but his wife didn't mind. Bill's horizontal thinking earned him enough money to buy his wife all the new waffle irons she wanted! Bill's horizontal thinking also earned him enough money to start his own company. He called it Nike!

QWERTYUIOP

Are you familiar with this configuration? It is the top row of letters on a standard typewriter or computer keyboard. It is known as the "QWERTY configuration," and it has a fascinating history.

In the 1870s, Sholes & Co., then a leading manufacturer of typewriters, received many complaints from users about the typewriter keys sticking together. In response, management asked its engineers to figure out a way to prevent this from happening.

While the engineers discussed the problem, one bright young intern got an idea. "What if we *slow* the *typist* down?" he asked. "If we did that, the keys wouldn't jam together nearly as much."

Management supported the idea, and the result was an inefficient keyboard configuration! For example, the letters O and I are the third and sixth most frequently used letters in the English language.

Yet the engineers positioned them on the keyboard so that the relatively weaker ring and little fingers had to depress them.

This "inefficient logic" pervaded the keyboard, and this brilliant idea solved the problem of keyboard jam-up.

Since that solution, typewriter and computer technology have advanced significantly. There are now electronic keyboards that can operate much faster than any human operator can type. Still, the QWERTY configuration continues to be used!

Why?

Because if left to ourselves, most of us don't ask enough questions. We accept things too easily. If left to ourselves, we think too vertically!

Carving Roast Beef

When my sister, Natalie, read the QUERTY story, she said, "This reminds me of the woman who watched her mother making roast beef so she could do it the same way."

First, her mother cut two inches off the ends of the roast and put the meat into the pan. Then she added seasoning, put the roast in the oven, and cooked it for a certain amount of time per pound.

For years, the daughter made roast beef this way every Sunday. One day, her mother came over as the daughter was preparing the roast. Her mother asked the daughter, "Why are you cutting the ends off the meat?"

"Because that is what *you* always did!" replied the daughter.

Her mother laughed and said, "I did that because, back then, my roasting pan was too small! Your pan is big enough to fit the whole roast!"

More assumptions; more vertical thinking. Shame on that daughter!

Have you got some more stories in you? Good! Read these then think horizontally and answer the questions!

Open Your Mind!

1. The Red Sox and the Tigers play five baseball games. They each win three games. There were no ties or rain outs. How could this happen? (The two teams did not play each other.)
2. A cowboy rode into town on Thursday. He stayed three days in a row and rode out of town on Thursday. How could this be? (The cowboy's *horse* was named Thursday!)
3. A man is found dead. He has a small hole in his suit. The hole caused his death, but he was not shot or stabbed. He has no wounds. How did he die? (He was an astronaut and died from lack of oxygen!)
4. Make a mental picture of this murder scene. The room is quiet. Romeo and Juliet lie dead on the floor in their castle. There are broken glass and a pool of water next to the bodies. Sir Lancelot, the killer, stands over them smiling. This murder did not happen on a stage, on a screen, or in the Middle Ages. It happened last week, in your neighborhood. Explain. (Romeo and Juliet were goldfish, and Sir Lancelot was a cat.)

How did you do?

Did you have trouble with the first question? If so, was it because you *assumed* that the Red Sox and the tigers only played each other?

If you had trouble with number 2, did you *assume* Thursday was a day (and not the cowboy's horse's name?)

In number 3 if you had trouble, was it because you *assumed* the man was wearing a dress suit (and not a space suit or a diving suit?)

In number 4, did you *assume* Romeo, Juliet, and Sir Lancelot were people (instead of two goldfish and the cat that knocked over the fishbowl and killed them?)

If you got any of your questions wrong, congratulations! You are human, which means from time to time, you think *vertically*! From time to time, you *make assumptions*!

I hope these questions and answers put muscle in our message to be creative. I hope they help you think horizontally!

Tractor Pulls

The United States started many programs in the 1960s to help underdeveloped nations grow. The founders of these programs had good intentions but no idea how firmly people "lock their thoughts in the box" and how hard it is to get them to change!

One group of developers, for example, identified some cultures that were not producing well because their work habits were outmoded and their equipment was outdated. Then the developers tried to help by introducing western technology and modern materials to these underproducing cultures.

After trying to update the areas of greatest need, the developers returned home. Some years later, they revisited the countries they had served and measured the impact of their efforts. They went to see, for example, if the tractors they had left behind with some under-performing farmers had increased the production of those farmers.

Alas, they found just the opposite. Instead of speeding farm production up, the tractors had slowed things down!

Why? Because the farmers who were given the tractors years before had attached their plows to the back of the tractors then hitched their oxen to the front of the tractors and plowed their fields (very slowly!) by having the oxen pull *both their tractors and their plows!*

Don't be like those farmers! Find solutions to problems by looking (and thinking!) "outside the box!" and "behind enemy lines!"

Von Ryan's Express

In that movie, Frank Sinatra played an American Air Force officer in World War II who led the war's largest escape from a Nazi prison camp. After their escape, Frank and his men stole a German train and were driving it to Switzerland.

As they approached the Swiss border, two German planes attacked. Their rockets missed the train but hit a ledge and dumped tons of boulders onto the track in front of Frank's train.

Frank's men cleared the boulders but found that the track had been destroyed by the falling rock. With lots of broken track in front of him and lots of unbroken track behind him, what did Frank do?

Right—he looked *everywhere* for a good idea and found one *behind* him! His men removed some good track from *behind* the train, used it to replace the damaged track in *front* of the train, and off they went to Switzerland!

Lots of other movies, plays, or stories made their money and built their box offices around a "surprise ending."

Which movies am I talking about?

Try these: *Charade, Spartacus, The Trojan Horse, Murder on the Orient Express, Citizen Kane, Sheer Madness, Psycho, The Usual Suspects*, and more!

Sometimes, show those movies to your followers, friends, or family. See if they can find or guess the ending! Doing so will make muscle for your message to "be creative!"

Flood Control

When floods threaten the United States and Europe, officials usually have the threatened areas lined with sandbags. These bags effectively stop floodwaters from leaving the desired course.

Once, there was a flood in Japan. It was so bad that Japanese officials were unable to get enough sand to fill their bags.

What did the officials do? Yes! They looked at the problem from outside the box and came up with a different filler that worked just as well, was much more abundant, and much cheaper than sand.

Instead of sandbags and *except* for rice, what did the Japanese use to stop the water?

Yes! They thought outside the box and filled the bags with *water*!

Now you are getting the idea!

Good Thinking

At lunch duty years ago, I was talking to a science teacher named Michael about his dad who had been in the hospital.

"He's in his mideighties," Michael explained, "and has lots of challenges. The biggest ones are high blood pressure and congestive heart failure. He is on a very strict diet that eliminates salt and saturated fat. Dad hates his diet," continues Michael, "and constantly complains about not being able to eat the foods he likes."

"What does he miss the most?" I asked Michael.

"Bacon!" Michael replied immediately. "It is the worst possible thing he can eat, but he *loves* it."

"One day," Michael went on, "Dad wouldn't stop talking about how much he missed his bacon. Finally, I caved and went to the hospital cafeteria to get him a piece. I figured, how much could it hurt him, right?"

When Michael gave the bacon to his dad, Dad thanked Mike, then opened the drawer to the little nightstand beside his bed. Then Dad took out a small brown paper bag that was in the drawer, opened it, and deposited his bacon in the bag.

"What are you doing?" Mike asked his father.

"Adding your bacon to my collection for later!" Dad confessed.

"Wait a minute," said Mike as he took the bag from his Dad.

An inspection by Mike revealed that there were *seven more pieces of bacon* in Dad's bag!

"Where did you get all this?" Michael asked.

His dad smiled and said, "You're not the only visitor I get, you know. Sooner or later, I squeeze a little bacon out of them all!"

Mike's dad got his bacon, and he made muscle for the message "Be Creative!"

Have you had enough creativity?

I hope not because I have more stories that will make more muscle!

Pick a Path

An architect built a cluster of office buildings that were set in a large open plot of onetime pasture land. When construction was completed, the landscaping crew asked the architect where he wanted the brick walkways connecting the buildings to be located.

"Don't set them in place yet" was the architect's reply. "Just plant grass throughout the pasture among the buildings."

This was done, and by late summer, the new lawn had grown in. It was lush and full, except for some pathways of trodden grass that had been created by people walking from one building to another all summer, using the same, convenient routes.

The architect called the landscaping crew together, pointed to the paths, and said, "Now you can install the walkways where the paths are!"

Smart architect! He let creativity design the pathways for him!

Hoodsies

Years ago, I attended the funeral for the brother of a friend. I had never met the man who died but came to know him very well, thanks to the wonderful service and send-off his close-knit family gave him. His nephew offered the eulogy. It was well done. One story stuck out. In fact, that story *jumped* out.

"My uncle Art fed his sick mother her dinner for a decade," the young nephew began. "That wasn't easy," he continued. "She lived in a nursing home and wasn't very happy about that or about anything else! No one could get her to eat but my uncle," the nephew explained. "He had a secret. Every night, he brought a Hoodsie with him to the nursing home. He would give his mom a spoonful of the Hoodsie at the beginning of her dinner, and she would smile. Then he would give a spoonful of dinner to his mother. She would eat it, thinking it was more Hoodsie, then frown when she found out it wasn't! When he saw his mother frown, my uncle would say 'Oh, Mom, I'm so sorry! I dipped the spoon in the wrong dish. Let's try again!' The next spoonful was from the Hoodsie again, and his mother would smile," the young speaker went on, "and the next was from the dinner, and she would frown. When she frowned, my uncle would apologize to her as before then give her more Hoodsie!

"He alternated some dinner and some Hoodsie until his mother finished them both, every night, for ten years."

Great story. Great son. *Great thinking!*

College Counseling

I faced another problem when I graduated from high school. That problem was where to attend college.

I agonized over several good schools then asked my father for his advice. He had an immediate (and creative!) solution!

"Carmen," he said with very little hesitation, "once a year, there is a second collection after communion at St. John's Church for some school that is called the Catholic University of America. I don't know anything about it," continued my dad, "except that it is Catholic, and it gets money out of me every year. Carmen," Dad went on after a pause, "I have been putting a buck into the basket for that place every year since before you were born. I think we should benefit from all that 'investing' and send you to that school!"

"I think only priests go there," I replied to Dad, not having a clue what I was talking about.

"If so, become a priest!" Dad replied. "And if not, go there anyway. Because they owe us something, thanks to all the money I put in their basket over all these years!"

No, I did *not* become a priest, but yes, I *did* go to the Catholic University of America, thanks to my father and our problem that was solved by his "out of the box" solution!

Dumb Whats?

My father taught me something every time we were together. Once, I went to visit him because he wanted me to empty his rain barrels. Dad had eight of them—fifty-five gallons each. He hooked them up to the downspouts of his house and garage. When it rained, they got filled! Those barrels saved Dad from having to pay for the water he used in the garden. His plan was really pretty neat!

But before winter, the barrels had to be emptied, or they would freeze and split. Dad did it every year, but this year, he just couldn't handle it, so I took over.

"I'll be right there," he said from his kitchen window when I pulled up. "Go out back and get started." I walked to the garden and reached to open its gate but saw a padlock hanging from it. I stopped and went upstairs to tell Dad.

"I can't open the gate," I said.

"Why not?" Dad asked.

"There is a lock on it," I explained.

"No problem," Dad said. "The lock is hanging there, but it's not locked."

"Why not?" I asked.

"Because my arthritis has been acting up, and if I close the lock, I can't use the key to open it."

I paused, got up my nerve, and asked Dad, "What good does it do to have a lock on the garden gate if the lock isn't even locked?"

Dad smiled, winked, and said, "It keeps dumb sh—ts like you out of my garden!"

Yes, Dad looked for a chance to teach me a lesson, and he found it!

Things are not always what they seem. Sometimes you have to look outside the lines or beyond the box to realize that!

Oak Street

One night, an ambulance dispatcher got a 911 call from a man living near a hospital.

"I need help," began the man. "My wife just fell. I think she is unconscious. I am very worried! Please send an ambulance right away!"

"Yes, sir!" replied the dispatcher, "What is your address?"

"It is 125 Eucalyptus Drive," replied the man.

"Could you spell that?" asked the dispatcher.

The man paused for a moment in silence, then replied, "I am not sure, Officer. Let me drag her over to *Oak Street*! You can pick her up there!"

Creativity strikes again! Muscle is made again!

Like Father, Like Son

One day, I drove my father to the hospital for an MRI. When we arrived, I got Dad settled in the MRI waiting room and asked how long he would be. The nurse said about an hour, so I wished Dad luck and left him in the waiting room.

(I had a touch of the flu and just wanted to visit my own doctor, whose office was also in that hospital.)

I was back in forty minutes, and Dad's chair was empty, so I sat next to it and waited.

Now waiting at the hospital is easy for me because I come prepared. I always bring a bag of books! So did my dad. Yes, we both liked to read—almost anything! But at the doctor's office, we always think horizontally and only read books—*our books!*

Why not magazines or newspapers? It all goes back to the first time we sat in a doctor's waiting room together. On that day, my dad watched as I picked up a magazine and began to flip through it. As he watched, he shook his head and smiled.

"What is it?" I asked.

"The first time I saw anyone read a magazine in a doctor's office," Dad answered, "he was sitting next to me with a runny nose and no handkerchief. He kept wiping his nose with his hand then using that same hand to turn the pages of the magazine. When I asked that man why he was seeing the doc," ended Dad, "he said he had the flu and diarrhea!"

Again, my dad thought horizontally and said, "It doesn't take a genius to know enough not to handle any of what these doctors leave their patients to read in their waiting rooms!"

Because of what my dad saw and thought that day, we both think horizontally and *only* read our *own books!*

So on this day, as on all days, I opened my bag and started to read. The time flew. When I looked up, it was two hours later.

I was surprised. I was nervous too. Dad's MRI was taking a long time! So I found a nurse and asked her if he was okay.

"Oh yes!" she said. "Luigi was only here for twenty minutes! He left a long time ago!"

Yes, I had been waiting for my dad for two hours outside of a room he had supposedly been in for twenty minutes. Where did he go when he finished?

I didn't know!

I checked the cafeteria and a few men's rooms, then for lack of a better option, I returned to my doctor's office. Dad was there, waiting for me!

I was sure he would be mad, but he wasn't.

"Mad? Why should I be mad?" Dad retorted. "I had my books with me!"

Yes, while Dad was upstairs reading in *my* doctor's office, I was downstairs reading in *his* doctor's office. Like father, like son!

Two Things

Shortly after my mother died, I asked my dad if he would like to come and live with DeeDee and me.

He said, "No, I am fine living alone. I can take care of myself. Besides," he continued, "your mother died in this house, and I will too."

"Okay," I replied. "You know best. But what can I do to make it easier for you?"

"Just two things," Dad replied.

"What are they?" I pursued.

"First, come to visit me when you can," he said.

"Of course," I promised. "What else?"

"Come because you *want* to, not because you *have* to."

My father had a high school education and was a genius.

He knew that having my *body* visit him meant nothing.

Having my *heart* visit him meant everything.

He thought out of the box and made his two requests. Thanks to those requests, I never visited my dad without bringing my heart.

Magic Drawer

When I was growing up, I had a drawer in my bureau that really was magical. I opened it every day and took clean underwear from it. I did that for a week—sometimes for longer. Each day, there was less underwear in the drawer than there had been the day before.

Until one day (always before the drawer was completely empty), it was full again with more clean underwear. It really was magical!

I never did a thing to make that magic happen. I just went to that drawer every day and took underwear from it. I did not clean, wash, pay, or even pray. I just took! Someone else *cleaned*. Someone else *washed*. Someone else *folded*. Someone else *gave*. That "someone else" was, of course, my mother. As I said, she gave and gave and gave.

Since I have been married, that "someone else" has been DeeDee.

She cleans, washes, and folds. She gives, and gives, and gives—just like my mother did.

I regret to admit that I never thanked my mother for that drawer. So I did want to thank DeeDee. One day, I got a "thank-you" card and put it in the magic drawer.

Dee said she liked the card. She told me how thoughtful it was. She told me how far "out of the box" it was too. If you have a magic underwear drawer like I do, leave a "thank-you" card in it someday.

If you do, someone will like how thoughtful you are. They will like how far "out of the box" you are too! Don't take that from me. Take it from DeeDee!

It's the Thought

Speaking of being "thoughtful" and "out of the box," some of the things my mother gave and gave were greeting cards. She kept piles of them in the house for every occasion.

If anyone ever asked her what all the cards were for, my mother would say they were for "a reason."

If anyone asked her "What reason?" Ma would reply, "Once you *have the card*, you will *find the reason*!"

One day, my mother *found* a reason but *had* no card, and that was a problem! You see, it was my birthday, and Ma was out of birthday cards! Undaunted, she found a card in her pile that said, "Happy graduation to my nephew!"

She then took a magic marker and scratched out the words "nephew" and "graduation." Next, she replaced those words with "birthday" and "son!"

"It's the thought that counts!' Ma then told me as I opened the envelop she gave me and reviewed her revisions.

My birthday was spared by my mother's thoughts *and* her creativity!

So what has been our most recent message?

Yes! It has been "Be Creative!"

And where do we hope to get that message's muscle?

Yes, again! From stories like the ones, we have just finished reading!

What message in need of muscle is next?

Welcome Failure!

Strange advice, right? It should read "*Avoid* failure" or "*Overcome* failure" or "*Learn* from failure," right?

Wrong. It *should* read what it *does* read!

It should read *welcome failure*!

Americans are proud of their rights and have paid dearly for them. Two of our most valuable rights are the right to be wrong and the right to fail.

Neither of those rights is embraced as much as it should be. Some of the most successful people in the world know that and show that.

One of my favorite expressions is "The biggest room in the world is the room for improvement!" Every house I know has one of those big rooms, and every family I know has the right to be wrong and to welcome failure.

"Examples?" you ask. Examples, here we come!

Walt Disney was fired by one newspaper editor for "having too little creativity!" The Beatles were turned away by a record executive who told them that "guitar groups were on their way out."

Someone once challenged Thomas Edison by reminding him that he had failed 25,000 times while experimenting with the storage battery. "No," rebutted Edison, "I didn't fail. I just found 24,999 ways *not* to make a storage battery!"

Be like Edison. Welcome failure. Make it your teacher, not your undertaker.

The Edsel

Henry Ford forgot to put a reverse gear in the first car he ever built!

Soon after building that car, Mr. Ford set out to build something better. Instead, he did the opposite! He built the Edsel!

Then Henry bragged about that car! He even called it "The Car of the Decade!" Henry's creation was renowned for doors that would not close, a hood that would not open, paint that would not stop peeling, a horn that would not stop beeping!

The problems started when the new Edsels were not even unwrapped!

The Edsel was meant to be Mr. Ford's crowning jewel. Instead, it became his most famous failure. Still, Henry Ford did learn from his mistakes and replaced the Edsel with the Mustang!

The "Pony" hit the streets in 1964 and has been in continuous production since then, making the Mustang the sixth-best selling Ford model in the corporation's history!

Take it from the Mustang, if failure finds you, do not fear it. *Welcome failure* just like Henry Ford and the Mustang did!

Robert Fulton

In 1802, Robert Fulton contracted to build a steamboat that would navigate the Hudson River. Five years later, Fulton's boat was barely ready for a trial run from New York City to Albany and back.

On an afternoon just before that run, trouble reared its ugly head. The *Clermont's* engine died shortly after leaving the dock. "It will never start! It will never start!" predicted several panicky passengers.

Seemingly to disprove such fears, Fulton's vessel belched flame and smoke as it powered two paddle wheels placed on either side of the hull. Then the *Clermont* began to move!

In response to such progress, other passengers warned, "It will never stop! It will never stop!"

In the words of Fulton's diary, "There was anxiety, mixed with audible fear, and even more *audible silence* among the passengers!

Then came murmurs of discontent, agitation, whispers, and shrugs. I could distinctly hear words like 'I told you this was a foolish scheme, and I wish we were not part of it,'" continued Fulton's diary. Those words were repeated by many voices speaking at increasing volumes!

If failure finds you, do not fear it. *Announce failure. Admit failure. Welcome failure* just like Robert Fulton and the Clermont did!

Failure's Disguise

When Winston Churchill was defeated as prime minister after leading Great Britain to victory in World War II, his wife tried to comfort Winnie by telling him that his defeat at the polls was "a blessing in disguise."

"If it is," replied Churchill, "then it is very effectively disguised!" Be like Mr. Churchill. Find success effectively disguised as failure!

West Pointers

Robert E. Lee didn't make it into West Point the first time he tried.

Jefferson Davis took his vacancy.

Pershing didn't make it in on his first two tries.

MacArthur couldn't get in the first time he tried, and Eisenhower had to spend an extra year in high school before he was accepted.

Patton took *three years* to get *in* and *five* years to get *out*!

All these heroes and patriots also found success effectively disguised as failure. So can you! When you do, welcome failure and give our "Welcome Failure" message some more muscle!

The Wright Brothers

Orville and Wilbur Wright have been credited with building and flying the first controlled motor-operated airplane. Admittedly, their first official "flight" was not exactly a success.

It lasted a mere twelve seconds with Orville positioned to pilot their craft (called the *Flyer*) on the morning of December 1903.

As Orville released the restraining wire, the aircraft began to move while Wilbur ran alongside and steadied the wings.

As momentum developed, the Flyer was unruly, pitching up and down as Orville overcompensated with the controls. He kept the plane aloft until it hit the sand about 120 feet down the runway.

The brothers took turns flying three more times that day, increasing their distance with each flight. Wilbur's second flight—the fourth of the day—covered 284 feet, or almost (and only) the length of one football field!

The good news was that *The Flyer* had flown. The bad news was, it would not fly again!

After that last flight, the craft was caught by a gust of wind, rolled over, and was damaged basically beyond repair. In fact, for future flights, the brothers decided to stockpile spare parts and tools on the runway to save steps back and forth to their hanger between crashes!

That left Wilbur and Orville to find success "effectively disguised" as failure and to *welcome* that failure!

It is true. People are not perfect. They make mistakes, missteps, messes, mischief, and more! They fail much more than they succeed. Still, the most valuable experience in life is not success—it is failure! So on your way to success, *expect mistakes* and *welcome failure*!

I hope the stories I just told will help you succeed by *welcoming failure*! I also hope the stories that *follow* will remind you that people not only fail, they *also make mistakes*!

Thanks, Honey!

Vince Lombardi was the legendary football coach of the Green Bay Packers. Occasionally, even he was wrong!

Occasionally, even he made mistakes.

"My father was constantly engrossed in some problem relating to his football team," remembered Mr. Lombardi's son. "One morning on Long Island," Vince's son recalls, "my mother drove my father to the train. A neighbor hitched a ride to the train with them. My father sat there, for the entire ride, lost in thought about football.

When they all got to the station, my father leaned over, said 'Thanks, honey,' kissed the neighbor on the cheek, and walked over to the platform!"

One night after practice, Vince drove himself home to the wrong apartment!

Then still consumed by thoughts of football, he walked through the apartment's front door and sat down at the kitchen table to eat while the woman who lived in the apartment began serving Vince his dinner!

When Vince finally looked up and saw that he didn't recognize the woman, he yelled, "Who are you?" and left the apartment!

Yes, even Vince Lombardi made mistakes. Everybody makes mistakes!

You will make mistakes. Expect your mistakes and *welcome your failures too*!

If you do, you will give muscle to both of those messages for your friends, family, and followers.

Another Mistake!

I fell in love with DeeDee when I was in my twenties. I asked her to marry me shortly after falling in love. She said yes, so I went to her father to ask for his blessing. Dee didn't think asking her dad was a good idea. I disagreed. "Why would he say no?" I asked, half kidding. "I have a job and am not in jail!"

"Don't get cocky," Dee warned me. I should have listened to her!

Some weeks after Dee and I talked about my "popping the question," I visited DeeDee's dad to tell him how I felt.

As Dee predicted, it did not go well!

I arrived at lunchtime on a Saturday, so Mr. F was eating a tuna fish sandwich and watching *Candlepins for Cash* when I arrived.

"Mr. Fagerlund," I began without overture, "I love your daughter" (I was so nervous I couldn't remember her name!) "and I want to marry her."

DeeDee's dad was bringing a wedge of his sandwich to his mouth when I made my announcement, and his arm seemed to freeze in midmotion. I waited for the arm to come alive and complete the "hand-to-mouth" gesture, but it never did!

It was as if his whole body became a tuna-fish-eating statue while it processed my news!

I waited on my chair in front of his television, hoping the sandwich would continue its journey in one direction or the other.

It never did. Instead, eventually (and unfortunately!), he spoke.

"Carmen, I don't think it would work for you and DeeDee," he said without ever taking his eyes off the bowling show or letting go of his sandwich. "You have very different backgrounds and come from very different...families."

I had not prepared a reply to a reaction like that, so I just sat and waited for him to rise from his chair. He did more than that. He left the chair (with remnants of his sandwich still in hand!), took the stairs to the kitchen, walked out the back door, and left the house.

To this day, I don't know where he went. Wherever it was, however, it must have been equipped with a bed and toilet because Mr. F did not return home for three days!

His reaction made me question my feelings for DeeDee, but I kept enough faith in them to marry her. It was not a perfect wedding, but it has become a close-to-perfect marriage. DeeDee locked herself in the bathroom during the rehearsal dinner among other difficult moments, but over time, our lives became one and our love became ours.

Many years later, on my father-in-law's eighty-fifth birthday, he and I were alone in his living room having a beer together. During a lull in our conversation, out of nowhere, he said, "Carmen, forty years ago, what I said to you was a mistake!"

Funny. I knew exactly what he meant.

Thank God for my faith and my feelings. Most of all, thank God for DeeDee. And yes, even fathers-in-law make mistakes. Everybody makes mistakes! So expect mistakes *and* welcome failure!

Did those stories give muscle to my message of "Welcome Failure"? If so, great and keep reading!

Our Mailman

While my dad was working at the shipyard in Quincy, one of my mother's brothers (Uncle Johnny) was our mailman.

Our house was on his route and close to the post office, so my uncle always made it the last stop of his day.

He got there by noon every day, gave my mother (his sister) our mail, then had lunch with Ma, and took a nap on the couch in our living room. Ma woke him just before quitting time (4:00 p.m.) so he could walk back to the post office and punch out!

This went on for months until one day when my father was pulling into our driveway on his way home from work. As he did, a woman who lived next door ran to his car and motioned for him to stop and roll down his window. When Dad did, the woman said, "Mr. Mariano, I just can't hold it in any longer. You need to know. For quite a while, your *wife has been having an affair with your mailman!*"

Dad kept from laughing and said, "It's okay. At least we always get our mail on time!"

Our neighbor (and our mailman!) made a mistake. Everybody makes mistakes.

In the words of an African proverb, "If mistakes were haystacks, there would be more fat ponies!" Everybody makes mistakes.

So expect mistakes *and welcome failure*!

A Small Parade

My cousin Frankie spent the night with me lots of times while we were growing up. We lived close to each other, so it was easy for us to get together.

On one really hot summer night, we sat together at the kitchen table playing cards with my father before heading to bed.

As the sweat poured off us all, I asked Dad if I could turn on the ceiling fan that hovered above the table.

"No!" Dad replied sternly. "It is broken. Don't touch that fan!"

Not long after giving me that directive, my dad rose from the table to use the bathroom. He looked at Frankie and me as he got up and decided he didn't like the little smiles both of us had on our faces, so he repeated his order.

"Don't either of you touch that fan while I am gone!" he said again. "It is not working, and you will make it worse if you try to use it."

The minute Dad closed the bathroom door, however, you know what happened. Yes, Frankie and I stood on our chairs beneath the fan and went to work!

I pulled the chain first, then Frankie did, but nothing happened.

Six more pulls got us nowhere, so we decided that Dad was right and the fan really didn't work. We then stepped down from our chairs and stood at the table to await Dad's return from the bathroom.

As we waited, the fan blade suddenly began to move, slowly at first, then faster and faster (and faster!) until it looked and sounded like an airplane propeller.

The blade was moving so fast, the kitchen ceiling started to vibrate, and the pole connecting the fan to the ceiling started to swing in a very large circle.

With all that came more noise—lots more noise!

"I think it's going to fly right off the ceiling!" yelled Frankie. "Those last few pulls must have sent it over the edge!"

"You are right!" I yelled back while hoping against hope that my father (who was still in the bathroom) couldn't hear or feel what was happening.

Seconds later, my hopes were dashed. Dad interrupted his bathroom business, threw open the door, and barged into the kitchen.

He had one hand holding up his unbuttoned pants, and the other holding up one of the kitchen walls that was by now beginning to lose plaster.

I was still standing by my chair, looking at the fan and at my father (both of which were out of control) at the same time. Frankie stood near me with his eyes screwed shut and his hands pressed hard against both ears.

My dad froze as he took in the scene. Then he shook his head, rolled his eyes, and said, "You two jerks would screw up a one-car parade!"

Everybody makes mistakes. Just ask Frankie and me. Just ask my father.

Frankie Continued

My cousin Frankie was the best man at my wedding and one of my closest friends. Frank's dad (my uncle Ed Faherty) was notably Irish, and his mom was my mother's sister, my aunt Millie. Frankie was also the source of many funny stories, including that big one we shared about Dad's kitchen fan!

Another laugh came when Frankie and I were in our midteens. We were then, of course, too young to drink…legally…but over time, Frankie was able to build a network of friends who worked in package stores in his neighborhood, and from time to time, he would visit one or more of those friends when they were working alone. In such a private environment, Frank purchased many a six-pack inside the store and outside the law!

My uncle Ed, of course, had no clue about Frankie's enterprise until one day when he needed ice from the same "packie" in which Frank just happened to be buying beer!

Frank entered on foot just before Uncle Ed pulled up to the small store. He winked to his friend, who was standing behind the counter, walked to the beer chest, slid a six-pack from the chest, and put it on the counter.

As Frank paid for his beer, he heard the bell hanging from the store's front door begin to tinkle, so he looked back. To Frank's dismay, he saw his father enter the store! As Uncle Ed turned right for the ice, Frank turned around for the door. As soon as he reached freedom, he ran like hell!

Uncle Ed still had no clue of what was happening, so he put his ice on the counter next to Frank's beer and reached for his money.

Then Frank's friend behind the counter, having never seen Uncle Ed before, looked at Frank's six-pack still sitting on the counter, stared up at Uncle Ed, and said, "Hey, go get Faherty! He forgot to take his beer!"

Still confused, Uncle Ed replied, "I *am* Faherty, and I came in here for ice, not beer!"

Then it all came together quickly for Uncle Ed. A chase ensued, and I didn't see Frank for a long time. Neither did his friend who worked in the package store!

The next time we met, Frank and I talked about that day and his beer, then we laughed…and laughed. Yes, everybody makes mistakes!

A Bank's Mistake

Fast-forwarding to the present, Frank was visiting DeeDee and me one night when his cell phone rang. Frank rolled his eyes as he recognized the phone number being displayed on the screen of the cell.

Then he cupped his hands on the phone and whispered to us, "It's a jerk who keeps calling me from the bank trying to float me a loan."

"Give him a chance!" I encouraged my cousin.

Frank pursued the banker to humor me.

"Okay, what kind of a loan are you selling?"

The man replied, and Frank rolled his eyes again, then put the phone on speaker, and told the banker to repeat his offer.

"Mr. Faherty" came the amplified voice, "Have I got a deal for you! I am prepared to offer you one more chance to pay off your *college student loans!*"

Frank paused, then replied like this, "I am seventy years old and graduated from college forty years ago! In fact, the school that gave me my degree has long since closed! Somehow, I don't think I have any loans left over! If I do, shoot me!"

Even banks make mistakes!

Big Parade

Uncle Johnny (our mailman, remember?) survived his "affair" with my mother. In fact, he got promoted! Yes, shortly after Ma's neighbor "squealed" on him, Uncle John became the superintendent of the Milton, Massachusetts, post office!

Not long after that, Tadone Raffaele's brother (my great-uncle Al) died. He had lived for years on Long Island, New York, with his wife and ten sons!

A contingent was sent from Quincy to the funeral with Tadone. It included my father, a few of my uncles, and me. One of the uncles was Johnny. He volunteered to drive because he had the biggest car and because that was the only way he was allowed to smoke his awful cigars on the ride!

It was a long way from Quincy to the funeral parlor and a long way from the funeral parlor to the cemetery! As we drove behind the casket and limos, Uncle Johnny made an announcement, "I have to take a pee."

"Hold it in" came Uncle Leo's predictable reply.

"I can't!" came Uncle John's equally predictable rebuttal.

They argued for a while at sixty miles an hour, and in the meantime, I noticed that Uncle Johnny's car was on a different road than it had been.

We had left the Long Island Expressway and were now on a small residential street. We had even lost track of the casket, flower cars, and limos! While I searched out the window for the funeral, Uncle Johnny searched for a gas station and its men's room!

Many blocks later, Johnny found what he was looking for. He parked in the station and ran from his car.

When he returned, he was relieved but not alone. Dozens of cars that thought Uncle Johnny was still part of Uncle Al's funeral procession had followed him from the highway to the men's room and were now lined up in the gas station's parking lot!

"Why did you leave the highway?" some asked.

"Where is the cemetery?" others inquired.

"What happened to the procession? Where is the priest?" still others wanted to know.

Uncle Johnny offered no answers and simply watched as the remainder of the funeral procession spun around in the gas station's lot and headed back toward the expressway.

By the time we got to Uncle Al's gravesite, he and his casket were underground, and his family was shaking their heads and calling us names. What a mistake!

Yes, everybody makes mistakes!

One day on a lark *the real* Charlie Chaplin entered a Charlie Chaplin look-alike contest. He came in third! Why?

Because the judges made a mistake!

Even judges make mistakes. Everybody makes mistakes.

Albert's Words

Albert Einstein once said, "I think and think for months and months, and still, ninety-nine out of every one hundred decisions I make are wrong!"

It's true. Even Albert Einstein made mistakes. Everybody makes mistakes.

A student stopped by my high school's office to turn in a lost sweater one day. My secretary gave it to one of our deans so he could look inside for some identification.

Moments later, the dean's concerned voice could be heard over the school's intercom, "Pardon the interruption," he said, "but would *Ralph Lauren* please come to the office? We found your sweater!"

It's true. Even deans make mistakes.

Even I make mistakes!

Everybody makes mistakes!

Their Names Have Been Changed!

Over many years as an educator, I have met some good friends who played important leadership roles within any number of school systems. One of those friends was (and is) a school committee member named Dave. I still see him once in a while and love to share memories and laughs with him.

One night while at a long late negotiating session with one of our unions, Dave and I waited in private for an answer to a proposal we had made. To kill time, Dave told me a story.

"It happened in grammar school," Dave recalled. "I went to parochial school back then and had a nun in the third grade. Her name was Sister Mary Catherine. Boy, she was tough," Dave went on. "On the first day of school, she went around the room and asked for our names. Then she wrote them into her seating chart. On the second day, Sister began to use that chart but not too well! She called on me three times that day, and every time, she called me Daniel. I corrected her respectfully every time. Still, she kept calling me Daniel!

On the third day, it happened again. She called me Daniel again and asked me to read the next problem out loud to the class.

"I replied with a courteous 'Yes, Sister, but my name is David.' As I spoke, Sister Mary Catherine walked toward me. Just as I finished saying my name, she reared back and whacked the palm of her hand with a ruler. No damage was done to Sister or me, but the sudden noise made me fall off my chair! As I collected myself, I could hear Sister say, 'Wrong answer. Your name is Daniel!'

"That night at supper, my father asked me how school went that day.

"'Okay,' I said, 'I got a new name!'

"'What do you mean?' asked Dad.

"'Sister Mary Catherine changed my name to Daniel today,' young Dave explained.

"'I know how you feel,' replied Dave's father whose name was Henry. "When I had that nun, she changed *my* name to Alfred!'"

Even nuns make mistakes. Everybody makes mistakes!

Color Television?

When "color television" was invented, my family was very excited. We watched a lot of TV and were hoping that seeing it in color would make it even more enjoyable than it was in black and white!

The first "colorized" show we planned to watch was the *Perry Como Show*. My mother had a crush on Perry, and the thought of seeing him in color made Ma "as giddy as a schoolgirl!"

True confessions, we should have caught on when we entered the living room and sat down in front of the same black-and-white television set we had owned and watched for years!

Still, we were caught up in the excitement of the moment enough to "color our judgment!"

As a black-and-white peacock appeared on the screen, we should have become suspicious. Instead, we held our breath for what we imagined would follow.

"We are going to see Perry in color right now!" my mother squealed.

The rest of us wiggled and clapped. Even my father watched from the edge of his recliner!

Then came Perry. He offered a welcome and started to sing. He wore a suit, dress shirt, and tie.

"Look!" Ma said, "His suit is dark navy, and his tie is gray!"

"His shirt is white, and his hair is gray as well!" noticed my sister.

"This is great! This is great!" I cheered.

Then light dawned on Italian marble heads!

"Wait a minute!" Natalie cautioned loudly. "This is our old regular black-and-white TV! How can its picture be in color?"

"It can't!" replied Dad also coming to his senses!

Thank God, the four of us were home alone! The whole thing could have been pretty embarrassing. Instead, it was pretty funny! Once again, my family made me laugh, and everybody makes mistakes!

How Many?

Many years ago, while I was the assistant superintendent of the Quincy Public Schools, I visited a first-grade class in one of our elementary schools.

As I entered the classroom, the teacher brought her little students to attention. "Class, come quietly to the front of the room, so we can give Dr. Mariano his surprise!"

Immediately, the class sprang into action.

They hurried up front, turned toward me, and formed their choir-like rows, one in front of the other.

On the teacher's cue and key, they broke into song.

Their song was long and contained just fifty words.

Those words were the names of the states.

Yes, these little geography students had learned the names of the states by singing them over and over to a catchy little melody.

When they finished, I applauded and applauded and applauded.

Then I spoke, "That was fantastic! It was outstanding! Why you knew the names of every state! You have learned them all."

Caught in the wave of my excitement, a little boy in the choir's back row jumped up and squealed, "That's right! We did! We learned *all 114 of them*!"

Even first graders make mistakes.

Everybody makes mistakes.

Tight Dress

When a bus arrived at its stop, a young woman at the head of the line tried to climb aboard but couldn't because of her tightly fitting dress. Thinking quickly, she reached back and undid her zipper a little to allow more movement. Still, her dress was too snug, so she lowered her zipper again.

Unable to climb aboard, she adjusted her dress' zipper a third time, but again, it wasn't enough to allow her to step up. Tired of waiting, the man behind her gently grabbed the woman around the waist and hoisted her onto the bus.

"Who do you think you are to touch me in that way?" asked the woman angrily.

"I'm sorry, lady," the man replied, "but after you *unzipped my fly* for the *third time*, I figured we must be pretty good friends!"

Everybody makes mistakes!

Everybody Still Makes Mistakes!

Two hunters hired a pilot to fly them into the far north for elk hunting.

They were quite successful in their venture and bagged six big bucks.

The pilot came back, as arranged, to pick them up.

They started loading their gear into the plane, including the six elk.

But the pilot objected and said, "The plane can only take four of your elk. You will have to leave two behind."

The passengers argued with him, claiming that the year before, they had shot six and the pilot had allowed them to put all aboard.

The plane was the same model and capacity as last year's, so reluctantly, the pilot finally permitted them to put all six aboard.

But when they attempted to take off and leave the valley, the little plane could not make the climb, and they crashed into the wilderness.

Climbing out of the wreckage, one hunter said to the other, "Do you know where we are?"

"I think so," replied the other hunter. "I think this is about the same place *where we crash-landed last year!*"

Too Many Engines!

Two hours into a flight, the pilot gets on the intercom and says, "Ladies and gentlemen, I am sorry to report that we just lost an engine." Then he continues, "It's all right, though. We have three more engines that are working, so we should make it home, but the trip will take an hour longer to complete with one less engine."

An hour of flying time later, the pilot reports as follows, "We just lost another engine, but have no fear, we still have two more good engines and will be fine, but it will take us another three extra hours to complete our flight."

After hearing that report, a nervous couple in the back of the plane looked at each other, rolled their eyes, and grumbled, "That is just great. At this rate, we'll be up here all day!"

Remember that couple and expect mistakes. Most of all, remember to *welcome failure* and tell stories that give that message more muscle!

Not Perfect

Sometimes, instead of making mistakes, people make trouble. They disagree. They argue. They quarrel. They even fight!

In fact, I know some people who have argued with each other for years, and I can't even remember why—and neither can they!

I know you will not believe it, but what is left of *my* wonderful family still argues! Some of the stories that follow tell the truth about those arguments. Other stories are a little less than true but still fun!

I hope you enjoy them all!

Divorced Mother

When it came to her children, my mother was sure of two things. She was sure that, as we became teenagers and beyond, my sister Natalie and I both ate too little and that we both worked too much!

Sometimes, my mother just accepted those facts. Other times, she fought back, and we argued! A Saturday morning some years ago was one of those "arguing" times!

I visited my parents for breakfast that day, and I ate a lot—not enough for my mother's liking but still a lot. By the time I got up to leave, it was midmorning.

"Where are you going?" my mother asked.

"I have to get to work," I replied.

"But it is Saturday," Mom reminded me. "You can't go to work on Saturday."

"I have to," I explained.

"You can't!" she repeated.

As I headed for the door, my mother said, "Carmen, if you go to work today, we are divorced!"

"You can't divorce me," I retorted. "I am your son, and a mother can't divorce her son!"

"I will be the first mother to do it!" she announced proudly.

Despite the threat of imminent separation, I went to work that day. When I got home, I called my parents. Dad answered the phone, and we talked for few minutes. Then I asked if I could say hi to my mother.

"I will get her," Dad said. He put the phone down and left me in silence for a while.

The next voice I heard was not my mother's. It was my Dad's. "She won't come to the phone!" he said.

"Why?" I asked

"She says you two are divorced!" he explained.

"What should I do?" I asked.

"You had better get over here and either make up with her or get a lawyer!" Dad replied.

Dear readers, you will all be glad to know that I listened to my dad! My mother and I reconciled shortly after. But if my mother was still alive, I am sure we would still argue! We would still not be perfect!

Great Question!

After an overnight flight to meet her husband back home, a woman arrived with her nine children, all younger than eleven. Collecting their many suitcases, they entered a cramped customs area. A customs official watched this entourage in disbelief.

"Ma'am," he asked, "do all these children and all this luggage belong to you?"

"Yes, sir," she said, sighing.

"They are all mine."

"Then I will do this as quickly as possible," replied the official, and he immediately began his interrogation of the mother.

"Ma'am," asked the official, "do you have any weapons, contraband, firearms, illegal drugs, or alcohol in your possession?"

The mother paused before answering. Then she smiled at the official and said, "Sir, look around! If I had any of those things with me, don't you think I would have *used* them all by now?"

The official allowed the mother to pass without opening a single suitcase!

Ladies and gentlemen, take it from that woman. People are not perfect!

It's true; families are special, but they are not perfect—and they are not quiet!

Families *do* argue. They do disagree. They make trouble, noise, mistakes, messes, mayhem, and more! They even say and do things to each other that are not pretty and *not perfect*!

Still not sure? Try these stories!

Ask My Son!

Shortly after Uncle Ed (Frankie's dad) passed away, Frankie, offered to buy a headstone for his grave.

"You have done too much already," replied Frankie's mother, my aunt Amelia, (a.k.a. Aunt Millie or "Auntie Mil.")

"Let me take care of it," replied Auntie Mil.

"Fine," said Frankie, relieved but nervous.

A month later, the scene repeated itself. Frankie had been to the grave many times but saw no stone.

"Ma, I'll be glad to buy one," he offered again.

"I told you, I will take care of it!" insisted his mother.

Days later, Frankie asked one more time for permission to buy a headstone for his dad.

"I told you I would do it! Now don't mention it again!" came Auntie Mil's stern reply.

Only days after that conversation, Auntie Mil was taken to the hospital with pneumonia. Frankie and I were with her when a visitor arrived.

"I was just at your husband's grave," said the visitor to my aunt. "How come it doesn't have a headstone yet?"

Auntie Mil rolled her eyes, shook her head, pointed at Frankie, and said, "Ask my son!"

No, families are not perfect. Just ask my cousin Frankie!

Where Were You?

Frank and his wife, Mary Jean, brought dinner to Auntie Mil for many years after Frank's father died. My aunt was constantly losing weight, and they wanted to bulk her up. So they brought dinner on Monday, Tuesday, and Wednesday. They brought it on Thursday, Friday, and Saturday too.

But Sunday was different. Because on Sunday, Frank and his wife brought *Frank's mother-in-law* dinner instead!

Now you might be able to guess what happened when Frank and his wife returned to see Auntie Mil on Monday night with dinner.

Yes, they walked into her house and were faced with a question. What question? That's right. "So where were you *last* night?" asked Auntie Mil!

It is true. People are not perfect! They argue. They make mistakes, and they fail. I hope the stories I just told will help prove that and give muscle to the message "Welcome Failure." I also hope the stories I have left to tell will give some muscle to our next and final message!

What message is that?

Believe in Yourself

Our next and final message is "Believe in Yourself."

I hope my remaining stories will put more muscle into that last message because that message is popular. Lots of speakers try to send that message to their audiences, and lots of leaders try to send that message to their followers, friends, families, supporters, and staff.

In fact, the commencement speaker I heard at that big Midwestern college tried to send *that message* to *his* audience on the day *I was in* his audience!

Yes, *his* message was the same as *your next* one will be. That speaker tried to convince his audience to "believe in themselves!"

If you think about it, isn't that what *most* commencement speakers try to convince their audiences to do?

Yes, that message is popular! A lot of speakers try to share it or sell it. Alas, the speaker I heard in the Midwest was not a good salesman!

How did I know that? Because I left his commencement address completely "unsold" on "believing in myself!"

I was simply not ready to do what the speaker had told me to.

And *why* was I not ready? Because the speaker's message *had no stories, so it had no muscle!*

You can do better. You *will* do better! Your "Believe in Yourself" speeches will have muscle because those speeches will have stories like these!

Close Call

I came to Quincy College at Plymouth, Massachusetts, more than thirty years ago. When I started, I was the campus director and taught a few courses.

Many of my students were single moms with little children, so they had many roles to play and many jobs to do.

Still, back then, with all their roles and all their jobs, many of my students were outstanding in school!

In fact, one single mom with three jobs and two children was the best student I have ever taught.

She was outstanding. She was exceptional.

One day shortly before her graduation, I was talking with this fine student in the school's main lobby, and I told her how much I respected her for being so busy and so good for so long.

She said, "Yes, it has been hard."

"What has been the hardest part of your life as a parent and as a student here at the college?" I asked her.

Her answer surprised me.

"The hardest thing I ever did here," she said, "was to walk through the front door of this building for the first time. I had spent almost an hour circling the block in my mother's car," she went on. "Finally, I got up the nerve to park, walk up the front stairs, go into the lobby, and register. I was sure I would fail," she confessed. "I was sure I would bomb. I was sure I would embarrass myself. If you must know, Doctor," she ended, "I almost never started at this school."

Someday, dear reader, if you haven't already done so, you will find a door that is hard to walk through. You will find a car that is hard to park, and you will find a set of stairs that are hard to climb.

When you do, think of this story and my student. Be like her. Believe in yourself in the face of failure. Believe in yourself in the face of fear.

Does that story put muscle in my message?

If not, try this!

Valedictorian

Two years after I had that conversation with my best student, I was back at the registration desk when a young man in his late twenties entered the lobby. He was wearing dark glasses and being led by a large German shepherd with a heavy harness.

It was obvious that the young man did not know where I was until I spoke.

"May I help you?" I asked, still standing behind the registration counter.

The young man responded to my voice by turning toward me and walking to the counter, still led by his dog.

"I want a degree in criminal justice," replied the young man.

"You'll need to submit an application," I said.

"Give me one, and I will take it home," he told me. "My family can help me fill it out."

I gave him the application. He then turned and left with his dog leading the way. After the young man was gone, I half hoped he would return and half knew that he would not.

One of my half hopes was answered. The next day, the young man was back at school with his family and his application!

As he handed it to me, I told him that I very much wanted him to try and to succeed but that I just didn't think our school could accommodate him.

The young man smiled and leaned over the counter toward me. If he had eyes, they would have burned right through me. "Oh yes, you can!" the young man assured me.

I was sure he was wrong but could not stand in his way.

I processed his application, and he began classes shortly after.

Some years later, that blind student graduated from Quincy College at Plymouth as his class valedictorian. Next, he earned a bachelor's degree in criminal justice.

After that, he earned a master's degree, and after that, yes, he came back to Quincy College to teach the *same courses* that I had been sure he could *never pass* when he registered so many years before.

What happened? Belief happened. Even in the face of my doubt, that young man believed in himself. Even in the face of my fear, that young man believed in himself. His belief brought him strength. His belief brought him success.

Be like that student. Believe in yourself.

Be That Good!

Some time ago, DeeDee came home from her last day of work.

She had just retired after forty years of working for Brigham and Women's Hospital.

She was depressed, and I knew it.

"What's wrong?" I asked.

"It just dawned on me," DeeDee said. "I spent forty years of my life in one place, and starting tomorrow, that place will go on as if I was never there. It's almost as if I stuck my hand in a pail of water then took it out." Dee continued, "My hand got wet while it was in the water, but once I took it out, the water acted as if my hand had never been there at all."

"You are forgetting something," I replied.

"What?" DeeDee asked.

"The water was at a higher level while your hand was in it," I replied.

"I know," said DeeDee, "but if I had really been that good, the water's level would have *stayed high* even *after* my hand was gone!"

You, dear reader, *can be that* good! Believe that. Believe in yourself.

Natalie's Journals

But don't take that from me; take it from the *real* doctor! Take it from Natalie! Since Natalie is a medical doctor, she reads medical journals! She gave me an article from one of those journals. It was about the brain. It said that the *average* human brain (not the exceptional, spectacular, or unbelievably intelligent but the *average* human brain!) has the capacity to learn over fifty languages, think faster than the world's fastest computer, and somehow memorize every word in every book on every shelf *in any college library*!

So tell me, how many languages have *you* learned lately? If it's less than fifty, you have yet to do your best. And how many shelves of library books have you memorized? If it's less than them all, you have yet to do your best!

Again, don't take that from me; take it from the real doctor. Take it from Natalie and believe in yourself!

Not a lot of my aunts and uncles went to college, but lots of my cousins did! They *believed* they could. They *knew* they could. So did their family. So did *our* family.

I felt the same way. As a student, a teacher, and a coach, I believed in myself because *my family* believed in *me*! One of my uncles even told me that the most popular saying in the Bible is "Be not afraid."

In fact, he *swore* to me that those words "appeared hundreds of times!" in the Bible. I believed my uncle. So I *was not afraid* to try *or* to fail. I was also not afraid to succeed! I was not even afraid to *excel*!

Listen to the Bible. Listen to my uncle. Listen to me! Be not afraid to try, to fail, to succeed, *or* to excel! Don't even be afraid of being smart *because you are*!

If you go fishing, go after Moby Dick and bring along the tartar sauce for when you catch him because you *will catch him*.

Believe that. Believe in yourself. Believe in what you can do.

Howard and Albert

Take what I just said from Howard Gardner or Albert Einstein! Howard has been a professor and an academic celebrity at the Harvard Graduate School of Education for many years. He gets credit for developing what he calls a "Theory of Multiple Intelligences," and Howard says *this* about being smart: "It is not *how smart* you are that matters. What really counts is *how you are smart*!"

In my words, Professor Gardner's theory says *every person is very smart in some ways*, but no person is very smart in *every* way!

Albert Einstein agrees with Howard, but Albert said it a little differently. According to Albert, "Everybody is a genius. But if you judge a fish by its ability to climb a tree, it will live its whole life believing that it is stupid!"

Both Howard and Albert are right. Elvis Presley could not play baseball, and Babe Ruth could not sing or play the guitar! Beethoven couldn't draw, and Picasso couldn't write music. Every person is some kind of smart, but no one is all of them!

Kinds of Smart

Yes, you and people like you have shown Howard and Albert that some people are *word smart*, and others are *number smart*, while still other people are other kinds of smart, like *body smart, picture smart, music smart, self-smart, people smart, nature smart*, and more!

Now I know what you are thinking. You are thinking, "If I *am* music smart, why does the church empty every time I join the choir in singing a hymn on Sunday? Or if I am body smart, how come I fall when I dance and trip every time I climb the stairs? And if I am word smart, why do I stare forever at a blank piece of paper every time I have to write a report or even a paragraph, and why do I have to read a book's first page ten times before I understand it enough to turn to page 2?"

That is because, according to Professor Gardner, we are all *lacking* in *some* kinds of smarts, and we are all *loaded* with *other* kinds!

And what about *you*?

Maybe you can't make music, but you can make friends like crazy. That means you are *people smart* and not *music smart*! Or maybe you pee your pants every time you have to attend your statistics class because you have no *number smarts*, but you draw a crowd every time you speak in public (because you are loaded with *word smarts*)!

Blind Side

Great movie. I watched it last winter. It is about Michael Oher, an all-star professional football player.

Michael was born to a broken home and soon after was left with no home at all. He was adopted by a well-to-do family who faced ridicule from their White racist neighbors for bringing a "big Black kid" into their home. Michael's strengths prevailed, and Michael grew inside and out.

He was placed in a pricey private school with the family's two biological children. At first, in Michael's world, he felt like a "black fly drowning in a glass of milk" at the school, but he worked hard and earned grades good enough to play football. He wasn't very good at football, though until his "new mom" had Michael tested.

"He got very low grades in reading and spatial relations," said the mom as she shared Michael's results with his new dad. "He did even *worse* in creativity and confidence. His lowest grade was in aggressiveness," reported Michael's foster mom after his tests. "Michael is not going to be a very good defensive football player no matter how big he is or how hard his coach pushes him."

"What did he score well in?" asked Michael's foster dad.

"Protection." His mom smiled. "Michael has a very strong protective instinct."

"Are you thinking what I am thinking?" asked the dad.

"Yes," replied the mom.

"Michael is going to make a *great* offensive tackle! He will protect any quarterback's *blind side*. He is built for that. He was *born* for that."

The rest is history. For many years, Michael Oher *shined* as a starting *offensive* tackle in the National Football League. He also *stunk* as a *defensive* tackle or as a defensive *anything*!

He *protects quarterbacks* very well. He *attacks anyone* very badly!

Moral? I have said it before. I will say it again. We all have weaknesses. So does Michael. We all have strengths. So does Michael. Each of us can be as good at something as Michael is at protecting his quarterback, and Michael is very, very good at that! There is *greatness* in us *all*.

The Impossible Business

Napoleon Bonaparte once said, "*Impossible* is a word to be found only in the dictionary of fools." Will Rogers mimicked Bonaparte by saying that "humility is the most overrated of all human emotions. In my opinion," Rogers said, "humility is unnatural. Life has no limits. Why should we pretend it does just so we can appear to be humble? What's the matter with knowing that we can do the impossible?"

As I mentioned many pages ago, when talking about my uncle Romey, the Battle of the Bulge was a major action of World War II. During that battle, an entire American division—eighteen thousand soldiers—became trapped at Bastogne, France. Four allied generals, including George Patton and Bernard Montgomery, were asked if any of them could march on Bastogne with his own army and rescue the trapped American forces there.

Montgomery and two other generals said no to General Eisenhower's request. After all, their men were already fighting a battle at the time. What is more, Bastogne was 125 miles away, the weather was terrible, and the roads were icy and snow-covered. All three generals were brave but realistic. Thus, all declined.

George Patton was *not realistic*! He said he could pull his men from their current battle, regroup, march to Bastogne, and rescue our forces in *two days*!

General Montgomery's aide told Patton that to try would be asking the impossible of his men. Patton's reply was "asking the impossible is what we are in business for."

It *was* unrealistic for Patton to think that he and his men could keep that promise. Still, Dwight Eisenhower let them try.

Patton did not attack Bastogne in two days as he had promised. He did so *in three*! During those three days, Patton led the largest and fastest forced march in the history of warfare. His men (including my uncle Romey!) marched in inclement weather for seventy-two hours without sleep or hot food.

When they arrived at Bastogne, Patton's Seventh Army immediately engaged in one of the fiercest battles of the war. Patton's army won that battle and rescued the American division.

General George Patton was right. He *was* in "the impossible business!"

So are the most successful bosses, leaders, coaches, parents, and people. They *ask* the impossible. Then they *expect* it, and they *get* it!

They believe in people. They believe in themselves.

Learn from Babies—Again!

Some pages ago, we called babies *relentless*, and they are! If you are still not sure of that, watch a baby learn to walk again (and again… and again!).

That will remind you that babies never, never, never give in!

Another scene from a movie (this time, Stallone's *Creed 2*) was about a baby as well. That baby was born to Rocky's son and his wife. She was beautiful and deaf.

"Do you love her anyway?" Rocky asked his son.

"Of course, I do! What kind of a question is that?" replied the offended dad.

"That's good," replied Rocky, "but do you feel sorry for her?"

"Of course not!" resisted the dad.

"Well, join the club!" replied Rocky. "Because I can guarantee that *she* doesn't feel sorry for *herself* either!"

So true. Babies *do not* feel sorry for themselves! No matter what they have or what they don't, whether it is a talent, disease, weakness, or strength, babies *accept* what they have and *adapt* to what they don't.

We should learn from babies (again!). We can always adapt, improvise, and overcome. We should be proud of that. We should be proud of our strengths and never ashamed of our weaknesses.

We should *believe in our strengths, in our smarts,* and *in ourselves*!

Get Off Your Buts!

No, not the buts in your seats—the buts in your *sentences*! When you are told to do the impossible and you reply with "I will try, *but* it might be too hard" or "*but* it might take too long" or "*but* I might be too tired," *get off your buts*!

That will help you *find faith* (there is that word of wonder again!). That will help you *believe in yourself*!

I have a big plaque hanging above my desk that some special friends gave me when I retired. It contains a quote by English author John Dryden. That quote's words are these: "They can who believe they can."

Are you feeling any muscle in your "Believe They Can" message? If so, great, and here come more stories!

Mark Wellman

There is a cliff in Yosemite National Park. It is made of granite and stands taller than *three* empire state buildings.

In 1989, a man named Mark Wellman climbed that cliff. Mark Wellman *has no legs*. He made the climb by pulling himself up with *his arms alone*—six inches at a time. It took him *nine days* to reach the top.

Impossible? Yes. Accomplished? Yes. Something is impossible only until it is accomplished, and people can accomplish anything. Just ask Mark Wellman. Just ask Zoe Koplowitz.

Success Is like Soup

Many years ago, marathoner Zoe Koplowitz was told that she had multiple sclerosis and could never run again.

In fact, her disease had made her muscles forget *how* to run! Still, eighteen years after she was told she had MS, Zoe *ran* and *finished* her first of twenty-four New York Marathons!

On average, it takes Zoe *thirty-four hours* to finish one marathon. Yes, she runs and walks day and night. She never quits. Instead of "*out-firsting*" the other runners, she *outlasts* them!

It has been said (by me!) that "success is like soup; it comes in cans!" *Zoe can*! She believes that. She believes she can. She believes in herself.

Mary Fasano

Mary Fasano's parents pulled her out of the eighth grade so she could work in a cotton mill in Rhode Island. Fifty-five years later, Mary decided to go back to school. She went to high school at night, and at seventy-one years old, Mary Fasano got her diploma.

Then Mary enrolled in Harvard University's extension program and took one course at a time. Mary commuted twenty miles to

Cambridge every week, every semester, every year *for seventeen years*! Then Mary Fasano graduated from Harvard University at the age of eighty-nine!

Impossible? Absolutely. Accomplished? Absolutely. Something is impossible only until it is accomplished.

Believe that. Believe in yourself.

Charles Lindberg

In 1927, Charles Lindberg flew alone from New York to Paris. He had no radar, no radio, no parachute, no automatic pilot. He could see nothing out of his front windshield because a spare gas tank had been welded to it.

Lindberg flew for over thirty-three hours without sleep. He could look forward only by using a periscope that was made from two pocket mirrors.

What Lindberg did was impossible until he did it. Something is impossible only until it is accomplished. Believe that. Believe in yourself.

Wilma Rudolph

Wilma was born in Tennessee. She was one of the twenty-two children. As a child, Wilma suffered from polio and had to wear a leg brace to walk to school.

In 1960, at the age of twenty, *that same* Wilma Rudolph *ran* in the Olympics. She won three gold medals, tying a world record in the process.

Impossible? Yes. Accomplished? *Yes!*

Are any of these stories making muscle for our message of "Believe in Yourself?" Good! Now keep reading!

The Brooklyn Bridge

In 1883, an engineer named Washington Roebling began work on the Brooklyn Bridge. Shortly after the project began, a tragic accident on the bridge left Washington with permanent brain damage. He was unable to walk or talk. The only part of his body that Washington could move was the index finger of his right hand.

But Washington developed a way to communicate with his wife by tapping on her arm with the one finger he could move. For *thirteen years*, Washington Roebling tapped out instructions on his wife's arm! Those instructions were transferred to the engineers at the bridge site. Thirteen years after it was started, the Brooklyn Bridge was completed under the direction of a *paralyzed and speechless Washington Roebling*.

Impossible? Of course!

Accomplished? Of course!

Believe in the impossible. Believe in Washington Roebling. Believe in yourself.

The Great Pyramids

There is enough stone in just one of the Great Pyramids to fill Fenway Park to the brim twenty times over. And all that stone was cut, moved, and laid without the use of animals or machinery—not even the wheel!

Impossible? For sure. Accomplished? For sure.

Something is impossible only until it is accomplished.

The most inspirational book in the library is the encyclopedia. There is no better proof of what people *can do* than the facts of what *others* have *already done*.

Sophia Hawthorne

One night, a heartbroken man went home to tell his wife that he had just been fired from his job and was a failure. His wife listened. Then she surprised him with a shout of joy.

"Now," she said proudly, "you can write your book!"

"Sure," replied the discouraged man, "and what will we live on while I am writing it?"

To his amazement, she opened a drawer and pulled out a substantial amount of money.

"Where on earth did you get that?" he asked.

"I have always known you were a man of genius," she told him. "I knew that someday you would write a masterpiece, so every week, out of the money you gave me for housekeeping, I saved a little bit. Here is enough to last us for one whole year. Now go write that masterpiece!"

That wife's name was Sophia Hawthorne. From her trust and confidence came one of the greatest novels of American literature, *The Scarlet Letter.*

Sophia Hawthorne had *faith* (here comes that word of wonder again!) in her husband. That faith moved mountains, wrote books, and made the impossible accomplished!

So Far, So Good

A farmer was planting his field one day when he noticed a little boy lying on his back with his feet sticking straight up in the air.

The farmer approached the little lad to see if he was hurt.

As he did, the farmer noticed that the boy's eyes were open, so he spoke to him.

"What are you doing lying there with your feet in the air?" he asked.

The little boy explained, "I heard that the sky was falling, so I decided to lay here and hold it up!"

"Oh," answered the farmer, "and I suppose your spindly little legs on your scrawny little body are strong enough to hold up the whole sky?"

The boy paused and looked up at the sky. Then he winked at the farmer and said, "So far, so good!"

Be like that little boy.

Believe in yourself.

The Little Engine

Steven Beering was the president of Purdue University for many years. A story about President Beering says he was once asked to name the one book that every college graduate should read to ensure success in any course.

What book do you think he named? No, he did not name *The Seven Habits of Highly Successful People* or *The World Book Encyclopedia.* He didn't even name *The Bible*, but he did name a book about faith. He did name a book about believing.

The president named *The Little Engine That Could!*

And what did the Little Engine say on its way up that big hill it was trying to climb?

"I think I can. I think I can. I think I can."

Be like that little engine.

Think you can. *Know* you can *because* you can.

Believe in yourself.

Failure Is Not an Option!

James Lovell flew Apollo 13 to the moon—almost.

As the movie of the same name depicts, an explosion onboard Lovell's spacecraft made it impossible for him and his two fellow astronauts to finish their mission. As Jim's family watched the fate of his capsule on live television, one of Jim's daughters began to cry at the thought of what might happen to her father if Apollo 13 was not able to return to earth.

At the sign of such tears, Jim's mother reached out and hugged her granddaughter, looked into her eyes, and said with a smile, "Don't worry, honey. If they could launch *a washing machine* into outer space, my Jimmy could find a way to land it!"

Believe in yourself as much as Mrs. Lovell believed in her son.

Picture of God?

A kindergarten class was having an art lesson one day. Their teacher asked one little girl what she was drawing. "I'm drawing a picture of God," the child replied.

"But, sweetheart," said the teacher, "no one knows what God looks like."

"They will in a minute!" said the little girl.

Think like that little girl. Have a childlike faith in yourself, no matter what challenges or odds you face. Believe in yourself.

The Impossible Is Accomplished!

During my first season as the varsity coach at Quincy High School, we wrestled many big schools with many strong teams. In that first season, the biggest and strongest of those schools beat us 60–0. That meant all twelve of our wrestlers lost their matches—four of them by a decision, and the other eight by either pin or forfeit.

After that meet, I was humiliated. I was embarrassed. I was devastated. So were my kids.

Most of our team members were sophomores that year, so after the meet, we went back to school and met in the locker room. I told every wrestler to stay strong and (of course!) *Believe in themselves*!

In fact, I made them a promise. It was a very dangerous promise, but I made it anyway! I promised those sophomores that if they stayed on our team until they were seniors, we would beat the school that had just humiliated us.

There was silence in the room for a few minutes, then one of the sophomores (whose mother was my uncle Romey's sister!) said something that all of them were thinking.

"Coach," he said, "*that is impossible*!"

I replied with, "Yes, it is, and *something is impossible only until it is accomplished.*"

At the time, I didn't know where those words came from, but I said them because I believed them!

Most of those sophomores *did* stay with me and *did* get better. I mean, *much better*! One year later, the team that had humiliated us the year before beat us again, but the score was much closer.

Then when those sophomores were seniors, we met a strong big team from that strong big school for the third time, and we *did* beat them!

I coached at Quincy High School for seven more years. We wrestled strong big teams from that strong big school in every one of those years, *and we beat them every year.*

So don't take it from me. Take it from my kids and from that big strong school. *Something is impossible only until it is accomplished.*

Different Name

In his book, *The First Day of School*, Harry Wong tells this story about faith.

A skinny old man went looking for a job in a logging camp. When he approached the camp foreman, the foreman took one look at his old body and tried to talk him out of the idea.

"Are you sure you want to be a lumberjack?" asked the foreman.

"Give me a few minutes, and I'll show you what I can do," said the old man.

The foreman said okay, and the two men walked to a grove of trees that needed clearing. The old man picked up an ax and proceeded to chop down a huge tree in record time.

"That's incredible," said the foreman. "Where did you learn to make a tree fall like that?"

"In the Sahara Forest," said the old man.

"You mean *the Sahara Desert*," corrected the foreman.

The old man smiled. "Oh sure, *that's* what they call it *now!*"

Be like that man. Show people what you can do. Believe in what you can do. Believe in yourself.

Another Test

Robert H. Schuller once posed this question to us all: *What great thing would you attempt if you absolutely, positively knew you could not fail?*

As you read this today—right now—ask yourself that question.

Then today—right now—*answer it!*

When you do, *know you cannot fail!*

Believe that. Believe in yourself!

Expect More

During the first parent conference I ever held as a teacher, I told a mother that her son was doing C work, but *that* was okay because "he was doing his best."

At the time, I was proud of my sensitivity. I was proud of my kindness. After all, I *was* being sensitive, wasn't I? I *was* being kind, wasn't I?

I *was* helping the mother feel good about her son, and her son feel good about himself, wasn't I?

No! I wasn't being kind. I was telling that mother that *at his best*, her son was *only average*.

I was giving that mother—and her son—a negative message about her son's potential. What *should* I have said to that mother?

I should have told her to be proud of her son because he *was* working hard and to be prouder still because he *could* work harder!

I should have told that mother and myself to be proud but not satisfied. I should have told that mother and myself to *expect more* from her son and me.

Jon Saphier and Bob Gower wrote an excellent book called *The Skillful Teacher*. The most powerful words in that book are these: "Nothing influences behavior more than the clear expectations of a significant other. "*You*, dear reader, are that significant other! Nothing influences your behavior more than *your expectations!*"

Set them high. Believe in yourself.

Awareness

A farmer found an eagle's egg and put it in the nest of a barnyard hen. The eagle hatched with the brood of barnyard chicks and grew up with them.

All his life, the eagle did what the barnyard chicks did, thinking he was a barnyard chicken. He scratched the earth for worms and insects. He clucked and cackled. He even thrashed his wings and flew a few feet in the air.

Years passed, and the eagle grew old. One day, he saw a magnificent bird soaring above him in a cloudless sky. It glided in graceful majesty among powerful wind currents with scarcely a beat of its strong golden wings.

The old eagle looked up in awe.

"What is that?" he asked of a nearby chicken.

"That's the eagle, the king of the birds," replied his neighbor. "He belongs to the sky. We belong to the earth. We are chickens." So the eagle lived and died a chicken, for that's what he thought he was (Source: Anthony de Mello).

Think you are an eagle. Expect to be an eagle. Believe you are an eagle. Believe in yourself. Give muscle to that message.

Jeopardy!

After my mother died, I visited my father every night. Among other things, we watched *Jeopardy!* together. Dad loved it because he knew so many of the answers. He especially liked it when I didn't know an answer that he did!

One night, the final Jeopardy answer was "This is what Ray Charles spent his whole adult life raising money to cure. Ray called it 'the most horrible deficiency any human being could suffer.'"

All three contestants said the question was "What is blindness?" because Ray was blind. I said the same thing. We were all wrong. What did my dad say? He said, "The question is 'what is deafness?' because Ray was a musician and would rather not see than not hear."

What We Have

What we *don't* have does not matter compared to what we *do* have. What we can't do does not matter compared to what we *can do*.

As we have said, Beethoven could not play baseball, and Babe Ruth could not write music. Michelangelo could not sing, and Elvis Presley could not draw or sculpt. What Beethoven, Ruth, Michelangelo, Picasso, Elvis, and more did *not* have *did not matter* compared to what they *did* have!

FDR's Images

More than twenty-five thousand pictures of Franklin Delano Roosevelt are on file at the Roosevelt Presidential Library in Hyde Park, New York. Most of those pictures were taken by news photographers who willingly adhered to a strict rule of the Roosevelt family that prohibited anyone from photographing the president in his wheelchair.

Because of that rule, only *two photographs* of FDR in his wheelchair have been known to exist until recently. It was only then that the number was sparingly increased to three!

Why?

Because FDR chose to remind the world that he was *presidential first and disabled second!*

FDR chose to celebrate his strengths first and to mourn his weaknesses later, if ever.

What FDR did not have *did not* matter compared to what he *did* have.

What FDR could not do did not matter compared to what he could do.

Much More Beautiful

Last year, a nun told me a story that took place shortly after Haiti suffered one of many horrible earthquakes.

"Two hundred fifty people died in thirty seconds," the nun told me. "I know. I was there," she continued, "and those who *lived* suffered more than those who *died*. One little boy's face was lacerated by falling rubble," the nun told me. "We found a surgeon to suture his wounds, but the little boy was left with many scars. It took days to find a plastic surgeon who finally did operate on the boy's face. Thanks to that doctor, the little boy would heal well this time," the nun went on, "and when his young mother first saw her son after the second operation, she cried with joy. Then she began to sing. Her voice was beautiful. So were her words. In Creole, she thanked God for healing her son. I listened. We all did." remembered the

289

nun. "As I listened, I turned to a nurse standing beside me. 'Isn't it beautiful?' I said. 'Her son is scarred for life, and she is thanking God for not making it worse.' 'It is much more beautiful than that,' said the nurse. 'What do you mean?' asked the nun. 'That woman has three dead children buried in the rubble she is singing beside' came the nun's reply."

Yes, what we *have* is always worth *more* than what we do not have. Just ask that young mother in Haiti.

Celebrate your strengths. Believe in yourself.

Kevin

The Golden Gate Bridge is breathtaking. It is beautiful. It is also destructive and dangerous.

Three thousand people have jumped from that bridge. Only thirty-six of those people have survived.

Kevin Hines is one of those survivors.

After jumping from the bridge, Kevin was in free fall for over 250 feet at more than seventy-five miles per hour.

When he hit the water, three of Kevin's vertebrae shattered and left him with no feeling or movement in his legs.

When Kevin's feet left the bridge, his mission was to die. Seconds later, his mission changed. Throughout his fall, he prayed to live.

Those prayers were answered.

Since his suicide attempt, Kevin has become a best-selling author, global public speaker, and award-winning documentary film-maker on behalf of mental illness.

Many factors contributed to his miraculous survival including a sea lion that kept him afloat until the Coast Guard arrived.

Kevin took a bus to the bridge when he was in his twenties. His plan was to exit the bus when it stopped on the bridge then run beside the rails and jump over them at the moment he was brave enough to do so.

Throughout his trip, Kevin hoped. He hoped for the one thing that would save his life and keep him from jumping.

"If even one person who met me along my way had asked me what was wrong or why I was about to take my life, I would have gotten back on that bus and come home," recalls Kevin. "And my odds of being noticed seemed good! As I rode the bus, I cried, shook, and hyperventilated. Some people did notice those things!"

Others even pointed Kevin's behavior out to others on the bus. Some of those made fun of him or called him names.

But no one cared enough to ask what was wrong. No one tried to "talk him down" from the bus or the bridge.

"The bus driver," remembers Kevin, "didn't ask me what was wrong or tell me not to jump. Instead, he told me to get off the bus so he could make his other stops."

One person who cared was all Kevin needed. One person's concern could have saved him from his jump, his despair, despondency, and desperation.

But that *person never came.* That person never asked. That person never cared. What would *you* have done for Kevin then?

What would you do for Kevin *now*?

Today, Kevin tells his story to anyone who will listen so others will give what Kevin needed but never got. Kevin's book is called *Cracked, but Not Broken.* Perfect title. Perfect words. Perfect story!

I have been told that (just) one meaningful relationship with (even) one caring adult will save a high school student from becoming a dropout.

Such a case for caring! Lives can be saved if one person cares. Lives can be lost with less. People have enough to be cared about. *Remember* what people *have.*

Believe in what people have.

Believe in what you have.

Chapter 3

Giving Magic to Our Memories

When I turned seventy, I remembered an entertaining warning my father had shared with me about a similar milestone he had "suffered" some thirty years before.

"Carmen," Dad said with a furrowed brow and half-closed eyes, "as you get older, two things go first. One is your memory, and I forget the other one!"

Like so many of life's challenges that my dad has prepared me for, that warning was prophetic!

At seventy-three, my memory has had its moments in both directions! I have encountered people after meeting them only once and remembered their names with no idea how. Then again, I bumped into friends after knowing them for years and their names were a mystery to me!

What gifts have helped me remember? What tools have helped me hold tight? Stories, of course! What stories? Here come some answers! *Here come more stories!* These stories, I hope, will help you remember.

Never Forget

Years ago, Natalie sent me an e-mail about the USS *New York*. It is a new class of warship, designed for a mission that includes special operations against terrorists.

Steel from the World Trade Center was melted down in a Louisiana foundry to cast the ship's bow section.

"When that melted steel was poured into its new molds in September 2003, those big rough steelworkers treated it with total reverence," recalled a Navy captain who was there. "It was a spiritual moment for everyone."

The ship's motto? *"Never forget."*

Stories have helped me obey that message. They have helped me never forget.

Making Magic

In the words of Rudyard Kipling, "If history were taught in the form of stories, it would never be forgotten."

This conversation tells stories about people who should never be forgotten, so it will help us make the "magic of memory" *through* the stories we tell!

Even the most modest pieces of a deceased person's life often find their way into the magic of memories that stories make.

A well-told story can help the world cling to a deceased friend or family member better than an album full of pictures, a closet full of videos, or a diary full of descriptions!

The Eulogist's Job

A eulogist is supposed to be sure that the world knows the deceased better *after* death than it did while that person was alive.

"Thus," continues Cyrus Copeland, "a great eulogy is both art and architecture. Its goal is to build a bridge between the living and the dead, memory and eternity."

What is more, there are many ways to build such a bridge!

One approach is to *describe* the person who died. That uses words, whose meaning may or may not be clear!

Other eulogies *tell stories* that are about the person being honored. Those stories almost always paint the clearest and warmest picture of the deceased.

Susan B. Anthony's eulogy was written by her friend and fellow suffragette, Reverend Anna Howard Shaw.

Reverend Shaw chose to *describe* Ms. Anthony rather than tell stories. Her words included these.

"Susan was harmoniously and well-poised in character. She possessed perfect self-surrender and splendid self-assertion. She was also unhindered in her service by narrowness and negative destructiveness. She was courageous, mightily intellectual, and home-loving. She possessed all that is best and noblest. Never did a more victorious hero enter into rest. Unnumbered generations shall rise up to call her blessed."

After wallowing in so many words with so many meanings, might you have given any advice to Reverend Howard if she had asked you how to write Susan's obituary?

Yes! You might have said *don't describe Susan's life.* Instead, *tell Susan's story!*

Examples? I will answer by reading some stories that come from the eulogy that President Obama offered for Senator Ted Kennedy some years ago.

See if those *stories* help you feel closer to Senator Kennedy than Reverend Howard's *words* helped you feel to Ms. Anthony. What is more, see if you feel closer to Senator Kennedy *after* reading those stories than you did while he was alive!

Remembering Ted

"When Ted's older brothers threw him out of their sailboat on Cape Cod because he didn't know what *a jib* was," began President Obama, "six-year-old Teddy got back in the boat and learned to sail!

"Much later, when a photographer asked the newly elected attorney general, Bobby Kennedy, to step back at a press conference because he was 'casting a shadow on his younger brother,' Teddy quipped, 'That will keep happening for as long as we are both in Washington!'

"There was also the time when Teddy courted Senator Orin Hatch for his support of a children's health insurance program by having Ted's chief of staff serenade the senator with a special song. Why was the song special to Orin? Because he had written it!"

"Another time," Mr. Obama continued, "Ted delivered shamrock cookies on a china plate to sweeten up a crusty old Republican colleague. Still another story tells of a Texan committee chairman whose vote Teddy needed on an energy bill.

"Ted walked into a meeting with a plain manila envelope and showed only the chairman that it was filled with the Texan's favorite cigars. While the negotiations were going well, Ted would inch the envelope closer to the chairman's place at the table. Anytime things turned and the chairman's position was losing ground, Ted would pull the envelop back. Before long, the deal was done!"

"Ted asked for my help with a bill I was sure would fail," recalled the president in another story. "The vote took place on Saint Patrick's Day, and it passed! It had no chance!" exclaimed the president after the vote.

"The luck of the Irish!" said Ted after a well-timed wink.

"But I am not Irish!" kidded President Obama.

"But I am!" kidded Ted. Ted was not lucky.

Still, he was loved, *and he loved*. In the days after September 11, he personally called each one of the 177 families from his state who lost a loved one in the attack.

Ted *kept* calling and checking on those families. He fought through piles of red tape to get financial assistance and grief counseling to those in need.

He invited them sailing, played with their children, and wrote them each a letter every time that horrible date cursed the calendar.

President Obama remembers complimenting Senator Kennedy on a seascape of Cape Cod he noticed in Ted's private office. Obama was a freshman senator at the time, and "Ted gave the seascape [which he had painted!] to Obama to welcome him to Washington!"

Ted also sent cards by the hundreds every year to help congressmen celebrate their birthdays and mourn their personal losses.

"The most common conversation that took place while Ted was in the Senate," recalls a colleague, "happened constantly between a senator in mourning and another senator. That conversation went like this. 'You won't believe who called me today!' The answer was always 'Ted Kennedy.'"

At the funeral of her husband, Jack, Jackie Kennedy mused, "They made him a legend even though he would have preferred to be a man."

Like any eulogist, President Obama's job was to make Ted Kennedy be remembered as a man. Did the stories that the president told make that happen? I wonder!

Remembering Todd

Do you recall Todd Beamer and his fellow heroes of Flight 93? If so, is it because of the words like brave, *strong*, and *faith* I used to *describe* those heroes earlier in this book?

Instead, might your memory have been made by their *story*?

Does their *story* help you *remember* Todd better than words?

I hope so. I hope their story will help you remember Todd and the brave passengers of Flight 93. Because *meaning*, *muscle*, and *memory* are what stories are for!

John Remembers

When a Marine named John returned home as a captain after his first tour of duty in the middle east, he and his company arrived in a huge welcoming crowd. His mother asked John if such a sign of support made him emotional. John said no.

His mom asked John if he was emotional when he saw so many buses drive along the main road leading to the base with all the *Welcome Home* signs everywhere. He said no again.

Next, John's mom asked him if he was emotional when he saw the huge crowd of families and friends as they came through the gates of the base, and he said no again.

"Were you emotional about *anything*?" Mom pursued.

John replied, "I got emotional when I talked with the families of all my men who came home safely with me."

To John, that was the best of emotions. To John, that was the best of memories!

John's memory of his second tour, however, was nowhere near his "best." While overseas, he won a bet on a football game but lost six of his men in battle.

One of those fallen heroes who was driving a Humvee while John sat beside him had a bet with John on who was going to go to the Super Bowl that year.

As a Bostonian, John, of course, bet on the Patriots. His driver (named Patrick) rooted for the Steelers.

Whoever lost the bet had to supply their entire returning company of marines with beer! John won the bet, but Patrick was tragically killed when the Humvee hit an IED.

Still, there was one more special piece of magic to be made by John's memory of that day. You see, in true Marine tradition, even the families whose love ones don't make it home are made part of the welcoming crowd as the surviving soldiers are greeted.

These families in mourning stand off to the side watching as the families of the returnees celebrate and give thanks to God. The ceremony is heart-wrenching, and guess who brought the beer to John and the other winners of the football bet?

Yes, Patrick's grieving family did.

I hope that story helps you remember John, Patrick, their friends, families, and fallen heroes. *It certainly helped John.*

Remembering Alfred!

The Nobel Prizes are presented for outstanding achievements in literature, peace, economics, medicine, and the sciences. They were created a century ago by Alfred B. Nobel, a man who amassed his fortune by producing explosives such as dynamite.

Let's try to remember Alfred with a *description*. Alfred Bernhard Nobel was born on October 21, 1833, in Stockholm, Sweden, the son of Immanuel and Andrietta Ahlsell Nobel. He was often sick as a child and had to be attended to almost constantly by his mother.

He attended St. Jakob's School in Stockholm in 1841 and 1842, but then the family moved to St. Petersburg, Russia, where Nobel's father, a chemist and inventor, had established an engineering school.

So much for *describing* the founder of the Nobel prizes. How much of that description might you remember?

Less than you would like? Me too!

What if I asked you what motivated this Swedish munitions manufacturer to dedicate his fortune to honoring and rewarding those who benefit humanity then turned my answer to that question into a story? Might you remember that story better than my description? Let's see! Here comes such a story!

When Alfred's *brother* died, a newspaper mistakenly ran a long obituary of Alfred's life instead, believing that it was *he* who had passed away. Thus, Alfred Nobel had an opportunity granted to few people; he got to read his obituary while he was still alive!

What Alfred read horrified him. The newspaper described him as a man who had "made it possible to kill more people more quickly than anyone else who had ever lived."

The obituary's author even called Alfred "a merchant of death."

At that moment, Nobel realized two things: first, unless he changed that awful image, it would be how he would be remembered forever; and second, that awful image was *not* how he *wanted* to be remembered! Thus, shortly thereafter, Alfred established his awards.

Today, thanks to Alfred, everyone is familiar with the Nobel Prizes while relatively few people know *the story* of how Nobel decided to dedicate them.

Shakespeare was right. "The good we do *does* live after us" and "What is done *last* is remembered *best*."

Most of all, stories give magic to our memories!

I hope you will remember Alfred and his prizes. I hope you will *remember my stories*!

Guess Who!

Once upon a time, there was a young Japanese automobile mechanic. He had a dream of designing a piston ring that would revolutionize the internal combustion engine. He spent all his time and money trying to make his dream come true.

But things did not go well for the young man. He ran out of money before realizing his dream and had to hock his wife's jewelry to continue.

He and his piston ring were rejected everywhere they went.

He spent the next two years trying to build a factory and make his rings better.

By the time his factory was finished, World War II had begun. The young man's factory was bombed and destroyed by the United States Air Force.

Somehow, the young man rebuilt his factory. This time, an earthquake destroyed it! That left the young man penniless. He could not even buy gas to drive his car to the grocery store!

As a last resort, to go food shopping, the young man took the engine from his lawn mower and attached it to his bicycle.

Pretty soon, friends started asking him to build them one of the young man's motorbikes. He sold so many bikes that he ran out of motors! So once again, he decided to build a factory; this time, to manufacture his own motors and his own motorbikes.

And the young man's motorbike sold like hotcakes, right?

No, it failed. People said it was too big and bulky. The young man redesigned the bike, making it much lighter and smaller. He called this bike the Cub.

The Cub became an overnight success and led the creative young man to fame and fortune.

By the way, what is this motorbike maker's name?

Yes, it is Soichiro Honda. What do you think? Would my telling his story help you remember him? Would Mr. Honda's story bring magic to your memory?

I hope so.

Remembering Helen and Anne!

Do you remember Helen Keller? Of course, you do!

Is it because of the words like *isolated, alone, lost, removed, revered, separate,* or *special* that has been used by many writers and speakers to *describe* her? Maybe, but those are words of wonder, which carry many different meanings for many different people.

Instead, might the magic of Helen's memory have been made more memorable by her *story*? What story?

You *know* the story of Helen Keller! Born healthy, she was left unable to see, speak, or hear when she suffered an illness as a child. For five years, she was isolated from the world, alone in the darkness. Then with the help of a special teacher, Helen fought back.

She learned to communicate; in *three* different languages. She graduated from Radcliffe College. She became an author and an ambassador and took an honored place in society.

There was *another* little girl who went blind when she was very young. That little girl's mother died, and her father disappeared. She lived with an aunt and uncle for a while, but they didn't want her. So she was placed in an orphanage with her sick brother.

As a teenager, with no formal education, she entered Perkin's Institute for the Blind. She graduated just six years later as her class' valedictorian.

This girl's name was Anne Sullivan.

Do you remember Helen? Do you remember Anne? Do you *remember their stories*!

Loved, Lost, and Remembered

Someone once wrote that when a person dies, it is as if a flower that had been planted on one side of a wall finds a hole in that wall and grows through it. Then the flower blossoms and blooms on the other side.

My friends Lucas and David are like that rose. So are Kate and Patrick. Their roots and their memories are still with me. So is their friendship. It always will be. And now their flowers blossom and bloom in heaven.

Yes, stories help us remember. So do people. This conversation has told many stories about people who have been loved, lost, and remembered.

Most of those people have left life against the world's will. No one on earth wanted them to leave. Only heaven did. It was as if heaven became impatient and could not wait to share them any longer.

I will end with stories about two Flowers on the Wall. I will end with stories about Kate and Lucas.

Remembering Lucas

First, let me tell you more about Lucas. We shared the same high school alma mater although he graduated more than fifty years after I did!

Lucas and I were very different people but still found a home at the same school. We were not alone in that. The ten thousand alumni who each spent four years at "Archie's" (a derivative of "Archbishop Williams, High School," our alma mater) had come there for different reasons.

We were all stars that shined in different skies. Many were athletes. More were scholars. Lucas was neither, nor was I.

He shined on stage, or should I say he shined *backstage?* Over time, he came to embrace the sound, lighting, props, and scenery that gave our drama program depth, dimension, complexity, and color.

After his graduation from Archie's, Lucas chose to attend Emerson College. For any New England "drama bee," Emerson carried credibility. It denoted *duende.*

None of that was lost on Lucas. He was as proud as he was humble. He was as confident as he was quiet. His life was not loud, but in the words of Russell Crowe in *Gladiator,* "His memory will echo throughout eternity."

On his way to his bachelor's degree from Emerson, Lucas had been a longtime volunteer at the college's radio station and a box office attendant at a Boston comedy club.

While walking home from a subway station after taking a Christmas shift at the club, Lucas was hit by a car in the hands of a drunken driver. He died a few days after that tragedy.

Lucas's mom remembers that she had agreed to donate his organs years before his accident, and she learned later that Lucas had already registered to be a donor while getting his learner's permit.

"He was twenty-one, so it was out of my hands," reflected his mom. "Needless to say, I've never been prouder of him!"

Based on conversations she had with Lucas about his future and his faith, his mother decided within the twenty-four hours following his death that five of Lucas's organs would be donated to people he had never met.

"This will be his gift to the world at Christmastime," said Lucas's mom. "In a week dimmed by darkness, my son brought some very sick people a little bit of light. Lucas would have wanted it that way. He was such a wonderful son," ended his mother, "and will continue to remind others of how precious life is."

It has been said that "you can count the number of seeds in an apple, but you can never count the number of apples in a seed."

Lucas and his organs will plant the seeds of many apples. They will serve as the soil of many lives. Those seeds and those lives will be remembered one at a time just as they were planted.

Likewise, Lucas's light will be remembered in small doses—one dose and one organ at a time. His memory and his light will remain bright enough to leave spots in our eyes as would an old-fashioned flashbulb. Each spot will remind us of one of the gifts Lucas gave and one of the lives Lucas saved.

Someone once said, "If you want to know what kind of person you are, find a piece of glass and hang it on a wall. Then ask yourself if you would like that glass to be a window or a mirror."

If you would rather the mirror, congratulations! You are *normal!* Your thoughts are of yourself and of how people see you. If you would rather a window, congratulations! You are *special!* You care most about what the world outside of you needs, has, wants, and deserves.

There is no doubt. Lucas would want a window. He is looking through one right now—from a place where sorrow will never find him and happiness already has.

Yes, stories give magic to memory.

Remembering Kate

Our school and her family lost Kate more than five years ago.

She was a special girl. In fact, she was more like an angel than a girl. She died in a car accident when she was a sophomore. Our world will never be as bright nor as beautiful.

Like my aunt Sadie, Kate's favorite color was purple. Perfect choice. Everything about Kate was regal. Everything about her was royal. Everything about her was revered.

Everyone who knew Kate felt cheated when she died. They felt incomplete. They felt unfinished. It was as if *their* lives had ended too soon because Kate's had. Kate's family, of course, felt those things most.

Still, Kate's family was *Kate's*, so they, too, were beautiful.

They inherited their beauty from Kate, and Kate inherited her beauty from them.

How did I know of their beauty? Stories like what follows told me.

In the fall after Kate died, I was at a golf match with our school's varsity team. Kate's brother, Liam, was on the team, so I gave him a hug before he hit off the first tee.

Just after that hug, Liam's (and Kate's) dad pulled up.

He brought his truck close to the tee then opened the back door of his double cab and took out a big cooler.

I went over and gave him a hand and a hug. As we embraced, we both leaned back a bit so we could look into each other's eyes. Then Kate's dad spoke.

"It's my day to bring lunch for the team," he explained. "Liam reminded me this morning."

I smiled and shook my head. "You would have been forgiven if you missed this time," I replied.

"By Liam, yes but not by me and not by Kate," he answered.

Yes, Kate inherited her beauty from her family, and her family inherited their beauty from Kate.

Beauty is another word of wonder. It is used too much and understood too little. When using *beautiful* to describe Kate, for starters, we should spell that word using only capital letters. Next (remember?), we should pretend we have never read or heard the word before.

Last, we should imagine a person who is so truly *full* of beauty that there is no room inside her for anything else! We should picture a table holding dozens of oversize roses overflowing from an under-sized vase.

Nothing less would do the word *justice*. Nothing less would do Kate justice. When it came to beauty, Kate's "cup runneth over!" People who hardly knew her felt her loss.

The lines at Kate's wake were never-ending. The throngs at her funeral made finding a seat in church impossible. Still, people looked for spaces to sit! They could not leave. They would not leave. They simply had to say goodbye ("for now") to Kate.

As the years pass, Kate's memory finds more ways into more lives and turns more sadness into more joy.

Family and friends by the thousands still run races and play games just to tell the world that Kate's heart has not stopped beating in theirs.

We thank Kate for the memories she made, the stories she lived, and the beauty she left behind.

Appendix

The Players and the Program

Dad's Family

Tadone Carmine
Nonna Pasqualina

Luigi (Lou)
Rose (Rosie)
Jenny (Cupcake)
Americo (Mac)
Donna (Donnie)
Peter (Wimpy)
Gloria (Glo)

Ma's Family

Tadone Raffaele
Nonna Lucia

Mary
Pasadea (Sadie)
Alfonse (Pop)
Angelo (Mike)
William (Bill)
John (Johnny)
Natale (Ned)
Amelia (Millie)
Helena (Lena)
Albert (Al)
Leo
James (Jimmy)
Jenny
Raffaele (Chick)
George (Jappa)
Gloria

In-Laws

Dad's Family

Uncle Alfred (Freddy)
Uncle Romaio (Romey)
Uncle Alfred (Freddy)
Aunt Ruth (Ruthie)
Uncle John (John)

Ma's Family

Aunt Julia
Aunt Eleanor (Eleanor)
Aunt Madeline (Molly)
Aunt Louise (Louise)
Uncle Ed (Eddie)
Aunt Marie
Aunt Susan
Aunt Marjorie (Margie)
Aunt Anna
Aunt Margaret (Margie)
Uncle Alfred (Al)

Nonnas' Recipes

They all came by way of heaven from my Nonna Pasqualina, Nonna Lucia, and my mother, Lena! If you use any of them, get ready for your family, friends, and neighbors to start fighting over them!

(Please note, amounts of ingredients are approximate and may vary according to taste or what's in the pantry!)

Italian Wedding Soup

Broth
- A fowl (or a big chicken if you can't find a fowl)
- Chicken broth (somewhere between 2–4 quarts, depending on how much soup you plan on making)
- A few carrots, peeled
- One onion, peeled
- 2–3 stalks of celery
- Bunch of escarole (added after the soup is cooked)

Put the fowl in a big soup pot and cover it with chicken broth.

Add the onion, whole carrots, and celery and simmer on the stove for a few hours (until the meat on the chicken is tender and falls off the bone).

Take the chicken and vegetables out of the broth, put them in a separate bowl, and refrigerate everything overnight. The next day, skim the fat off the chicken broth, strain it through cheesecloth, and put it back in the soup bucket. Cut up the carrot and add it to the broth. Throw away the onion and the celery.

Meatballs for Wedding Soup

- 1 pound of hamburger
- 2 eggs
- 1/4 grated Romano or Parmesan cheese
- Salt and pepper
- 2 slices of stale white bread soaked in warm water and squeezed dry
- About a tablespoon of dried parsley

Put everything in a bowl and mix it with your hands until well blended. Roll into balls, about the size of marbles, and place on a cookie sheet. Bake in a 350-degree oven for about 12 minutes and drain on paper towels. Add to the soup.

After adding the meatballs, take a bunch of escarole, rinse it, and chop it up fine. Add it to the soup and simmer the soup until the escarole is soft and wilted.

Ceci's for Wedding Soup

- 3 eggs
- 1/2 c. grated Romano cheese
- 1 tsp. baking powder
- 2 tbsp. chopped parsley
- 1/2 to 1 c. of flour

Beat the eggs with cheese and baking powder. Add the flour slowly, beating well until the batter reaches the consistency of pancake batter. Stir in the parsley. Heat about 2–3 tablespoon oil in a big frying pan. Drop the batter by the tablespoonful into the frying pan and cook until brown on one side. Flip over and cook the other side. Drain on paper towels. After cool, slice into little squares. Add to the soup right before serving.

Somewhere before adding the Ceci's, take a bunch of escarole, rinse it, and chop it up fine. Add it to the soup and simmer the soup until the escarole is soft and wilted.

Meatballs for Spaghetti Sauce

Please note, amounts of ingredients are approximate and may vary according to taste or what's in the pantry!

Ingredients
  - 1 pound of ground beef (some people use equal parts of pork and beef)
  - 2 eggs
  - 2 stale hot dog rolls that have been soaked in warm water or milk and then squeezed dry
  - 1 clove of garlic, minced
  - 1 tbsp. dry parsley
  - 1/4 c. grated Romano (optional)
  - 1/2 tsp. salt
  - 1/4 tsp. ground black pepper

- Preheat oven to 350 degrees.
- In a large bowl, mix all the ingredients using your clean bare hand until well mixed.
- Form mixture into balls, about the size of golf balls or larger.
- Place in an ungreased baking pan.
- Back for 20–30 minutes until meatballs are firm and juices are clear.
- Drain on paper towels.
- Add to sauce.

Cheese Ravioli

Dough
   2 1/2 c. AP flour
   1/2 tsp. salt
   2 eggs
   1/4 cup water
   1 tbsp. olive oil

Note: You may be tempted to use a mixer or food processor to make this dough. That's fine, but if you do, your ravioli will *not* be Helena's ravioli, which were always made by hand.

- Mound flour on a clean dry surface.
- With your fist, make a well in the middle of the mound.
- Beat eggs with oil and salt and add to well in the center of the flour.
- Gradually add flour into to the eggs by using the fingers of one hand, bringing the flour into the center, and gradually mixing it into the eggs until all the flour is incorporated
- If the dough feels too dry add a little water, a few drops at a time, up to 2 tablespoons. If the dough feels too wet, add a little more flour.
- Knead for about 10 minutes until the dough is smooth and elastic.
- Place in an oiled bowl and cover with a clean dish towel.
- Let it sit for at least one hour.
- Cut dough into sections, each about the size of your fist.
- Roll each section by hand or with a pasta machine, making thin strips, about 4-inch wide.

This is the most difficult step of the procedure. My mother, Helena, was known to lose her temper and even swear during this step! (Please don't tell that to Nonna Lucia!)

Filling
Mix together
    2 lbs. ricotta cheese
    2 eggs
    1/2 c. grated Romano cheese
    1/2 tsp. ground black pepper

Assembly
- On a flat surface, work on one strip of dough at a time.
- Place dobs of filling, each about one tsp, along the center of the strip.
- Fold dough over filling by flipping it and press around each mound, using cupped hands.
- Cut around the edge of each of the ravioli with a pizza or ravioli cutter.
- Seal edges well by pressing together with a fork.
- Place on cookie sheets until ready to serve.
- Cook in boiling salted water for ten minutes.
- Remove from water using a slotted spoon.
- Place on platter or bowl and cover with hot tomato sauce.
- Top with grated Romano.

Spaghetti Sauce

1 tbsp. olive oil
1/4 pound salt pork, minced fine
2 bone-in country spare ribs or one fatty pork
1 medium onion, peeled
2 cans crushed "Kitchen Ready" tomatoes
2 cans tomato paste

- Place olive oil and salt pork in a large pot on medium-high heat.
- When salt pork has started to render its fat, add spare ribs and onion.
- Brown pork and onion, stir to avoid burning.
- Add crushed tomatoes and simmer covered over low heat for about 1 hour.
- Add two cans of paste and stir in.
- Fill each empty paste can with warm water and add to the sauce, carefully scraping every last molecule of paste into the sauce.
- Stir well.
- Uncover and simmer on low heat for about 90 minutes.

Periwinkles

Wash enough periwinkles to half fill a 3-quart saucepan

1 can crushed tomatoes
1 small onion, diced
2 cloves of garlic, minced/crushed
3 bay leaves
Olive oil

Pour olive oil pan to cover the bottom.
Simmer onion and garlic for a few minutes.
Add tomatoes and bay leaves.
Simmer about a half hour.
Add the washed periwinkles and simmer for about a half hour.
Eat and enjoy.

Linguine with Anchovies

1 lb. linguine
1/2 c. pure olive oil
2 cans of anchovy fillets chopped into tiny pieces
2 cloves of garlic, crushed
Grated Romano cheese

Cook and drain linguine.
Heat olive oil and add garlic. Sauté for about 1 minute. Add anchovies to the oil. Cook until the anchovies are dissolved.
Pour the anchovy sauce over the cooked linguine. Toss well.
Top with Romano cheese.
Eat and enjoy

Pizzelle with Filling

Pizzelle Batter
   3 eggs
   3/4 c. of sugar
   3/4 c. of margarine, melted
   1 1/2 c. sifted flour (approximately)
   1 tsp. baking powder
   2 tsp. vanilla or if desired
   1 tsp. of anise

To make pizzelle batter, mix all the ingredients together.
Heat a pizzelle iron and drop by the teaspoonful onto the heated pan; close the lid and cook for 30 seconds until the steam stops. Remove with a fork and cool on a rack or towel.
Store pizzelle in an airtight container.

Pizzelle Filling
   11 oz. package of seedless raisins
   6 oz. dark chocolate bar
   1/2 c. grape jelly
   1 c. of chopped walnuts

Soak the raisins in water overnight; drain and mince well.

Chop the chocolate and place in a saucepan; add the jelly and raisins. Cook for 1 1/2 hours over low heat; cool and stir in walnuts.

Before serving pizzelle, top with a scant amount of filling and cover with another pizzelle, and serve immediately.

Potato Gnocchi

Boil 4 baking potatoes; cool.

Rice potatoes to make them mashed.

When potatoes are cool, place them into a bowl.

Add one egg; mix thoroughly.

Add 1 cup of flour and knead as if making bread. Use more flour if needed. Remember, you always want to taste the potato, so do not add too much flour to make them too heavy like a dumpling!

Divide the dough into quarters.

Take one of these pieces and roll it back and forth and stretch until it is a long rope (1 inch to 1 1/2 inch in diameter).

Cut into 2-inch pieces and make a finger curl by placing the middle and index finger on top and press down as it rolls backward one complete turn to create the gnocchi. The little hole or indentation holds the sauce!

Gnocchi with Ricotta

1 c. ricotta cheese
1/2 c. of flour
1/2 c. grated Parmesan cheese
1/2 c. Romano cheese
1 large egg/beaten
Salt and white pepper

Mix together all ingredients working together to form a soft ball of dough.

Then repeat the steps to make the gnocchi!

To cook gnocchi, add to boiling water, watch them rise to the top, and continue to boil for 1 minute. Drain.

Eat and enjoy!

Italian Almond Bars (Biscotti)

1 c. of dark brown sugar
1 c. white sugar
2 eggs
1/3 c. Crisco Oil
1/2 tsp. powdered cloves
2 tsp. cinnamon
2 tsp. baking powder
2 3/4 c. of flour
2 c. of chopped almonds

Glaze (optional): 1 egg yolk mixed with 1 teaspoon of water

Beat eggs. Add brown and white sugars. Add oil. Mix almonds with 2 tablespoons of flour and add to batter. Slowly add flour mixed with baking soda, cloves, cinnamon, and water.

Roll dough into 2 logs and place on 2 greased cookie sheets. Brush with glaze mixture and bake at 375 degrees for 30 minutes. Cool and cut into bars.

Story Titles

Chapter 1: Giving Meaning to Our Words

Landscaping	Lumber	Washing Machine
Dog Bites	Election Day	What Bill?

Words of Wonder

Faith

The Rope	I Knew You Would Come	Faith in the Truth
It's Your Turn	Faith in the World	Faith in Friends
Faith in God	Todd	Faith in Each Other

Family

The Express	Another Special Movie	Out of Ham
The Porcupines Dilemma	Blossom, Bloom, Share	Tadone Carmine
The Puzzle	Every Goodbye	The Tailor
Thomas Edison	The Hawthorne Effect	Screwier Results
Brad	Morris and Esther	Why They Live
Holding Hands	Everything They Had	My Blanket
Home	The Gift of Language	Bad News
Lord Nelson	The Other Puzzle	Our Invisible Thread

A Hundred-Hundred Proposition

Safety Patrol

Beautiful Flowers

Albert Einstein

Quantity and Quality

The Players and the Program

Nonna's Help

Special Sandwiches

Nonna's Words and Wonder

Math Class

Not So Poor

Family Grave

Nonna's Embrace

Special Stories

Candy Canes?

The Changing Room

Salt Water

Relentless

Bad News

Victor's Uncle

The Little Flower

Aunt Minnie

Christmas Eve

Caviar

Extravagant, Extreme, Extraordinary

Mother Teresa

FDR's Funeral

Nonna's Glass

Another Special House

Their Families' Eyes

Lucky Not To Care?

Anthony's Hat

Take Responsibility

Dr. Seuss

Babies

Rudy

"Pray For Them All"

Nonna Lucia

16 Blocks

Our Daily Bread

Our Future President

A Special House

Just Be Happy

The Cost of Eating Less

Maypo's Walk

Another Question

More Sand

Friends

Friend or Father

June Is Tough

Don't Be Too Great

My Cousin Vinnie

Good Kid, Good Friend

How Do I Look

Paddy and Elly

Blood or Not

Anne Marie

The Belly Button

Inclusion

Amazing Grace

Footprints

Brian

A Place to Pray

Too Many Cards

Family by Another Name

Timing Is Everything

More than Players

Wrestlers

Love Grows and Love Shows

All That Matters

New Friends

The Best is Yet to Come

Tim

George

Come, Sit, Eat

David

Loose Change

Feelings

Happiness Is a Victory

DeeDee's Bag

Always Hers

Favorite Pastime

Better Wheels

Let Feelings Lie

The Goalies Father

Feelings Change

John Patterson

Grandchildren Are Different

Inflatable Love

A Mother's Love

The Best

More Good in All Bad

More Victories

Still More Victories

Irregulars

Infected

Perfect T-Shirt

I Love You Too

Tender and Tough

Crystal Ball

Cinderella Man

The Love of (Another) Father

Find Your Keys

Good Kid

Hal

Always Mine

Aida

Feelings Forever

DeeDee Fagerlund

Grand Canyon

Silence Is Golden

My Uncles and Others

More Crystal

More of Love

Student of the Week

The Candle

Good in All Bad

Food

Definitely Not Italian	Great Cooks and Great Food	The Master's Hand
Left Field	Leave Some Beauty Behind	That Good
That Depends	Good Things	Filled Pizzelle
Ma's Secret	Fussy Fathers	Jay's Grandpa
Nonna's Polenta	The Kitchen Table	

Fun

One Man's Work	Dinner with a Hero	Big Buttons?
Susan	On the Road	Short Meeting
Old Speaker, Older Audience	Aunt Sadie	Aunt Mary
Uncle Albert	Uncle Romey	Uncle Romey, Again
Uncle Mike	The Blindfold Experiment	Help Me
Reflection	Number 12?	Pardon the Interruption
Dad's Pills	Nice Sweater	

Strength, Success, and Sacrifice

Dad's Shopping List	More Perfect Vision	Patrick
Palmer	Joe	Nick
Sylvester Stallone	Two Gardeners	Ronald's Gift
John Quincy Adams	*The Last Supper* and More	Special Sacrifices
Safety at Any Cost	More than Their Lives	

Chapter 2: Giving Muscle to Our Messages

Work Together

Walk Your Talk

Never Give In

Work Hard

The Butterfly	Michelangelo	His First Words
		Beautiful Plumbing
Cousins and Teachers	Work and Pride	Calluses and Collateral

Stay Positive

Happiness	*Hamilton*	From the Ashes
No Less Beautiful	Always Good	Mourn or Celebrate
Pearl Harbor	God Will Provide	No Waves
Father Bob	The Bright Side	Medical Mastermind
Gotta Be a Pony	Tree Tragedy	The Kids Today
In Good Hands	Last Gasp	Good Grace
A Reason to Smile	Young President	Classmates?
Smart Smile	Life Is Difficult	
Possessions or Privileges	Beauty Is…	Win Some, Lose Some
Happy Anniversary	Dinner	
Flat Tire	Aunt Gloria	Dad's Blood Test
Different Sisters	More Good Kids	In Charge
Another John, Another Plum	Janet	The Accident
Still A Smile	Shoe Salesman	Show Business
385 Smiles	Look Inside	Small Tools
Reticular Activation System	Bad Luck	Sleeping In
Not Yet!	Good Business!	Grandma Moses

Have Direction

| Dan | Lost Knight | Lost Company |
| Wrong Way? | Walt Disney | Burn the Boats |

Run to the Roar	The Wall, Not the Ball!	Poor Dog
A Matter of Life	It Was the Fog	Another Test
Loud and Clear	Important Days	

Be Creative

Picky Men	Baxter	Inmates of Imagination
Wheaties	Stadium Lighting	Lots of Rocks?
Sticky Burrs	Rubber Waffles	QWERTYUIOP
Open Your Mind!	Tractor Pulls	Carving Roast Beef
Carry the Scale	Flood Control	It's the Thought
Good Thinking	Pick a Path	Magic Drawer
Hoodsies	College Counseling	Dumb Whats?
Oak Street	Like Father, Like Son	Two Things
Von Ryan's Express		

Welcome Failure

The Edsel	Robert Fulton	Failure's Disguise
The Wright Brothers	Thanks, Honey!	Another Mistake
Our Mailman	A Small Parade	Frankie Continued
A Bank's Mistake	Big Parade	Albert's Words
Tight Dress	Their Names Have Been Changed!	Color Television
How Many?	West Pointers	Everybody Still Makes Mistakes
Too Many Engines!	Not Perfect	Divorced Mother
Great Question!	Ask My Son!	Where Were You?

Believe in Yourself

Chapter 3: Giving Magic to Our Memories

Loved, Lost, and Remembered

About the Author

When Carmen Mariano was six years old, his father gave him some advice. He said "Carmen, whatever you do, stay in school!"

Carmen listened to his dad. He did stay in school; for 67 years! That's right, Carmen is 73 years old and has been in school as a student, teacher, coach, or administrator since he was six!

In that time, Carmen has earned a Bachelor's Degree from the Catholic University of America, a Master's degree from Harvard University, and a Doctorate from Boston College.

He has also taught classes or spoken to audiences in 25 states and five countries.

All of that learning, teaching, and speaking, has taught Carmen a lot about the strength of a story!

What has Carmen learned? "He thought you'd never ask!" Get ready to enjoy Carmen's answers!